D0484206

first light

WOMEN'S DAILY DEVOTIONAL & JOURNAL

Oxmoor House®

first light

WOMEN'S DAILY DEVOTIONAL & JOURNAL

Book Division of Southern Progress Corporation
P.O. Box 2463, Birmingham, Alabama 35201

This edition created especially for *Southern Living At HOME* ™,
the Direct Selling Division of Southern Progress Corporation.

For information about *Southern Living At HOME* ™, please write to:
Consultant Services
P.O. Box 830951
Birmingham, AL 35283
www.southernlivingathome.com

ISBN: 0-8487-2649-9
Printed in the United States of America
Fourth Printing 2004

Previously published as
First Light Devotional and Journal for Women © 2000
by Oxmoor House, Inc.

OXMOOR HOUSE, INC.
Editor-in-Chief: Nancy Fitzpatrick Wyatt
Executive Editor: Susan Carlisle Payne
Art Director: Cynthia R. Cooper
Copy Chief: Catherine Ritter Scholl

Women's Daily Devotional and Journal
Editor: Lauren Caswell Brooks
Designer: Melissa Clark
Contributing Copy Editor: Adrienne S. Davis
Director, Production and Distribution: Phillip Lee
Book Production Manager: Theresa L. Beste
Production Assistant: Faye Porter Bonner

Contents

Weeks 1–4

Weeks 5–8

Weeks 9–12

Weeks 13–16

Weeks 17–20

Weeks 21–24

Weeks 25–28

Weeks 29–32

Weeks 33–36

Weeks 37–40

Weeks 41–44

Weeks 45–48

Weeks 49–52

Acknowledgments

Throughout the Year

Face to Face

date:

In C. S. Lewis's mythical novel, *Till We Have Faces,* the central character, Princess Orual, provides a striking visual image of the necessity for us to come to God with an understanding of ourselves.

Angry with the gods, Orual veils her face for many years and never lets her countenance be seen. Finally, near the end of her life, the princess comes to a reconciliation of her anger. And she writes: "How can [the gods] meet us face-to-face till we have faces?"

We cannot meet God face-to-face till we have faces.

Till we know ourselves,

Till we take the time to discover who we really are,

Till we acknowledge our need for grace.

And then we realize that we aren't called to be super Christians after all. We aren't asked to do everything. We aren't responsible for meeting everyone's expectations. We aren't required to be perfect.

We're invited to come.

Come into an understanding of your own soul, of your capacity for good and evil, of the fruitlessness of your frantic activity and performance. Come into the place of authenticity, where you know yourself and are comfortable with who you are in God. Come into the deep waters of the Lord's presence, where you will be healed and made whole, lifted up and transformed.

When your countenance is unveiled and your soul revealed, you can meet God face-to-face and find peace in becoming the person you were created to be.

Your *self* in God. —Penelope J. Stokes, *Beside a Quiet Stream: Words of Hope for Weary Hearts*

Will you come into the presence of God—face-to-face—completely as yourself?

"Your face, Lord, I will seek."
Psalm 27:8 NIV

Making Your House a Home

Bill and I still live in the house we built thirty-some years ago when we were both high school English teachers. Three children have grown up here.They were cradled and diapered here, celebrated and congratulated here. Now four children of the new millennium generation hide in these trees, roll down the hillside, and fish in the same creek their parents did. The newly married school teachers who planned and built this house now answer to "mamaw" and "papaw."

The house has metamorphosed over the years into its present size, shape, and function. The original two-car garage became the first office/shipping room for Gaither Music Company, and then matured into a big, warm family room. The original family room is now the master bedroom. The kitchen became a dining room when a two-story kitchen and playroom addition was built. Finally, after all three kids got through college, we added a private bath with two well-lit walk-in closets. Now Bill can tell on a Sunday morning whether the suit he pulls out is navy or black!

Dogs and kids and lots of friends have snuggled in daybeds, curled up in window seats, and sipped lemonade on the front porch. Sooner or later, though, everyone seems drawn to the old brick fireplace in the kitchen (the brick came from the building where Bill went to high school) where in three seasons of the year there is a log fire burning. In the summer I line the hearth with big chunky candles. Spring, summer, fall, winter—the hearth seems to be the heart of this place. And if that hearth could talk it would sing the anthem of our lives. —Gloria Gaither, *By This Fire: Fireside Moments at the Gaither House*

If the walls in your house could speak, what would they say about your family?

date: ....

"Unless the Lord builds the house, its builders labor in vain."
Psalm 127:1 NIV

Memories

date:

Do you remember when? We all have important events, answered prayers, and precious moments that can easily get lost in the blur of everyday busyness—lost and sometimes, sadly gone forever!

The memories of these special times are important reminders of God's love and goodness in our lives, and they need to be recorded for His glory and our encouragement.

I have a collection of friendship memorabilia—cards, letters, photos, birth announcements, ticket stubs, and more. From the laughter shared at a retreat to the tears shed when we move away, many treasured memories are marked with a memento.

We all have the opportunity to capture and preserve memories, not only for ourselves but as gifts of love for our friends. I once had a lot of fun creating a small scrapbook album for my friend Katherine. A remembrance of her baby shower held in my backyard, it was a gift from my heart and hands that she could treasure long after her son had outgrown his diapers!

Take a walk down memory lane. As you pause along the path to enjoy those special moments from days gone by, take time to thank God for each blessing and ask Him how you might give the gift of a memory to a special friend.

—Karla Dornacher, *The Blessing of Friendship: A Gift from the Heart*

What friend could you honor and thank God for through a memorable gift?

"How can we thank God enough for you in return for all the joy we have in the presence of our God because of you?"

1 Thessalonians 3:9 NIV

FROM GLORY TO GLORY

The Lord is calling—you, me, all of us—to something different, something deeper, something better than we've ever known. A metamorphosis is on its way, a transformation that will make all the difficulties of the journey—the dark nights, the stormy days, the rapids, whirlpools, and riptides of human experience—seem like tiny ripples on the surface of the stream.

The change doesn't come because we work at it, because we grit our teeth and will it into existence. It doesn't happen because we pray for it night and day or make it happen by the force of our conviction.

It's a gift from the heart of the Creator, a grace bestowed by the One who loves us.

We are being transformed from one degree of glory to another. This is God's promise.

It's not a promise based on our worthiness, our work, or our spiritual insight. It's not a reward for good deeds, a gold star for doing our homework. It comes from the Lord, the Spirit. It's free, part of our inheritance from the One who adopted us into the Divine family.

God knows how hard you've tried. How tired you get, how empty your soul can feel even when your days and nights are crowded with all you do in the name of the Lord. God knows the longings of your spirit, the unfulfilled places of your heart.

To you who are weary, the Spirit whispers:

Lay down your burdens. Rest. Look into my face, and behold the image of One who loves you more than you could possibly imagine. One who cares enough to lift you up and give your soul new life.

Let the reflection of Christ shine like the morning sun on the water and be transformed. —Penelope J. Stokes, *Beside a Quiet Stream: Words of Hope for Weary Hearts*

date: ....

How has God transformed you as you rest in Him?

"Do not conform any longer to the pattern of this world, but be transformed by the renewing of your mind."

ROMANS 12:2 NIV

Being Set Apart

date: ....

To be holy means to be separated, set apart for God. We have an instinct for holiness. That is, if we've experienced the new birth. An instinct must grow, and so we learn about holiness through experience just as the Lord Jesus did when he "learned obedience from what he suffered" (Heb. 5:8).

Living more than thirty years as a quadriplegic, I'm acquainted with the "suffering" part. It's the "learning" I'm still working on. I learn not only from God's Word, but from watching others. I've met people in the oddest places who have served as an example of holiness to me. I've watched them drastically obey. I've seen them survive tough, cramped choices to become shining examples of the Master who learned obedience from what he suffered. I'm not imitating the holiness of these people, just how they got there!

I want to "get there," too. I'm learning to love this rugged life of being set apart for God. My soul stirs, and I feel courage rise when I choose to follow God in the small decisions, the stop-and-start successes, as well as the failures. Yes, the path to holiness is painful and at times unpleasant, but its pleasures and rewards are matchless and utterly superior. My wheelchair has shown me that the path of holiness is not an easy journey . . . but it's the right—no, the righteous—one.

You will find holiness where you least expect it: in the most unlikely people and in the most hidden places. You will find it in humility. You will even see glimpses of it in glory.

And you'll discover holiness in the hidden places of your life. —Joni Eareckson Tada, *Holiness in Hidden Places*

Do you desire holiness in your life?

"But just as He who called you is holy, so be holy in all you do."
1 Peter 1:15 niv

Peace

"Peacemakers who sow in peace raise a harvest of righteousness."
James 3:18 niv

How can you sow peace in your life and in those around you today?

"Make every effort to live in peace with all men and to be holy; without holiness no one will see the Lord."
Hebrews 12:14 niv

What efforts do you need to make to live at peace with others in your life?

Mother Made God Real

date:

The Pledge of Allegiance states that we live under God's benevolence. Our country was founded on Christian principles, and uses the "In God We Trust" inscription on our coins to prove it. Congress prays to invoke God's wisdom for its day's work. My English teacher quoted Scripture along with Shakespeare in class discussion. Our community has a church on every corner.

In short, the concept of God somehow seeped into my consciousness along with the fact that water tasted good on a hot summer day and that the sun rose each morning. I don't remember when I did *not* know of God's existence.

But it was Mother who made God real and faith personal. At meals and during family devotions, she prayed for us individually as children, for her sick friends and for guidance about jobs and financial decisions. She read her Bible every morning, day after day after day. She hummed praise songs as she ironed. She and Dad took us to church on Sundays, even when she wasn't feeling well or was tired. She did the morally right thing in times of conflict. She dealt with disappointment without despair. Mother took God from a religious theory to a relationship right before my eyes. —Dianna Booher, *Mother's Gifts to Me*

How can you make God real to someone today?

"So whether you eat or drink or whatever you do, do it all for the glory of God."
1 Corinthians 10:31 NIV

"SHOULD-BE-DOINGS"

Someone once compared the daily task of caring for small children to stringing beads. At the end of the day you expect to find quite an impressive strand considering your efforts; then you come to realize there was no knot at the end of the string! All your hard work is strewn across the floor in spilled juice, Cheerios, toys, and dirty diapers.

After the birth of her third child, Joy could easily relate to the "stringing beads" analogy. Every day she cared for a preschooler, a toddler, and a nursing infant—three needy little humans. Although she felt blessed beyond measure to be entrusted with these children, she found herself mostly exhausted, frustrated, and overwhelmed.

In a rare moment of quiet one afternoon, Joy cried out to God, "What are my priorities? Quiet times?" (Those were hard to come by.) "Scripture memorization?" (She could hardly remember where she put her purse!) "Exercise?" (How about pull-ups; she would pull the covers up over her head each morning.)

"Joy," He seemed to say, *"if you'll quit looking for significance in your circumstances and accomplishments and simply rest in your assignment, I will accomplish My agenda through you each day. This important season of your life may not look like you think it should, but by serving these little ones you are serving Me."* Sure enough, when she let God's plans dictate her "doings," her life was filled with peace and contentment. Some days that divine agenda consisted simply of three meals and snacks, spills and cleanups, diapers and laundry, but always, God's love.

—Cheri Fuller, *Quiet Whispers from God's Heart for Women*

What "doings" in your life will you allow God to dictate?

date: ....

"Though I walk in the midst of trouble, you preserve my life; . . . with your right hand you save me. The Lord will fulfill his purpose for me."
PSALM 138:7–8 NIV

A Bouquet of Believers

date:

Every flower has its own personality—a uniquely beautiful shape, color, and texture. When you gather these "personalities" together and arrange them in a bouquet, they create a wonderful harmony of beauty and fragrance.

God created you just as beautiful and unique as any flower. There is no one else like you. He has designed you with a unique combination of gifts and talents, strengths and life experiences. But He never designed you to stand alone. You are an important and valuable "flower" in His bouquet.

When you allow the Master Gardener to take the single "stem" of your life and place it in the beautiful bouquet of the Body of Christ, something extraordinary happens. God's church needs the shape, color, and texture that only you can give. Perhaps you fit best in the nursery or in a Sunday school class or in the choir. Perhaps you enjoy cooking meals for those in need or ministering in prayer. As you come together with other believers in worship and service, God creates a fragrance of love and kindness that can be poured out abundantly on the world!

—Karla Dornacher, *Down a Garden Path To Places of Love and Joy*

Are you allowing yourself to be used as part of the bouquet?

"In Christ we who are many form one body, and each member belongs to all the others. We have different gifts, according to the grace given us."
Romans 12:5–6 NIV

Commitment

New Year's Day has come and gone. People are talking about their resolutions. Talk, as the old adage says, is cheap. It's now two weeks into the new year, and most of those resolutions have already gone into the recycling bin. The spirit may be willing, but the flesh just can't seem to keep up. We slip back into our old comfortable patterns.

date: ....

Why is it so difficult for us to keep the commitments we make? Perhaps because the changes we seek are external rather than internal. We can make vows but unless true commitment is rooted deep in our hearts, we are bound to fail, to disappoint our loved ones and ourselves.

We live in a society where lack of commitment is the accepted norm. If the road to marital bliss gets a little rocky, bail out and start over with someone new. If a job's tougher than you planned, turn it over to someone else—or just abdicate it altogether. If you're always late for appointments—hey, no big deal. They'll wait. Commitment, in the modern world, simply isn't a very high priority.

To God, however, commitment is the very bedrock of faith. And it begins, not with our external efforts to change our outward patterns, but with a profound inward conviction that draws us into a commitment to Someone greater than ourselves.

When we commit our lives to God, we begin to see the spiritual truth in everyday life, to realize that keeping our word is not just a matter of making a good impression, but a matter of being true to the One who created us and redeemed us. Commitment is not an outward effort, but an inner transformation. It's not a New Year's resolution; it's a gift of grace. —Penelope J. Stokes, *Simple Words of Wisdom: 52 Virtues for Every Woman*

What commitments do you need God's help to fulfill?

"I will lift up the cup of salvation and call the name of the Lord. I will fulfill my vows to the Lord in the presence of all his people."
Psalm 116:13–14 NIV

The Desires of Your Heart

date:

Sometimes God whispers through His Word and other times through singing birds, autumn trees, or a blue heron on the beach. He can speak through a friend, through a book, through a crying infant, or through His still, small voice in our minds.

God whispers to women of all ages and in all seasons of life: high school and college girls, mothers and grandmothers, working women, single women and married women. As I talk to women, I discover that while God speaks to some in their quiet times of devotion, more often He whispers in the middle of their life experiences.

One thing is sure—when God whispers from His heart to ours, something changes. Healing begins or an attitude is transformed. A relationship is restored. We're infused with hope and energy when we're just about out of steam. Sometimes God whispers vital direction for a job or other change in life. And sometimes His whispers are meant simply to reassure us of His love.

My prayer is that stories, quotes, and Scriptures will encourage you to listen and know that God wants to speak to you. He is speaking all the time, but sometimes the clattering culture around us drowns Him out.

Pay attention when He taps you on the shoulder in the middle of your drive time or while you're at your computer or taking a walk. God doesn't waste words. He can change your life with but a few. As you listen and respond to His quiet whispers, your heart and life will be blessed beyond imagination. —Cheri Fuller, *Quiet Whispers from God's Heart for Women*

Are you listening for God's whispers?

"My sheep listen to my voice; I know them, and they follow me."
John 10:27 NIV

Thankfulness

"Therefore, since we are receiving a kingdom that cannot be shaken, let us be thankful, and so worship God acceptably with reverence and awe."
Hebrews 12:28 NIV

How will you respond to God for what He's done for you?

"So then, just as you received Christ Jesus as Lord, continue to live in Him, rooted and built up in Him, strengthened in the faith as you were taught, and overflowing with thankfulness."
Colossians 2:6–7 NIV

Are you overflowing with thankfulness?

God's Perfect Design

date:

A few years ago a forget-me-not, with its tiny blue flowers, appeared amidst my deep pink azalea border. I had not planted this little charmer, but I greeted it as a gift from God—delivered most likely by one of my flying friends.

Every year the forget-me-not has multiplied and even though I never considered planting these two together, the harmony they create today is breathtaking! I delight to confess to all who compliment me on its beauty that this striking combination is God's design, not mine!

God also has a special design for each of our lives. Sometimes He allows "seeds" of circumstance or relationships to take root that we would never have chosen for ourselves. But He knows what is best for us. And though we may not be able to see its beauty or purpose today, we can be confident that whatever God allows in our lives will be for our good, to help us become more like Christ.

—Karla Dornacher, *Down a Garden Path To Places of Love and Joy*

Can you trust God's design for your life today?

"And we know that in all things God works for the good of those who love Him, who have been called according to His purpose."
Romans 8:28 NIV

Heart Connections

Through my artwork and books, I have met many women and enjoyed many new friendships across the country. In fact, the way I figure, if you read and enjoy my books, we are friends. Maybe not talk-on-the-phone, share-the-deepest-secrets-of-our-lives, come-on-over-for-coffee-type friends, but then, we don't know what the future holds either, do we?

I do know this though: If you are being blessed by these words, we are connecting at a heart level. There is a good chance that if we ever met for lunch, we could visit and laugh for hours, and maybe even share a tear for good measure. Heart connections are often formed as we share an interest or an activity.

Moms tend to naturally connect with other moms at the playground, as they homeschool, or when they attend a PTA meeting. I have one friend who regularly gathers with a small group of women to do needlework—something normally done alone becomes the link that allows them to share their lives and their needs with one another. Your heart connection may be with a Bible study group, a walking partner, or a woman at work. It's not as important where it happens, as long as it happens.

If you are presently needing heart connections, ask God to show you where to look. He not only knows you and your needs better than you do, but He also knows of another woman who is praying for someone to call a friend—and it might just be you! —Karla Dornacher, *The Blessing of Friendship: A Gift from the Heart*

Who are your heart connections?

date: ....

"As iron sharpens iron, so one man sharpens another."
PROVERBS 27:17 NIV

Encouraging Teenagers

date:

Being a teenager today is not easy. The world woos, tugs, and pulls from every direction. Yet God's desire for our young people is that no one would have opportunity to despise or criticize them, but would respect them because of their godly lifestyles.

He calls our teens to be an example, not only to their peers but to the whole church, by their words, their faith, and their conduct. That's a tall order! A good question might be . . . who are their examples?

Ultimately, the greatest example is Jesus Himself, but teens also need to see the reality of Christ in the lives of their parents. No one has more influence.

Be a godly example and a source of strength for your teens (or any young person you know). Love them unconditionally. Encourage them not to neglect but to exercise the gifts God has given them. Be their loudest cheerleader! Cheer them on in the race they're running both in the Lord and in their daily lives. Reward them by letting them know they are #1 in your book, no matter what. Teach them God's truths in practical ways (without preaching). Prepare them to stand on their own, and prepare yourself to eventually let them go—and trust God. —Karla Dornacher, *Love in Every Room*

What kind of example of Christ are you to others? How can you encourage teenagers you know to live like Christ?

"Don't let anyone look down on you because you are young, but set an example for the believers in speech, in life, in love, in faith, and in purity."

1 Timothy 4:12 NIV

A Chance to Laugh and Dance

Monica's cancer was back with a vengeance, and that frail ten-year-old was the saddest child to watch as she pulled an IV pole around the clinic at Children's Hospital. In just ten short years, Monica had suffered more pain than most of us experience in a lifetime. One of her legs had been amputated, and although she was fighting valiantly, she was losing her battle with cancer. That's what made the party Kay and Marsha gave for her so special.

As I entered the art center, fifties music blared from a boom box. Dressed up in a poodle skirt with a scarf around her neck, Monica was serving root beer floats to other children from the clinic. A smile lit up her face. This party was a gift of time, carefully planned by volunteers to lift Monica's spirits.

It was just a pocketful of time—but it gave her a chance to laugh, to dance the twist and, for a short while, to feel like a normal kid again. —Cheri Fuller, *The Fragrance of Kindness*

How can you bring a smile to someone you know who is suffering?

date:

"A cheerful heart is good medicine. . . ."
Proverbs 17:22 NIV

WHO YOU KNOW

date:

We've all heard it—this sage and depressing bit of advice given to anyone dependent upon public opinion for career success: Listen, kid, making it in this business doesn't have anything to do with talent or genius or what great things you can do. You gotta get in with the right people, develop a network. It's not what you know, it's who you know.

Success sometimes does depend upon getting the attention of the right people—people in a position to push for that promotion, to market that talent, to get an audition, to make the critics sit up and take notice.

If we turn that advice around and apply it to our spiritual lives, however, it takes on a whole new—and much more positive—meaning. It's not what you do or what you know, but who you know.

As Christians, we often get caught up in the quest for knowledge and the obsession with activity. We study the Bible, investigate various doctrinal perspectives, work hard to get our theological ducks in a row. We give ourselves to good works and pride ourselves on our spiritual accomplishments. But underneath, we're tired.

Sure, it's important to know the right stuff. It's important to do the right things. But in God's sight, something else surpasses knowledge—love, and an intimate relationship with Jesus Christ.

Spiritual depth is not based on an accumulation of facts, but on a profound connection with the Lord of the Universe. Gaze into the still pool of God's love and let the healing, renewing waters refresh you. It's worth a little down time to go deeper with the Lord. After all, it's not what you know . . . it's who you know. —Penelope J. Stokes, *Beside a Quiet Stream: Words of Hope for Weary Hearts*

Are you intimately acquainted with the Lord?

"And I pray that you, being rooted and established in love, may have power . . . to grasp how wide and long and high and deep is the love of Christ, and to know this love that surpasses knowledge—that you may be filled to the measure of all the fullness of God."
EPHESIANS 3:17–19 NIV

LOVE

"Above all, love each other deeply, because love covers over a multitude of sins."
1 PETER 4:8 NIV

Which sins could your love cover for someone?

"For God so loved the world that he gave us his one and only Son, that whoever believes in him shall not perish but have eternal life."
JOHN 3:16 NIV

How will you respond to God's ultimate act of love?

A Narrow Escape

date:

It was night time. Right under a dark overpass, my handicap-equipped van conked out. Everything went dead: the engine, the lights, and, to my horror, the brakes and steering. I yanked violently on the braking mechanism, but my puny shoulder muscles were no match for the weight of a three-quarter-ton van rolling forward.

Oh, God, help me, help me! Just as I quit struggling and hunched over, waiting for a crash, I spotted Ken's truck. I knew he'd been driving somewhere behind me, but I didn't expect him to be the first to reach me out of the pack of traffic.

As cars zoomed by, he jumped out of his truck, bolted into the van, and manhandled the braking mechanism to a stop. Weeks later, my nerves are still rattled.

Something else bothers me: my vulnerability. I've always leaned hard on God's protection for "the helpless," but in my most helpless moment, when I could do absolutely nothing for myself, what happened to my trust in Him?

When I read "The Lord is my light and my salvation—whom shall I fear?" (Ps. 27:1), my answer is "I fear dead batteries and no brakes." That's why, to shore up my faith, I've been re-reading a few biblical accounts of the way God helps His people. I keep coming back to the story of Jesus calming the storm.

I have to admit I used to scoff at the disciples being so afraid. Now when I read the account in Luke, I notice words like, "the boat was being swamped" and "they were in great danger." The narrow escape out of that storm was a horrifying experience for each of them. Their fear was real, and their lack of trust in God understandable.

—Joni Eareckson Tada, *Holiness in Hidden Places*

From what are you trusting the Lord to deliver you?

"He who dwells in the shelter of the Most High will rest in the shadow of the Almighty."

Psalm 91:1 NIV

The Power of Forgiveness

Every morning Mother would give me an extra nickel with my lunch money, telling me that I could spend the nickel for a Popsicle or ice cream only if I ate all my lunch first. I didn't eat all the lunch, but I typically spent my nickel. When I would come in from school, I always dreaded the days she remembered to ask pointedly, "Did you spend your nickel? Are you sure you ate a good lunch?" Sometimes I avoided the feeling of guilt when she phrased it that way, because even in my seven-year-old mind, I could rationalize that she had asked about eating "a good lunch," not "all my lunch." *Good* was relative; *all* was not.

But guilt got the better of me one particular evening. Mother kissed me, tucked me in bed, and left me in the darkness for my prayers. Head under the covers, I started to sniffle and then sob. When I finally called out for her, she came back into my room.

I made my confession.

"I see," is all she said for a moment. Then, "Well, lying is wrong." I nodded agreement. "But I'm glad you told me. Have you asked God to forgive you?" I nodded again. "Good. Then He has and I forgive you, too." Instead of the anticipated spanking, she merely reached under the covers and pulled me up close for a hug.

Ten thousand pounds rolled off my tiny shoulders. Then I said to myself more than to her, "But I guess I still don't get any more nickels."

She swallowed a smile. "I think eating a good lunch rather than all your lunch will be good enough." With that, she hugged me again for good measure and left the room. That was my first understanding of the power of forgiveness.

—Dianna Booher, *Mother's Gifts to Me*

date: ....

Who taught you about the power of forgiveness?

"Be kind and compassionate to one another, forgiving each other, just as in Christ God forgave you."

Ephesians 4:32 NIV

Devotion

date:

The religious disciplines—prayer, Bible study, worship, meditation, fellowship—have value, of course, in the quest to know God better. But what we do can never substitute for who we are, on the inside, in the secret places that only God sees. The inner virtue of devotion is ultimately a private matter, between you and God.

Let's face it—when you fall in love, your time with your beloved is not limited to a prearranged schedule: 15 minutes to touch base in the morning, lunch twice a week, and an extended date for a couple of hours on the weekend. Whether you're together or apart, throughout the day your thoughts drift to the one you love. Your beloved is the last thought on your mind as you fall asleep and your first memory upon waking.

So it is when we fall in love with Christ. "O God, you are my God," David says. "Earnestly I seek you; my soul thirsts for you. . . ." (Ps. 63:1-4).

This is devotion. No scheduled list of activities can ever take the place of such all-consuming love.

And lest you're tempted to argue that David was a special case, God's anointed, a "man after God's own heart," remember David's darker side: He was a murderer, an adulterer. A sinner.

Just like you and me.

True devotion to God isn't some special grace given to saints and prophets.

Devotion to the Lord is your soul reaching out and finding God's heart reaching back. —Penelope J. Stokes, *Simple Words of Wisdom: 52 Virtues for Every Woman*

What does it mean to be truly devoted to God? In what ways do you reveal your devotion to God?

"O God, you are my God, earnestly I seek you; my soul thirsts for you. . . . I have seen you in the sanctuary and beheld your power and your glory. Because your love is better than life, my lips will glorify you. I will praise you as long as I live, and in your name I will lift up my hands."

Psalm 63:1–4 NIV

Stop and Smell the Roses

Georgia dashed upstairs to her room at the conference center and grabbed some notes for the seminar she was presenting. It was only the first day of the conference, but already she felt caught up in the whirlwind of activities, workshops, and time pressures. On her way out the door, she glanced quickly out the window across Chesapeake Bay and noticed a blue heron standing on the shore. Elegant and beautiful, the heron's long neck jutted out as it moved slowly along the shore. The bird paused gracefully between each step, like a bride walking down the aisle.

It was the end of October and there were no people on the shore—just an incredible stillness, water shimmering like diamonds, and the stately blue heron. Looking out at the sea and the bird, Georgia heard God whisper, *"You were going so fast you almost missed the beauty of the heron. Stop and watch—notice how it doesn't strive or hurry."* It was a Father's gentle admonition. "Be still, and know that I am God" (Ps. 46:10).

As she watched, mesmerized by the scene, Georgia felt the tension melt away. Her spirit settled as she realized what a direct contrast the heron's deliberate movement was to the fast-paced whirlwind of the conference—and to much of her life. Caught up in busyness, she was missing the beauty around her.

In a matter of moments, God had adjusted her priorities, almost like a spiritual chiropractic alignment. For the rest of the conference and for weeks afterward, the image of the lovely blue heron came to her mind, reminding her to slow down and be still, to brush off the clamoring hurry of the world. —Cheri Fuller, *Quiet Whispers from God's Heart for Women*

date: ....

Is God reminding you to slow down and be still?

"Be still, and know that I am God."
Psalm 46:10 NIV

Thirsting for God

date:

Thirst scares us. We can live without food for weeks, but without water, we die in a matter of days. How many of us, however, experience the same kind of immediacy in our thirst for God?

When we begin to go deep with God, we start to recognize our own need. Need for quiet times of peace and restoration in the presence of the Lord. Need to quench our thirst from the springs of living water.

But many of us don't take the time we need for refreshing. We keep going and keep doing, sweating it out for God. Our spirits get weak and shaky. We don't realize that we're depriving our souls of what they need to sustain spiritual life.

We can't survive long without water. We can't expect to take a sip or two one day a week and have our thirst quenched until the next Sunday rolls around. We need a constant infusion—every day, every hour—of the water that brings life to our souls.

When you're physically thirsty, your body tells you: your tongue swells, your mouth goes dry, and you can think of little else but getting a drink.

Spiritual thirst demands attention, too. When anxiety rules your heart, when frantic activity crowds your days, when the voices around you drown out the still small voice of God, it's time to stop and take in divine water.

Listen to your inner thirst. Take time to drink deeply of God's grace and mercy. Your thirst will be quenched, but you will find yourself longing for more.

—Penelope J. Stokes, *Beside a Quiet Stream: Words of Hope for Weary Hearts*

How will you quench your thirst for God today?

"As the deer pants for streams of water, so my soul pants for you, O God. My soul thirsts for God, for the living God. When can I go and meet with God?"
Psalm 42:1–2 NIV

Wisdom from God

"For the Lord gives wisdom, and from his mouth come knowledge and understanding."
PROVERBS 2:6 NIV

What type of wisdom are you pursuing?

"If any of you lacks wisdom, he should ask God, who gives generously to all without finding fault, and it will be given to him."
JAMES 1:5 NIV

Have you asked God for wisdom?

Magnetic Love

date:

Marsha told me that she knew me before we even met. But how could that be? We live thousands of miles apart. She said she "knew me" through some magnets she bought at a store in Texas. Who would have imagined that God had gone before us, to prepare the soil of our friendship, by sending my artwork to Texas and placing a magnet in Marsha's life?

But that is the way it is with God and friendships. He goes before us to prepare the soil of our hearts—not only for our friendships with other women, but also for friendship with Himself. God knew you before you were even born, and, like that magnet, He sends you His love and draws you to Himself through the circumstances of your life.

For various reasons, our friendships with others may not survive the years, but once you meet Jesus and call Him Friend, there is nothing that can separate you from His powerful, magnificent, magnetic love!

—Karla Dornacher, *The Blessing of Friendship: A Gift from the Heart*

Have you ever considered that nothing can separate you from Jesus and His love?

"For I am convinced that neither death nor life, neither angels nor demons, neither the present nor the future, nor any powers, neither height nor depth, nor anything else in all creation will be able to separate us from the love of God that is in Christ Jesus our Lord."

Romans 8:38–39 NIV

Being Hospitable

We are each called to hospitality—to open our homes, our cupboards, even our guest rooms, to share with others the blessings we have received. You do not have to have fine china and the budget to serve steak, but you do need to offer the gifts God has given you to serve and bless others. The Lord loves a cheerful giver, so give yourself away generously and joyfully to others—your time, your compassion, your open door.

Your guest room suggests a pleasant refuge, a place of acceptance, comfort, and love. A cup of tea represents a time of refreshing and rest. Cookies remind us that as we are hospitable to others, they will "taste" and see that the Lord is good. Flowers suggest the reflection of Christ's beauty through a generous heart. Books remind us to share not only our lives but the Good News of new life in Christ. Our lamp symbolizes that Jesus is the light of the world. Our clock reminds us to make the most of every opportunity to reach out to others in love. —Karla Dornacher, *Love in Every Room*

Do you understand the difference between hospitality and entertaining?

date:

"Share with God's people who are in need. Practice hospitality."
ROMANS 12:13 NIV

A Mother's Blessing

date:

When Heather Whitestone lost most of her hearing at 18 months of age, the doctor told her mother that the little girl would probably never learn to speak or go beyond third grade. But her mom patiently encouraged her during the six long years it took Heather to learn to say her last name correctly.

Mrs. Whitestone enrolled Heather in a clinic that advocated ocoupedics—learning to listen and speak rather than using sign language—and took her to dance classes where Heather fell in love with ballet.

Years later she achieved what many said was impossible—she became Miss America 1995. Heather attributes her success to her mom's encouragement: "One of my biggest blessings has been my mother, who looks at me as a person with a heart, not a disability," she says.

—Cheri Fuller, *The Fragrance of Kindness*

How did your mother shape the way you perceive yourself?

"[Love] always protects, always trusts, always hopes, always perseveres."
1 Corinthians 13:7 NIV

A (Really) New Mind

People will buy anything that's labeled "new." Sadly, we do it in our Christian lives, too. We latch onto the newest methods of prayer, Bible study, child-rearing, and relationship enlightenment as if we were sliding off the deck of the *Titanic* and that new idea were the only flotation device in sight. We see the need for change, so we turn over a new leaf. We make resolutions. We want to do something now to bring freshness, newness to our walk with God.

The problem is, repackaging and relabeling accomplishes little, except perhaps to make us look more spiritual in the eyes of those around us. We end up changing the outside, while the inside remains untouched.

God has a better plan. "Be renewed in the spirit of your minds," Paul writes to the church at Ephesus. "Clothe yourselves with the new self, created according to the likeness of God in true righteousness and holiness" (Eph. 4:23–24).

We don't get a new mind—as Paul describes it, "the mind of Christ"—by slapping a new logo on an old product. It's a transforming process that happens over time as we immerse ourselves in the presence of the One who created and redeemed us. We don't just wake up one morning to find ourselves spiritually mature, instantly re-created in Christ's image. It happens so gradually that we may not even be aware of it. But those around us will see the difference.

Transformation is God's job, and it will never be accomplished by human effort. Instead of looking for results, focus on the Lord, who is the source and completion of your renewed mind. —Penelope J. Stokes, *Beside a Quiet Stream: Words of Hope for Weary Hearts*

date: ....

Do you want to be repackaged or transformed?

"You were taught, with regard to your former way of life, to put off your old self, . . . to be made new in the attitude of your minds; and to put on the new self, created to be like God in true righteousness and holiness."

Ephesians 4:22–24 NIV

A Glimpse of Glory

date: ....

I look for God in lots of places. Especially when I'm on the road. I look for Him when a flight is canceled or when a gate agent gives me a hard time about the batteries on my wheelchair. Long trips on the road make me long for Him.

It's easy to see His glory in warm and inviting settings such as churches or conferences; but it's in those in-between places, such as car rental parking lots and airport terminals, that I long to feel His presence, sense His nearness, and see His hand at work.

Like last week. I was in the home stretch of a long journey, flying into Memphis to change planes. Thoughts of heaven filled my mind as I looked out the airplane window.

As our plane began its approach, I leaned against the window and peered ahead to see a cemetery. I noticed there were only brass plates marking each grave.

As we flew over, suddenly the sun exploded off the tops of hundreds of different brass markers in a quick-fire succession of sparkling light—bam! bam! bam! I gasped and squinted against the dazzling light. In an instant, it was over.

The metaphor wasn't lost on me. I'd been looking out the window, looking for God, dreaming about heaven, wondering when, oh when, I might be called home. The Lord answered, opening the eyes of my heart to gain a glimpse of glory. I got a bird's-eye view of 1 Corinthians 15:51-52 when "we will not all sleep, but we will all be changed—in a flash, in the twinkling of an eye, at the last trumpet. For the trumpet will sound, the dead will be raised imperishable, and we will be changed."

—Joni Eareckson Tada, *Holiness in Hidden Places*

When and how has God given you a "glimpse of glory" during a routine part of life?

"I keep asking that the God of our Lord Jesus Christ, the glorious Father, may give you the Spirit of wisdom and revelation, so that you may know him better."
Ephesians 1:17 NIV

TEMPTATION

"Because he himself suffered when he was tempted, he is able to help those who are being tempted."
HEBREWS 2:18 NIV

In what ways are you being tempted lately? Will you ask Jesus for help?

"No temptation has seized you except what is common to man. And God is faithful; he will not let you be tempted beyond what you can bear."
1 CORINTHIANS 10:13 NIV

How has God been faithful to you—protecting you from suffering more than you can bear?

Will the Real Child Stand Up?

date:

Once the "I Do's" were said, Mother demonstrated the same love and acceptance toward her sons-in-law and daughters-in-law that she showed to her own children.

There are never unkind words to the child about the spouse. There are never exclusions when family secrets surface. There are never differences in the value of gifts given. There are never concerns expressed for one without the other. Should a stranger stumble into one of our family gatherings, he'd have a difficult time identifying the children from the children-in-law.

One of the greatest gifts mothers can give their children is warm acceptance and impartial love for their children's spouses. —Dianna Booher, *Mother's Gifts to Me*

How do you love your sons-in-law and daughters-in-law? How does your mother-in-law show you love and acceptance?

"Everyone who believes that Jesus Christ is the Christ born of God, and everyone who loves the father loves the child as well. This is how we know that we love the children of God: by loving God and carrying out his commands.

1 John 5:1–2 NIV

Balance

Juggling—when it's done with rubber balls—can be an amusing pastime. But sometimes we feel as if our life depends on our juggling skills: husband, children, parents, friends, money, church, jobs. Everything is important; everything vies for our attention. If we lose our rhythm for an instant, chaos ensues.

date: ....

But God does not call us to be jugglers. God calls us to be people of balance.

Martha, in the Bible, was an accomplished juggler. When Jesus brought his disciples to her home, Martha scurried around making sure everything was just perfect. Mary, Martha's sister, sat at the Master's feet and listened to what he was saying.

Finally, Martha began to lose her rhythm. Her juggling act was falling apart, and she panicked. "Lord," she said to Jesus, "don't you care that my sister has left me to do the work by myself? Tell her to help me!" (Luke 10:40).

But Jesus had a different agenda. He responded: "Martha, Martha, you are worried and upset about many things, but only one thing is needed. Mary has chosen what is better, and it will not be taken away from her" (41-42).

Does God care about all the responsibilities we have to juggle in our daily lives? Of course. But he cares more that our lives demonstrate balance, the ability to discern what is essential and give ourselves fully to it.

Our spiritual life, our connection with God, is the solid footing that enables us to fulfill our responsibilities. We may be able to juggle a lot of things at once, but we can only hold a few things at a time. Our Lord. Our loved ones. Our inner lives. Our outward calling. —Penelope J. Stokes, *Simple Words of Wisdom: 52 Virtues for Every Woman*

In what ways do you think your life is out of balance? How can you make God your solid footing?

"But Martha was distracted by all the preparations that had to be made. 'Martha, Martha,' the Lord answered, 'you are worried and upset about many things, but only one thing is needed.' "

Luke 10:40–42 NIV

Expectations

date: ....

Burdened by the demands on her day, Laura talked to God. "Lord, why doesn't my life have more joy? I can barely manage an occasional smile." God spoke to her in a quiet whisper. Very clearly the word *expectations* popped into her mind.

Suddenly clear thoughts filled her mind. *"Remember when you were a little girl? You were always dreaming you would marry a man like your dad; you would have two handsome boys and two darling girls; you would live in a cottage with red geraniums at the window."*

"Lord, what are you getting at?" Laura interrupted. "I'm not sure what my lack of joy has to do with expectations."

His answer was perfectly clear. *"Hanging onto imaginary expectations has stolen your joy.*

"You expected a husband like your dad, who could fix anything. But I chose a pastor to be your husband; one who would fix his eyes on me and preach and teach my Word.

"You expected two little girls. But I entrusted you with five boys. Instead of putting bows in little girls' hair, I've called you to put my Word in the hearts of young men who will grow up to be mighty warriors for my kingdom.

"You expected a cottage in the country, but I gave you a four-bedroom home in the suburbs. Your cul-de-sac is filled with children who need to know my love."

Yes, Laura had to admit it. "Forgive me, Lord. And help me to trust You and the plan You have for my life. Your designs are far superior to my dreams."

A glow suddenly filled her heart. Perhaps the joy had been there all along—hidden under that load of *expectations.*

—Cheri Fuller, *Quiet Whispers from God's Heart for Women*

How have your own expectations stolen your joy?

"Many are the plans in a man's heart,
but it is the Lord's purpose that prevails."
Proverbs 19:21 NIV

The Importance of Celebration

My garden was in all its glory—full bloom, neat, and tidy. We covered the tables with lace tablecloths and quilts and placed a fresh bouquet on each one.

With colorful ribbons, I tied pansies and sprigs of ivy to the hand-lettered placecards.

As the women arrived, with garden hats and gifts, the air was filled with the joyful sounds of love and laughter.

We were rejoicing in the birth of a baby! We were celebrating life!

God's Word encourages us to celebrate all the wonderful things He has done for us, even the everyday things like friendship, a beautiful sunset, or a job well done.

You don't have to wait for a birthday or anniversary to celebrate. And you don't need to have lace or quilts or gifts. You can pull out the barbecue, have a potluck, or just do a dessert.

The important thing is to celebrate!

—Karla Dornacher, *Down a Garden Path To Places of Love and Joy*

What good thing has God done for you? Or for someone you know? What can you do to celebrate what God has done?

date:

"Let them give thanks to the Lord for his unfailing love and his wonderful deeds for men, for he satisfies the thirsty and fills the hungry with good things."
PSALM 107:8–9 NIV

Caught Ya!

date: ....

It all started with that distinguished man who had taken time to visit our office. One comment he made kept echoing in my mind: "It's important to be obedient not just in big things, but in little things as well." I felt inspired. I want to be more obedient in the little, yet important things.

That evening, at the beginning of my usual prayer time, I focused my heart and embarked on what was sure to be a glorious time of praise and intercession.

Just then, Ken opened my bedroom door and asked, "Joni, remember you wanted me to remind you about that special on Genghis Khan? Want me to flick on the television?"

"Yeah, thanks, turn it on." I quickly breathed an apology: Lord, let me put our prayer time on hold.

I quieted a twinge of guilt as the opening credits appeared on the screen. At that instant, the phone rang. Ken picked it and yelled, "It's for you. It's Bunny!"

"What's up?"

"You tell me, darlin'," Bunny said. "I was just sitting here when the Holy Spirit said to me, 'Call Joni.' I said, 'You mean now, Lord?' And He said, 'Yes, now!' so here I am calling you. I don't know why, but . . ."

I burst out laughing. I told her about how I had asked the Lord to remind me to be obedient even in little things.

"Caught ya!" Bunny laughed.

That was the night the Spirit grabbed me by the collar before I took a step of disobedience. Gotcha! He whispered. Off went the television. Back I went to a glorious time of prayer. Before I closed my eyes in sleep, I whispered, Thanks, Lord. Grab me by the neck anytime you want.

—Joni Eareckson Tada, *Holiness in Hidden Places*

How has the Lord caught you before you've been disobedient?

"And this is love: that we walk in obedience to his commands."
2 John 1:6 NIV

God's Omniscience

"For God is greater than our hearts, and he knows everything."
1 John 3:20 NIV

Do you believe that God knows everything? How does this fact affect the way you trust Him with your life?

"For a man's ways are in full view of the Lord, and he examines all his paths."
Proverbs 5:21

Do you behave as if God is examining all your ways?

The Keeper of Your Home

date: ....

A house is a physical building, walls that shelter, protect, and sometimes even divide. A home is the invisible structure, radiant love that embraces each member of the family and reaches out to draw in friends, neighbors, and strangers.

God has called you, as a woman, to be the heart and the keeper of your home. It is a position of influence and responsibility, as well as honor and great reward.

This high calling is an expression of God's own heart, for as you allow His love to fill your life and spill over to touch the lives of others, that same love will warm your home and the hearts of all who enter there.

God in you—the heartbeat of the home.

—Karla Dornacher, *Love in Every Room*

In which ways are you the heart and the keeper of your home?

"A wife of noble character who can find? She watches over the affairs of her household and does not eat the bread of idleness. Her children arise and call her blessed; her husband also, and he praises her."

Proverbs 31:10, 27–28 NIV

The Gift of a Smile

As teachers we can easily think that our instruction is the best thing we offer our students. But the day I received this letter, I realized that it's the little things—like the way we look at students—that lift their hearts:

"Dear Mrs. Fuller, I really appreciate your coming. I hope you like our classroom! You have taught me so many things about writing, but what I love is the way that you always walk in our class with a smile on your face. Thank you so much! From Sara Hawkins."

—Cheri Fuller, *The Fragrance of Kindness*

How often do you smile during the day? What does your countenance convey to those who see you each day?

date:

"A cheerful look brings joy to the heart. . . ."
Proverbs 15:30 NIV

True Love

date:

Although St. Valentine has been adopted as the patron saint of lovers, the Feast of St. Valentine has nothing to do with candy hearts or roses or romantic dinners. Valentine, a third-century martyr, was beheaded for his faith on February 14, 269 A.D. He died for love, but not the kind of love we celebrate.

He died because he loved God more than life.

The society in which we live is obsessed with romance—or, more specifically, with sex. We are bombarded on all sides with romantic imagery—some positive, some negative, but all centering on only one kind of love. Eros. Physical love. Sensuality.

Well, *love* does make the world go 'round. But not that kind of love. *Agape* love, God's selfless love, set the world in motion and keeps the stars in place.

No matter what the world may try to tell us, God's love is the foundation for all other loves. We as Christians are called to "love as the Lord loved us,"—that is, selflessly, sacrificially. To offer ourselves to others as God offered Christ to us.

True love, the Godlike kind of love, does not bargain or manipulate or seek to control. It gives itself freely as a gift, not as a bribe for something in return. Real love has its beginning and its consummation in the Divine.

Perhaps it's time for us as Christians to reclaim love and bring it back where it belongs—to wrestle it away from the songwriters and the movie producers and the greeting card vendors and return it, worn and battered as it might be, to the lap of God. Perhaps it is time for us to do a re-evaluation of our own loves, and bring them, too, under the canopy of God's grace. —Penelope J. Stokes, *Simple Words of Wisdom: 52 Virtues for Every Woman*

What kind of love are you most thankful for in life?

"If we love one another, God lives in us and his love is made complete in us."
1 John 4:12 NIV

Encouraging Your Husband

If you find yourself becoming critical of your mate, make a list of 10 things about him for which you are grateful. Then let him know how much you appreciate these qualities. Here are tips on encouraging your husband:

- Avoid criticizing him in front of other people.
- Be his most enthusiastic cheerleader.
- Affirm your unconditional love, commitment, and acceptance of him.
- Extend forgiveness regularly and quickly.
- Affirm his positive character qualities and talents.
- Pray for him!

—Cheri Fuller, *The Fragrance of Kindness*

Will you follow these tips and encourage your spouse today?

date:

"A wife of noble character who can find? She is worth far more than rubies. Her husband has full confidence in her and lacks nothing of value. She brings him good, not harm, all the days of her life."

PROVERBS 31:10–12 NIV

Strong and Tender

date:

My younger brother, Keith, had polio at the age of two. He had just been dismissed from Texas Scottish Rite Hospital for Children in Dallas, and Mother and Dad had brought him home to care for him, with instructions to give him hot baths for his muscles.

Only moments after my mother dipped him into the hot water for that first bath, his eyes closed and she could not rouse him. He lay lifeless in the tub. Grabbing him up in a blanket, she laid him in the backseat of the car, and she and Dad sped off to the nearest doctor—their family doctor who practiced in a rural community a half hour away.

For the entire trip, mother sat stoically while Daddy kept his eyes on the road. They pulled into the driveway of Dr. Girzzaffi's home, and Daddy jumped out to summon his help. The doctor opened the car door, and pulled back the blanket. My brother opened his eyes for the first time since he'd been slipped into the bath water, and smiled.

Only after the doctor explained that the hot bath had simply put him into such deep relaxation that he'd gone to sleep, did my mother break into hysterical tears.

It was not the last time my mother displayed both strength and tenderness.

I've seen her wash and clothe an abused mother and small children. And I've seen her tell an itinerant troublemaker to get off our property.

The lessons weren't lost on me. Life is all about the right mixture of strength and tenderness of heart.

—Dianna Booher, *Mother's Gifts to Me*

In what ways have you displayed tenderness? In what ways have you displayed strength?

"For when I am weak, then I am strong."
2 Corinthians 12:10 NIV

Kind Words

"Reckless words pierce like a sword, but the tongue of the wise brings healing."
Proverbs 12:18 NIV

In conversations, are you careful to choose kind, wise words that uplift others?

"With the tongue we praise our Lord and Father, and with it we curse men, who have been made in God's likeness. Out of the same mouth come praise and cursing."
James 3:9–10 NIV

How have you contradicted yourself with your mouth—praising God and cursing men?

AUTHENTICITY

date:

I received an offer in the mail the other day—an opportunity to purchase a strand of "genuine faux pearls." We live in a world of genuine fakes and authentic reproductions. But God—our genuine, unique, unadulterated Lord—calls us to something more than the appearance of authenticity.

When Jesus was choosing his disciples, he came upon Nathanael and exclaimed, "Here is truly an Israelite, in whom there is nothing false" (John 1:47).

Most of us, if Christ were to give us such a compliment, would put on a semblance of humility and protest, "Aw, not me, Lord."

Nathanael's response was more straightforward: "How do you know me?" Jesus responded, "I saw you while you were still under the fig tree before Philip called you."

I saw you, Jesus' words imply, when you didn't know I was watching. I saw the reality of your deepest soul. You are who you claim to be.

Authenticity is a hallmark of true faith, a living demonstration of the belief that God knows us as we are. We can't hide from God. The Lord created us, redeemed us, understands us. We can't masquerade as something we're not.

With Christ, we have nothing to hide. We don't need to camouflage ourselves in a mantle of spirituality. We are revealed. We are loved. We are forgiven. We don't have to pretend any more.

Authenticity with God and within our own souls brings great liberty and great power. We can be ourselves. We can admit our shortcomings and allow God to work within us. And then a miraculous transformation begins to occur. We begin to look more like Jesus. —Penelope J. Stokes, *Simple Words of Wisdom: 52 Virtues for Every Woman*

How or what do you try to hide from God?

"Nothing in all creation is hidden from God's sight."
HEBREWS 4:13 NIV

Unconditional Love

Caroline has an unusual job for a young woman. She manages a night shelter for the homeless in Bedford, England. Naive at times, Caroline can still be shocked when she finds out exactly who has been staying with her.

date:

One day, a police officer telephoned and inquired whether George was staying at the shelter. "Yes," Caroline answered, "George has been here for some time."

"Then you'd better be extra cautious. He is a known sex offender."

The next time Caroline saw George, she struggled to love him as freely as she had before the telephone call. She discovered fear, anger, and judgment lodging in her heart.

A short while later, Helen came to the shelter. Caroline's heart softened during a long conversation with the homeless woman. Caroline liked her immediately. After Helen left the shelter, Caroline read in the newspaper that her latest resident had just been arrested for serial murder! Caroline felt so vulnerable. How will I feel when I see her again? Will I be able to feel compassion for her?

Talking to a friend a few days later, she shared what a struggle it was to love people when she knew the horrible things they had done. "It's so hard to look at them and love them. Instead, I look at them and judge them."

In the middle of her sentence, she heard God's passionate whisper, *"Caroline, I see all your offenses, and I still love you—unconditionally!"*

From that moment Caroline began praying that God would empower her to love others—even murderers and rapists—without condition. Just as God loves her!

—Cheri Fuller, *Quiet Whispers from God's Heart for Women*

Who can you love unconditionally instead of judge?

"But God demonstrates his own love for us in this: While we were still sinners, Christ died for us."
Romans 5:8 NIV

A Simple Note

date: ....

A few words of encouragement in a simple note written by a teacher on a student's composition or on the manuscript of a fledging writer can make a tremendous difference. That single positive comment can be like a signpost that points the person in the right direction. Notes of hope spur on one's dreams. Words of faith are like a shot in the arm when it is desperately needed.

A simple written note can brighten the receiver's day or motivate him to persevere when things are difficult. It doesn't have to be long. It can even be tacked on to an office report, a student's exam paper, or slipped under someone's coffee cup.

Make it short and sincere, and add a specific compliment or word of praise. A few lines not only lift the spirits but can also be kept for other days when a boost is needed. They can even change a life. —Cheri Fuller, *The Fragrance of Kindness*

Who around you deserves or needs a note of approval, affirmation, or encouragement? A vote of confidence or a simple expression of kindness?

"Therefore encourage one another and build each other up. . . ."
1 THESSALONIANS 5:11 NIV

Words for the Wise

The Bible spares no ink in teaching and warning us of the power of our words! We are told that words hold the potential for life and death! They have the ability to lift a spirit, transform an attitude, instill hope, and alter eternity!

Thoughtlessly said, they can also wound the heart, destroy a vision, instill fear, and distort the truth!

We need to have friends and be friends who will speak wisely.

Our conversations should always be to build up and encourage, never to tear down. Our counsel should always be preceded by prayer and showered with grace. Our commitment should always be to speak truth with love and integrity.

And remember that Jesus is your ever-present friend, the unseen guest in every conversation. May the fragrance of your words be pleasing to Him and a blessing to all.

—Karla Dornacher, *The Blessing of Friendship: A Gift from the Heart*

What do you think your words instill in others? What kind of fragrance do your daily conversations hold?

date: ....

"Do not let any unwholesome talk come out of your mouths, but only what is helpful for building others up according to their needs, that it may benefit those who listen."
Ephesians 4:29 NIV

Quilted with Love

date:

The attic is a place for hiding things. Perhaps in your house it's the basement or a closet. You hide things there that you don't want others to see; things that once had value but now seem outdated, broken or useless.

Do you ever feel broken? Outdated? Of little value? Tossed in a corner like an old worn out quilt?

In a sense, you are like a quilt, pieced together with the fabric of your personality, your experience, and your choices. When you first come to God, your quilt may not be very pretty. It may show wear from being tossed around and neglected. It may bear the stains of rejection and the marks of a broken heart. Torn by unfulfilled dreams and broken relationships, soiled by bad habits and poor choices, you may find it difficult to believe that God truly loves you and has a special plan for your life. But He does!

You are not hidden from God's eyes. He sees you and wants to hold the quilt of your life close to His heart. He knows the story of your quilt and wants to wash away every stain and blemish with His mercy and grace. He will not take away the old, worn places for they are part of your character. Instead He will touch them with new life through Christ and restitch the pieces of your quilt together with the beautiful threads of love and compassion.

You are God's workmanship, a quilt of beauty to behold. He wants to use you to bring glory to His name, to wrap a blessing around others who need your love.

—Karla Dornacher, *Love in Every Room*

What does your quilt look like right now? Will you allow God's love to repair it?

"For we are God's workmanship, created in Christ Jesus to do good works, which God prepared in advance for us to do."
Ephesians 2:10 NIV

Hope

"Always be prepared to give an answer to everyone who asks you to give the reason for the hope that you have. But do this with gentleness and respect."
1 Peter 3:15 NIV

What answer would you give to explain the hope you have? How would you display gentleness and respect?

"And hope does not disappoint us, because God has poured out his love into our hearts by the Holy Spirit, whom he has given us."
Romans 5:5 NIV

How has God's love in your heart by the Holy Spirit given you hope beyond disappointment?

My Time Is Yours

date:

When Cyndi's husband, Steve, lay in a coma in the intensive care unit after being hit head-on by a drunk driver, the doctors told her he might not make it through the night. Earlier that day, friends and family had crowded in the emergency room and surgery waiting room, but now everyone had returned to their own homes for the night.

So at 11:00 p. m., Cyndi paced the hall outside the unit and faced a long, lonely night.

Suddenly, she looked up and saw Debbie—loaded with pillows, blankets, and sandwiches—bound through the heavy doors. Although Debbie's children were hosting their first-ever sleepover at her house, Debbie had left the festivities to join Cyndi in her hospital vigil.

"I'm here to wait out the night with you. My time is yours," Debbie whispered, hugging her friend around the neck. A huge wave of relief rushed over Cyndi, sweeping away the nagging anxiety about being alone all night. Debbie's presence gave Cyndi the courage to get through one of the hardest nights of her life.

—Cheri Fuller, *The Fragrance of Kindness*

How can you offer your time to a friend in need? Whose burden can you share?

"Carry each other's burdens, and in this way you will fulfill the law of Christ."
Galatians 6:2 NIV

Both Sides of the Picture

I tried to keep a straight face as the pastor gave the children's sermon. "What does Jesus look like?" he asked. He was going to show each child a mirror, and tell about how we don't know what Jesus looked like, but how Christ should be reflected in all of us.

date:

The point got railroaded by a child. "Of course we know what Jesus looks like," she protested. "We've got a picture of him. He's sick looking, with long hair and sad eyes."

Many artistic renderings of the Savior do make Christ look anorexic, anemic, and profoundly depressed.

Certainly the Bible adds validity to that picture. Jesus, the gentle shepherd, the suffering servant. But there's another side to Jesus we need to embrace if we hope to reflect the Divine Image in our own lives. Immanuel is also an agent of justice, a defender of the weak.

"The Spirit of the Lord is upon me," Jesus declared, reading from the scroll of Isaiah, "because he has sent me to proclaim release to the captives and recovery of sight to the blind, to let the oppressed go free. . . ." Then, he said, "Today this scripture has been fulfilled in your hearing" (Luke 4:18–21).

And Jesus stood up for the weak, healed the sick, defended the abused and neglected, protected the afflicted. He gave us an example to follow from the heart of God.

Consider the scriptural picture of the one we call Savior and Lord. Gentle? Yes. Loving? Certainly. But Jesus was no wimp. He was committed to justice, righteousness, and truth. When Christ's reflection shines in us, we will be, too.

—Penelope J. Stokes, *Beside a Quiet Stream: Words of Hope for Weary Hearts*

What do you think Jesus looks like?

"And we, who with unveiled faces all reflect the Lord's glory, are being transformed into his likeness with ever-increasing glory, which comes from the Lord, who is the Spirit."
2 Corinthians 3:18 NIV

The Meaning of Hospitality

date:

A friend once said, "You can't really know me until you've been in my home." There is some truth to this statement.

We meet and enjoy each other in a variety of places—church, community meetings, our place of business, or school. These are generally safe, nonthreatening environments where we can reveal only as much about ourselves as we desire—places where we can keep people, even our friends, at arm's length.

God does not desire that we hold our arms out in front of us to keep people at a distance, but that we hold them wide open to invite people into our lives and our homes.

Hospitality is not about how big your house is or how it's decorated. It's not about how good a cook you are or how you set the table.

Hospitality is about opening your heart and your home and sharing what God has given you. It's about giving yourself to someone else, to let them know you care about them.

So put on the soup or fix some sandwiches. Pick up the phone and invite a friend! —Karla Dornacher, *The Blessing of Friendship: A Gift from the Heart*

How do you keep people at a distance? To whom can you open your heart and home?

"Offer hospitality to one another without grumbling."
1 PETER 4:9 NIV

Meddle Moments

How very tempted our mothers must be—tempted to meddle in our marriages and in the way we raise our children and grandchildren. Tempted to tell us how to spend or not spend our money. Tempted to chastise us for not using our God-given talents and time wisely. Tempted to offer us advice when we did not ask for it.

Instead, they somehow manage to keep their mouths shut all through our adult years, and just be there for us, supporting us, giving guidance only when asked, and offering opinions only when solicited.

What courage our mothers have had simply to trust us to God's hands. —Dianna Booher, *Mother's Gifts to Me*

How have you seen your mother resist the urge to meddle?

date:

"The Spirit of the Lord will rest on him—the Spirit of wisdom and of understanding, the Spirit of counsel and of power, the Spirit of knowledge and of the fear of the Lord."
Isaiah 11:2 NIV

Healthy Humility

date:

Humility is a virtue often undervalued by the world in which we live. We are taught that we have to look out for Number One, to climb the ladder of success no matter who we have to step on in the process. We are encouraged to be our own best friend, to blow our own horn because nobody else will.

God, however, seems to have a different perspective on self-aggrandizement.

Jesus approached the subject with a parable: When somebody invites you to a wedding, he advised, don't take the place of honor. Someone else more distinguished than you might come in, and then you'll be embarrassed when you're asked to move to the cheap seats. Instead, seat yourself among the lowly, and when your host sees you there, he will insist that you move to a place of greater honor. But we need to be careful to understand what humility is, and what it is not. Humility, Jesus implies in the parable, is knowing the truth about yourself—not pretending to be something you're not. Often pride masks itself as false humility, the kind of worm theology that says, "Woe is me; I am worthless!" Translation: Look at me; I need attention. We are not worthless—God in Jesus Christ has rendered us worthy. We can hold our heads up, believe in ourselves, be strong without violating the principles of humility. The key lies in understanding the source of our worthiness.

We are worthy because God loves us, loved us even before we accepted that love. We are valued members of God's family because God reached down to us in grace and mercy. We are redeemed, beloved in God's sight, not because of what we have done, but because of what Christ has done on our behalf. —Penelope J. Stokes, *Simple Words of Wisdom: 52 Virtues for Every Woman*

Do you have a balance of humility and worthiness in your life?

"For everyone who exalts himself will be humbled, and he who humbles himself will be exalted."
Luke 14:11 NIV

Faith

"Now faith is being sure of what we hope for and certain of what we do not see."
Hebrews 11:1 NIV

Is your faith such that you are certain of what you don't see?

"Therefore, since we have been justified through faith, we have peace with God through our Lord Jesus Christ, through whom we have gained access by faith into this grace in which we now stand."
Romans 5:1–2 NIV

How are you justified through faith?

Spring Arrives Again

date: ....

I walked down the lane near our house. Everything was frozen. The bare trees stood stark against the white fields. The sky was gray— again. In the entire month there had been only 24 hours of sunshine—something very depressing for a transplanted Southern girl. My soul felt as drained and as gray as the sky.

Just then I noticed a rose bush that had been severely cut back. Ice was frozen solid around its branches. That forlorn rose bush reminded me of our family. We've been pruned, too, I thought. We're 2,000 miles away from family and friends. Holmes' building projects are on a downhill slide. Our savings are gone, and money is tight.

In the midst of my thoughts God seemed to whisper. *"Like the rose bush, you will bloom again and be fruitful if you sink your roots deep into Me. This rosebush wasn't cut back by accident. Someone pruned it purposefully so there would be abundant roses next summer. Trust Me in the winters, too!"*

God did bring us through that long winter, and as we saw Him provide again and again, our trust in Him deepened. We grew a hardy endurance and perseverance as Holmes worked an all-night job at a printing press and I substituted at the high school by day and wrote magazine articles at night. God taught us invaluable lessons, like thanking Him for the gift of life itself and for our children's smiles as they played in the woods behind our house.

By the next spring, though we still faced many difficulties, we were back home in Oklahoma. Eventually, Holmes had construction projects again, and God opened new doors for me in writing and speaking. Slowly, imperceptibly at first, the blooms began to appear. As surely as God had promised, spring did come again. —Cheri Fuller, *Quiet Whispers from God's Heart for Women*

Are you able to rejoice in difficult seasons of life?

"Though the fig tree does not bud and there are no grapes on the vines, though the olive crop fails and the fields produce no food, . . . I will rejoice in the Lord. . . ."
HABAKKUK 3:17–18 NIV

Mapping Out Life's Journey

As Christians, we're trained to "seek God's will." We search the Scriptures, pray, seek counsel, listen for a voice from above.

We expect God's will to be some kind of celestial career counseling, where we take a spiritual-gifts inventory, evaluate our possibilities, and begin moving along the "right" course for our lives. Then we get frustrated and resentful—sometimes outright angry—when the wind shifts or the river bends and we find ourselves going in a different direction.

We're looking at what we do rather than who we are. We're more concerned about where we're going than who we're becoming.

So, what exactly does Scripture say about God's will? More to the point, perhaps, is what Scripture doesn't say about it. It exhorts us to follow God's will wholeheartedly, to pray "thy will be done," to delight in doing God's will. But it doesn't tell us, "this is the one path to your spiritual destination." It gives us general principles to live by. It doesn't give us a detailed travel plan.

For those of us who live in fear of making a mistake—who want to be told where to go, what to do, who to marry, what church to attend, what job to take—the Bible isn't much help. But for those who long for the liberated, abundant life, the Scripture brings very good news.

The Lord's perceptions about the journey into God's will are a little different from our own. We are concerned about the outcome—covering the most distance in the least amount of time, and tying up at the right dock at the end. God is concerned about the process—letting the journey itself be the goal, what it can teach us, and the character it can form within us. —Penelope J. Stokes, *Beside a Quiet Stream: Words of Hope for Weary Hearts*

date:

How has the Bible guided you in your journey?

"Be joyful always; pray continually; give thanks in all circumstances, for this is God's will for you in Christ Jesus."
1 Thessalonians 5:16–18 NIV

Patience

We are an impatient people, even those of us who claim the name of Christ. We have a hard time seeing beyond our schedules, our responsibilities, our well-ordered plans and goals.

date:

Patience is the kind of character trait that everyone wants to possess but no one wants to develop. And it's no wonder. The Bible tells us that suffering brings patience, so we don't dare pray for patience lest suffering come. The truth is, we want what we want when we want it. We don't like sitting in traffic. We're frustrated and demoralized by delayed gratification and unanswered prayer. We want patience, but we want it right now.

But patience is, by its very nature, a future-oriented virtue. "If we hope for what we do not yet have," Romans 8:25 tells us, "we wait for it patiently." Hebrews encourages us to "imitate those who through faith and patience inherit what has been promised" (Heb. 6:12).

Patience, it seems, is developed in the Christian life through two processes—delay and interruption. Neither is very attractive to goal-driven, product-oriented people like us. But our responses to both are based on faith. Faith in God's timing, and faith in God's priority system.

If we want to be people of patience, we need to trust that God is in control of the outcome. What we call a detour may be the Lord's scenic turnpike. When our plans are delayed by gridlock or interrupted by unanticipated rerouting, God knows the best way home. —Penelope J. Stokes, *Simple Words of Wisdom: 52 Virtues for Every Woman*

Do you trust that God is in control of all outcomes?

"But if we hope for what we do not yet have, we wait for it patiently."
Romans 8:25 NIV

One of a Kind

When you take time to smell the roses, gaze at the stars, or delight in the colors of fall leaves, you will find that the Creator of the universe made no two alike. The same is true of His children. Each one is special, as distinctive as the bolts of fabric on the shelf.

date:

God made you one of a kind! He knit you together in your mother's womb. There is no one on the face of this earth like you. No one else has your unique combination of personality, gifts and talents, strengths and life experiences. There is a path before you that you alone can walk. There is a purpose that you alone can fulfill.

When you begin to accept and embrace this truth about yourself, it will truly set you free. When you learn to accept yourself as God's design, you will also be more willing to accept your husband, your children, and others around you as the people God created them to be.

Ask God to give you the desire and the wisdom to accept and nurture each person's individuality, including your own. Help those you love to be all that God designed them to be instead of trying to mold them into someone they are not—into someone you think they should be. Remember that God has the perfect plan for their lives as well as for your own. —Karla Dornacher, *Love in Every Room*

Have you asked God to help you accept and nurture your individuality?

"For you created my inmost being; you knit me together in my mother's womb. I praise you because I am fearfully and wonderfully made; your works are wonderful, I know that full well."
PSALM 139:13–14 NIV

A Lifeboat of Love

date:

A teacher who listens and cares can be a lifeboat to a child who is "drowning" on the seas of life. A woman I once met told me her third-grade teacher was this kind of listener. During that time of her young life, the child was very frightened and alone. Her mom was a single parent who worked two jobs to support the family and was too exhausted at night to spend time listening to her daughter. During that year, the eight-year-old was being molested by a neighbor and family member, but she couldn't find a way to tell her mother.

"I didn't know how, but my teacher listened to me, encouraged me, and saw me as a real separate person. When she talked to me, she always got down on my eye level and really listened, something no other adult in my life ever did. That is something I've never forgotten—that at least once in my childhood, I mattered." —Cheri Fuller, *The Fragrance of Kindness*

Will you be the kind of person who listens to others?

"Everyone should be quick to listen, slow to speak and slow to become angry."
James 1:19 NIV

Joy

"I have no greater joy than to hear that my children are walking in the truth."
3 John 4 NIV

What brings you great joy?

"May the God of hope fill you with all joy and peace as you trust in Him, so that you may overflow with hope by the power of the Holy Spirit."
Romans 15:13 NIV

Are you full of joy?

Tranquility

date:

I have a dozen people coming for dinner—most of them vegetarian—and haven't even begun to think about what to serve. The house needs cleaning; the guest room hasn't seen a dust rag in over a month.

Martha, Martha, you are upset about many things.

Make that obsessed about many things. Hurry, hurry. Worry, worry. It's easy to miss that still, small voice:

"Peace I leave with you; my peace I give to you. I do not give it to you as the world gives. Do not let your hearts be troubled, and do not let them be afraid" (John 14: 27).

Fine for you to say, Jesus—you don't understand the pressures I'm facing. You don't know what it's like, bearing all this responsibility.

And amid all my agitation, I hear that Voice again:

Sit down beside the quiet stream, and listen. Look into the pool, and see my character reflected there.

The image of Christ is a picture of tranquility, not of turmoil. But sometimes it's hard for us to stop and heed the quieting voice of God. Our narrow, limited experience makes us believe that the Lord could never understand the obligations and pressures of modern life.

But Jesus does understand. He spent a good part of his earthly ministry with crowds pressing around him, clamoring for bread and healing. In the last days of his life, he was pursued by the authorities, who sought to put him to death. And what did he do? He went away to a quiet place—to the mountains, to the sea, to the Garden. He spent time alone with God. He found refreshing and renewal and strength to go on in the presence of the One who had sent him. —Penelope J. Stokes, *Beside a Quiet Stream: Words of Hope for Weary Hearts*

Do you find renewal and strength in the One who sent you?

"A heart at peace gives life to the body. . . ."
Proverbs 14:30 NIV

Shame on Me

We were behind a closed door in the restroom, so I felt free to ramble on to my friend as she helped me. I should have kept my opinions to myself. After all, it was a public place. And—yikes—the woman with whom I had disagreed, unbeknownst to me, was standing beyond the door by the wash basin!

date:

When I exited the stall, I came face-to-face with her. Thankfully, her face was lit up with laughter. "Gotcha!" she said good-naturedly. "I'm assuming you were about to come back to the table to tell me your opinion, right?"

I was red as a watermelon. "Right," I said, relieved. But was I ashamed!

I had just displayed an inflated idea of my own importance, a pompous know-it-all attitude. Most of all, I blushed because of my shame in misrepresenting my Lord.

Shame can be one of God's best tools in refining us. Think about a time when you were ashamed of yourself. Perhaps you were sitting, sophisticated and nicely dressed, with a new friend over coffee. As the conversation flowed, you felt witty and interesting. But then it happened. You knocked your cup and coffee spilled all over you. Instead of laughing, you felt stupid, embarrassed, and ashamed.

God exposes the things we idolize. The conversation was flowing . . . you felt witty and charming. What idol did the feeling of embarrassment expose? Pride in your appearance. Smug self-confidence in conversational skills. An inflated idea of your own importance.

Shame is a good thing. Embarrassment isn't bad. It helps us detect the idols in our life.

I'm relieved that God keeps exposing them. It's worth the embarrassment. It's worth the shame.

—Joni Eareckson Tada, *Holiness in Hidden Places*

How has God exposed your sin through an embarrassing situation?

"All who worship images are put to shame, those who boast in idols—worship him, all you gods!"

Psalm 97:7 NIV

In Your Spare Time

date:

My mother has been in perpetual motion since she was wheeled out of the delivery room. To attend four ball games a week, church services three times a week, and at least one community function each week took planning and determination. My earliest memories include seeing my mother hanging clothes on the clothesline at dawn before she left for work, folding clothes while she cooked dinner, addressing get-well cards at a ball game, canning beets while she drilled us on fractions, baking cookies for school while she prepared to teach her Sunday school class, and listening to the news while she mopped the floor. When others said they didn't have time to volunteer for this or that project, mother made time.

She modeled personal productivity that would make the experts pale. Can I do less? —Dianna Booher, *Mother's Gifts to Me*

How could you make better use of your time?

"The sluggard craves and gets nothing, but the desires of the diligent are fully satisfied."
PROVERBS 13:4 NIV

Godliness

Those ancient family photos tell the tale: my ancestors in sepia tones, peering out at me from the cracking pages of an album that dates back to the Civil War. I don't know their names, but I know they trace their lineage from the Stokes clan. The family resemblance is remarkable.

date:

I pray that, as I mature, the "family resemblance" that marks me as a daughter of God will be equally evident.

For that is what we're called to, after all—to take on the characteristics of the One who created us in the Divine Image. The prime directive of spiritual life is not what we do, but who we are. It is the passion to become increasingly like Jesus Christ. It is the invitation to godliness.

The problem is, some of us mistake godliness for god-likeness. Like Adam and Eve, we fall prey to the temptation of wanting to "be like God." Then when we get a little spiritual truth under our belts, we start acting as if we're omnipotent and omniscient.

True godliness, however, isn't a spiritual trump card that enables us to exalt ourselves over others. It is the quiet, secret, inner longing to become more like Christ, to imitate our Lord and cultivate the fruit of the Spirit.

If Jesus Christ was, as the Bible claims, the earthly incarnation of the Divine Nature, his life and ministry should give us an example to emulate. And what an example it is!

Jesus reached out to those on the fringes of acceptable society. He fraternized with outcasts, embraced lepers, fed the hungry, offered hope to the despairing. He healed the sick, gave sight to the blind, set the captives free. He lived in grace, in forgiveness, in integrity.

This is the ancestral portrait. This is our spiritual gene pool. —Penelope J. Stokes, *Simple Words of Wisdom: 52 Virtues for Every Woman*

Do you resemble your heavenly Father?

"Be imitators of God, therefore, as dearly loved children and live a life of love, just as Christ loved us and gave Himself up for us. . . ."
EPHESIANS 5:1–2 NIV

Your Dwelling Place

date:

I walked around the block that had been our neighborhood for the last three years. We had bought our first house there, had wallpapered the kitchen a cheerful yellow print, grown red roses in the garden, and built a fort for the boys in the backyard. For the first time in our marriage I felt truly at home.

Sadness filled my heart at the thought of our impending move. I wanted to be like Abraham who said "yes" to God's call to travel to unknown places and live as a stranger camping in tents because he was keeping his eye on an unseen city with eternal foundations —the home designed and built by God Himself (Heb. 11:8-10). Although I sensed that God wanted me to be flexible instead of being stuck on some earthly dwelling, I was struggling.

Lord, You know I'm a nester by heart. I'd just love to stay right where we are. I don't even need to move the furniture to be content, much less change houses.

He gently whispered, *"Yes, I know you'll miss the house, but remember I am your dwelling place—not the house you live in or the rooms where you eat and sleep. You'll live in other houses here on earth, but don't get attached to any of them; they are all temporary. I am your permanent dwelling place!"*

Fortunately, I had no idea how many other houses God was referring to! When we moved again last summer for the ninth time, storing some furniture and giving our children other pieces, I heard God's gentle reminder once more, "I am your dwelling place." It makes me grateful, too, for the home He's making me in heaven—where I'll never have to pack again! —Cheri Fuller, *Quiet Whispers from God's Heart for Women*

Where is your dwelling place?

"By faith Abraham, when called to go to a place he would later receive as his inheritance, obeyed and went, even though he did not know where he was going. By faith he made his home in the promised land like a stranger in a foreign country; he lived in tents, as did Isaac and Jacob, who were heirs with him of the same promise."
Hebrews 11:8–9

Righteousness

"But now a righteousness from God, apart from law, has been made known, to which the Law and the Prophets testify. This righteousness from God comes through faith in Jesus Christ to all who believe."
Romans 3:21–22 NIV

Have you received God's righteousness?

"I do not set aside the grace of God, for if righteousness could be gained through the law, Christ died for nothing!"
Galatians 2:21 NIV

Are you striving to obtain your own type of righteousness?

WISDOM

date:

Solomon, the Bible tells us, was the wisest man who ever lived. Early in his reign as King of Israel, God came to him in a dream and made him an offer he couldn't refuse: "Ask for whatever you want me to give you."

Solomon asked not for wealth or honor, but for wisdom. "Give your servant a discerning heart to govern your people, and to distinguish between right and wrong." God was pleased with the request, and gave Solomon wisdom that set him apart from all others—and great wealth and power in the bargain (1 Kings 3: 5-13).

Solomon obviously realized something we often forget: Knowledge can be cultivated through study; power can be gained by conquest; honor can be acquired by deeds of greatness. But wisdom is a gift from God. Anyone who lacks wisdom, James 1:5 reminds us, should ask God, who "gives generously to all without finding fault."

Perhaps the key to Solomon's wisdom lay in his awareness that he needed it. Too often we depend on ourselves—our instincts, our training, our education, and our reputation—rather than looking to God for wisdom. But being wise doesn't mean knowing everything, memorizing large portions of Scripture, or having a list of degrees after your name. It means being able to see situations from God's point of view—and having the capacity to discern our own limitations.

What do we get when we ask for wisdom? Most of the time, we get questions—lots of them. Hard questions. Many more questions than answers.

But the questions drive us back to God. And dependence upon the Almighty is the ultimate wisdom.

—Penelope J. Stokes, *Simple Words of Wisdom: 52 Virtues for Every Woman*

Have you asked the Lord for wisdom?

"If any of you lacks wisdom, he should ask God, who gives generously to all without finding fault, and it will be given to him."
JAMES 1:5 NIV

Mourning with Others

I have a friend who endured a terrible loss. Her grief clung to her like a heavy shawl around her shoulders. I could not take the shawl from her, but I could come alongside her and lift a corner of the shawl upon myself to help her bear its weight. More than once she apologized for being a burden, but I assured her—that's what friends are for.

It's not always easy, at least for me, to develop the ability to listen and embrace without offering advice or correction and without sharing my own equally traumatic experiences. And I must confess that there were moments when I wanted her to put it behind her. I yearned for days to come when we would share more joy than sorrow. But grief must be walked out, step-by-tearful-step.

The Bible tells us that we are not to grow weary in doing good because joy returns to those who wait patiently on the Lord! Never quit praying and never give up . . . on your friend or your God.

There is a time to speak, to embrace, and to encourage. And there is a time to quietly come alongside, lift the shawl, and be a friend. —Karla Dornacher, *The Blessing of Friendship: A Gift from the Heart*

Are you waiting patiently on the Lord or growing weary?

date:

"Let us not become weary in doing good, for at the proper time we will reap a harvest if we do not give up."

Galatians 6:9 NIV

DON'T FORGET THE LORD

date:

Even though you may have a great devotional time with the Lord in the morning, it can be easy to "forget" Him as you are challenged throughout the day with children, chores, and everyday cares.

But just as you cherish and display old photos and memorabilia around the house to remind you of important people and special events, why not hang Scripture on your walls to remind you what a great God you serve—to remind you what He has done for you, and what He has promised for your future.

Be encouraged to place God's words of encouragement and direction first in your heart and then prominently in your home—on wall plaques, refrigerator magnets, even scribbled scraps of paper taped to the bathroom mirror. This will demonstrate to your children how much you value God's Word and will be a tool to teach them as well.

—Karla Dornacher, *Love in Every Room*

What could you put in your home to remind you of God and His Word?

"These commandments that I give you today are to be upon your hearts. Impress them on your children. Talk about them when you sit at home and when you walk along the road, when you lie down and when you get up. Write them on the doorframes of your houses and on your gates."

DEUTERONOMY 6:6, 9 NIV

A Boomerang Blessing

Every Thursday for many years, my friend Cynthia headed across town to visit Maureen, a ninety-year-old woman who was crippled by arthritis. Cynthia took her out to lunch and ran errands each time she came. Yet the blessing of encouragement Cynthia gave to the elderly woman boomeranged right back to her own life—Cynthia knew few people in town and had no family around to share her pregnancy or the joy over her newborn child, so Maureen's interest and motherly wisdom were a special blessing. This "pocketful of time" shared between a younger woman and an older woman turned out to be a blessing for them both!

—Cheri Fuller, *The Fragrance of Kindness*

Who could you be a blessing to by spending some time with them?

date:

"Freely you have received, freely give."
MATTHEW 10:8 NIV

POURED OUT LIKE WATER

date:

Don't we lie to ourselves, to others, even to God? We claim that everything's just fine, even when we're struggling with depression. We mouth "spiritually correct" platitudes about trusting God and knowing that the future is in good hands, even when we're anxious or frustrated, or so angry with the Lord we could scream. As if we believed that God didn't know better.

Reflecting the image of God in our lives, being conformed to the likeness of Christ, includes being honest with ourselves and with the Lord, even if that honesty makes us look less spiritual in the eyes of those around us. Jesus was open with God, after all, when he prayed in the Garden of Gethsemane, "Let this cup pass from me." He was honest when he rebuked the disciples and displayed anger with the money changers in the temple. The prophet Jeremiah was candid enough with the Lord to write an entire book of lamentations over the destruction of Jerusalem. He was angry, and he let God know it.

Our hearts cannot be healed and liberated when they're filled with unexpressed bitterness, anger, or despair.

Are you frustrated, confused, mad at God? Go ahead, say it out loud. God already knows what you're feeling. You won't be struck down for your honesty. Being open with the Lord is not just a catharsis, but an expression of trust. It is reaching out in faith to One who listens and loves.

Be honest, with yourself and with the Lord.

Pour out your heart like water. It can become a cleansing, healing flood.

—Penelope J. Stokes, *Beside a Quiet Stream: Words of Hope for Weary Hearts*

What do you need to be honest about before the Lord today?

"Pour out your heart like water in the presence of the Lord."
LAMENTATIONS 2:19 NIV

Anger

"A gentle answer turns away wrath, but a harsh word stirs up anger."
Provers 15:1 NIV

Are your responses to others gentle or harsh?

"Do not make friends with a hot-tempered man, do not associate with one easily angered, or you may learn his ways and get yourself ensnared."
Proverbs 22:24–25 NIV

Do you surround yourself with people who help you control your anger?

THE *TITANIC*

date:

Even after it received 11 Academy Awards, I refused to see it. But my birthday was last week and guess what—someone gave me a video of *Titanic*. So three nights ago, I had Ken pop the cassette into the recorder.

The movie was a powerful metaphor of a frightening reality. This tiny planet has been given a mortal blow, a gash in its side. Rebellion against God has set it on a crash course with hell, and whether we like it or not, it's going down and dragging a lot of people with it.

Some refuse to believe it. Surely if we hate suffering, God must hate it worse and could never have founded an institution as horrible as hell. But the same Jesus who gave heaven a five-star rating also described an otherworldly chamber of horrors.

Had the Bible not told us otherwise, we might think this life was the only life there is. We'd continue to arrange our days as though rearranging deck chairs on the *Titanic*. We'd clink our brandy glasses and toast our fate, as though we were facing only a soul-sleep—a dull, gray existence without God, who, as a matter of fact, was a bit of a bore on Earth anyway.

Don't misunderstand. God didn't make hell for people. Jesus said it was "prepared for the devil and his angels" (Matt. 25:41). It's unnatural for humans to be there—as unnatural as turning our backs on a Creator who loves us. As unseemly as shrugging off the Father's kind arm while we caress Eden's serpent, coiled around our hearts.

God takes no joy in anyone heading for eternal misery. And His Son is the lifeboat—big enough and wide enough to rescue all of the perishing. —Joni Eareckson Tada, *Holiness in Hidden Places*

How will you express thanks for being in the Son's lifeboat?

"For God so loved the world that He gave His one and only Son, that whoever believes in Him shall not perish but have eternal life."
JOHN 3:16 NIV

In the Cleft of the Rock

Moses needed a little reassurance. God had instructed him to lead the people from Mount Sinai toward the Promised Land. And so Moses said, "Show me your ways; show me your glory" (Exod. 33:13, 18).

date:

What he got was what we all get when we make such a request—a glimpse of the glory, a fleeting glance. "I will make all my goodness pass before you," the Lord responded, "but you cannot see my face; for no one shall see me and live." And so the Lord put Moses into a cleft of the rock. "I will cover you with my hand until I have passed by," God said, "then I will take away my hand, and you shall see my back; but my face shall not be seen" (Exod. 33:19–23).

We long to see the face of God, to be assured of the Lord's presence in our lives. But the glory and the power are too much for us; we cannot behold God's face and live.

So where do we get a glimpse of God? We may not look upon the Lord's face directly, but in righteousness we get a pretty good picture of God's character. We see where the Lord has been; we see the results of the Divine Presence.

When Moses came down from the mountain, he "did not know that the skin of his face shone because he had been talking with God"(Exod. 34:29).

When we've been in presence of the Lord, the likeness of the Almighty will shine within us and out from us, illuminating the darkness and giving off a reflection of holy love and grace.

The face of God is revealed in righteousness. It's the holiest of close encounters, a transforming experience that will leave you changed and full of light.

—Penelope J. Stokes, *Beside a Quiet Stream: Words of Hope for Weary Hearts*

Do you desire to see the Lord? Do you want that likeness to be reflected in your life?

"And I—in righteousness I will see your face; when I awake, I will be satisfied with seeing your likeness."
Psalm 17:15 NIV

FORGIVENESS

date:

True forgiveness, biblical forgiveness, is not an external accomplishment, a white-knuckled, force-yourself-to-do-it-whether-you-like-it-or-not act of imposed self-righteousness. When Jesus forgave the sins of the woman who anointed his feet, he explained to his host the nature of real forgiveness: "Her sins, which were many, have been forgiven; hence she has shown great love. But the one to whom little is forgiven, loves little" (Luke 7:47–48).

Forgiveness that extends outward to others begins inwardly, in the heart. It begins with comprehending how deeply we ourselves need to be forgiven.

The woman who anointed Jesus' feet understood this. She was conscious of her sins, aware of her unrighteousness before God. She knew her need. And when her sins were forgiven, she responded with an outpouring of love so great that it shamed those who called themselves followers of the Messiah.

In the Lord's prayer, Jesus set forth a radical pattern for living: "Forgive our sins, as we forgive those who sin against us." The key to "forgiving as we have been forgiven," I believe, lies in spiritual self-awareness, acknowledging just how much mercy we need—and have received—from the Lord. If I am mindful, on a daily basis, that the sinless Christ endured death on the cross for my sins, I'm likely to be less judgmental and more forgiving toward those who cause me pain.

Forgiveness is not so much an action as an attitude—a virtue of the heart. A perspective of gratefulness toward God and love toward others. —Penelope J. Stokes, *Simple Words of Wisdom: 52 Virtues for Every Woman*

As you reflect on how you've been forgiven, who do you need to forgive?

"Bear with each other and forgive whatever grievances you may have against one another. Forgive as the Lord forgave you."
COLOSSIANS 3:13 NIV

NO FEAR IN LOVE

Jodi's husband, Bill, left for Vietnam in October. While Bill was in battle in Southeast Asia, Jodi was battling her own enemy—fear—and was losing. She asked God for peace in her heart and for Bill's safety, but the truth was she didn't feel she deserved Bill and saw no reason why she should be spared grief when so many other wives were losing their husbands.

date:

One night as Jodi was reading the Bible, she came upon 1 John 4:18, "We need have no fear of someone who loves us perfectly; his perfect love for us eliminates all dread of what he might do to us" (TLB).

That's me, she thought. I'm dreading what might happen to me and worrying whether God will take Bill.

In that moment God whispered, *"You don't believe I love you. You don't believe that even if I take Bill, I still love you and have a plan for your life."*

Suddenly Jodi realized that the problem was more than her fear of Bill's death and the dangers he faced in Vietnam. It was a lack of trust in God and His love for her. As the truth of His Word sank in, she knew she could trust Him—with her husband, with her life, with everything. From that moment on, the issue was settled. Peace replaced fear.

Although Bill didn't come home for many months, Jodi was no longer afraid of tragic telegrams or telephone calls. She quit worrying and started trusting.

This experience transformed Jodi's spiritual life. She learned that God could minister to her by His Word and His Spirit. Never again would she forget that He cared deeply for her and would meet her every need—she simply had to trust Him. —Cheri Fuller, *Quiet Whispers from God's Heart for Women*

Do you trust God to meet your every need?

"There is no fear in love. But perfect love drives out fear, because fear has to do with punishment. The one who fears is not made perfect in love."
1 JOHN 4:18 NIV

A Well-Watered Garden

date:

As we were cleaning the brush for our garden in Alaska, I knew this would be my most challenging garden ever. In addition to the short growing season, we had no water on our property. I would have to haul the water in by barrels and hand water each plant individually. I worked the soil beneath each plant and built up a reservoir around it so not a drop of water would be lost. Each thirsty plant from seedtime to harvest received my undivided attention as I poured life-giving water onto its roots and tended to its needs.

Every garden requires water to give life to the seed, develop a deep root system, grow strong, and bear fruit. Without water a garden dies.

Are you thirsty? Is your garden wilted and weak? Is your heart soil dry and parched? Jesus says, "Come to Me, I will water you with living water." The Master Gardener calls you by name. Go to Him and tell Him your need. Spend time with him and feel the touch of His tender mercy. Pray and ask Him to water you deeply with His presence. Let your roots soak up His life-giving love. Don't waste a drop, and your soul will be like a well-watered garden. —Karla Dornacher, *Down a Garden Path To Places of Love and Joy*

Will you ask the Lord for living water today?

"The Lord will guide you always; he will satisfy your needs in a sun-scorched land and will strengthen your frame."
Isaiah 58:11 NIV

Being Christlike

"Whoever claims to live in Him must walk as Jesus did."
1 John 2:6 NIV

Does your life resemble Christ's life?

"Clothe yourselves with the Lord Jesus Christ, and do not think about how to gratify the desires of the sinful nature."
Romans 13:14 NIV

How will you clothe yourself with Christ today?

Rejoicing with Others

date:

It can be hard when you've wanted something for so long only to see a friend receive the blessing instead of you. Maybe it's a new house, a promotion, or a position of leadership in the church. Even worse, it might be when your friends get married and you're still single or have babies and you're still barren.

Your thoughts and emotions naturally become confused. You love your friend, but why is God choosing to bless her and not you? As difficult as it may be at times, God asks us to rejoice with those who rejoice—without being jealous or bitter. God desires us to trust Him even when we don't understand. When we are confident in His perfect plan for our lives, we will want the best for our friends as well. I have experienced the pain from both perspectives. But I also know the joy and peace that comes when you are able to trust God and rejoice in His goodness—even when it's not happening to you!

When something good happens in our lives, we want a friend who can truly feel glad with us. Let's choose to be that kind of friend. —Karla Dornacher, *The Blessing of Friendship: A Gift from the Heart*

Do you rejoice in God's goodness to others as well as to yourself?

"Rejoice with those who rejoice; mourn with those who mourn."
Romans 12:15 NIV

An Inviting Atmosphere

The family room is the focal point of the home, the gathering place where all are welcome. Here lives are shared and memories are made. This is the room known for its warmth, filled to overflowing with love, joy, and laughter. Whether we're playing games, singing songs, reading stories, or watching videos, this is where the family gathers and friends are welcome.

This is also the room that invites a party! Birthdays. Anniversaries. Holidays. A lost tooth or a new found friend! Find reasons to celebrate! Turn the ordinary into extraordinary!

Although a hearth is inviting, the true warmth of a home is created with open arms and loving kindness.

Make time to enjoy old family traditions and even create some new ones. The memories you establish now will refresh the hearts of future generations. Let their hearts recall times of reflecting on God's goodness, reading Bible stories, singing praises, and sharing together in the joy of the Lord. —Karla Dornacher, *Love in Every Room*

Is your home an inviting place where people can sense the Lord's presence?

date:

"Above all, love each other deeply. . . ."
1 Peter 4:8 NIV

YOUR KINDNESS MATTERED

date:

When Clara's school took 100 sixth-grade students to Washington, D. C., she went along as a sponsor. The last day as they toured the national aquarium, Brittney, a new student whom Clara knew only slightly, collapsed. Brittney felt alone and scared when she woke up in the ambulance, without her parents or anyone she knew. But soon after arriving at a hospital emergency room, she saw Clara peek through the door into the room. Instead of going on with the group to lunch and more sightseeing, Clara had taken time to find Brittney at the hospital. Later Brittney said, "I'd never been in an emergency like that before. Your kindness mattered. You held my hand. You prayed with me. It was powerful. You were like my grandmother. I remember the peace I felt when you said, 'If we have to stay a few days longer while the other students return home, I'll stay with you because I'm your friend. I'm here for you.' " —Cheri Fuller, *The Fragrance of Kindness*

Will you go the extra mile to show kindness to someone today?

"An anxious heart weighs a man down, but a kind word cheers him up."
PROVERBS 12:25 NIV

Too Busy Doing

We human beings have a spirit—a central core that connects us to truth beyond ourselves. God's Spirit, Romans 8:16 tells us, "bear[s] witness with our spirit that we are children of God." As humans with free will, we can choose whether or not we will allow our spirits to be empowered by the Spirit of Christ, but whether we do or not, we still have a spirit that governs our lives.

date: ....

Ironically, a lot of people who would never identify themselves as Christians seem to be more in touch with that inner self than we are. Many of them find a center of peace and tranquility that sustains them. We may not agree with their motives or their conclusions, but we have to admit that they've found *something* that brings them joy and strength.

How much more should we, whose spirits are linked to the Spirit of the Almighty, find that inner place of peace? How much more should we be aware of the very marrow of our beings, the key to who we are and how we relate to God and others?

Unfortunately, we don't always take the time or effort to explore the inner self. We're too busy *doing* to think very much about *becoming*.

Still, if we're honest with ourselves, we have to face the truth that becoming is important to God. Do you want the reflection of the Lord to shine from your life? Do you want to see the image of Christ developed more fully within you? Then look to Jesus, who was in touch with that inner self. Jesus, according to John 13:3, knew who he was, where he had come from, and where he was going. And that knowledge enabled him to wash feet, to serve, to live as an example of a gentle and quiet spirit. —Penelope J. Stokes, *Beside a Quiet Stream: Words of Hope for Weary Hearts*

Have you developed or identified your inner self?

"It should be that of your inner self, the unfading beauty of a gentle and quiet spirit, which is of great worth in God's sight."
1 Peter 3:4 NIV

Somebody Needs Help

date:

I had come to cut the ribbon on Joni And Friends Ministries' Wheels for the World restoration center where prisoners refurbish used wheelchairs for our teams to deliver overseas to disabled children and adults. The inmates had seen our video of disabled children who lived on straw mats or in wheelbarrows. Each child was given a new set of wheels—wheelchairs refurbished by these prisoners.

I flashed a smile at four inmates who stood proudly by their workbenches, polishing chrome and screwing on new leather backing to chair-frames.

"Uh, mind if I ask you to do a bit of detail work on these leg rests of mine?" I asked as I gestured toward the chipped paint on the legs of my chair. I could have had the wheelchair repair service back home spruce up my wheels, but I needed a bridge to these inmates.

"I'll have it done in 30 minutes," said Jorge. With that, he began sanding my leg rests and preparing the paint.

I watched for a moment, and then asked, "Why are you doing this?" He gave me a funny look. "No, I mean this," I gestured toward the wooden shelves, racks of tools, and wheelchairs waiting to be worked on.

"Because somebody needs help," he said simply. "It makes me feel good to do something that's gonna help somebody. Like those kids in that video."

I left the prison that day with a fresh resolve to "do something that's gonna help somebody." I can do something useful. I have something to share with someone in need, and you do, too! —Joni Eareckson Tada, *Holiness in Hidden Places*

What could you share with someone in need?

"He who has been stealing must steal no longer, but must work, doing something useful with his own hands, that he may have something to share with those in need."

Ephesians 4:28 NIV

KNOWING GOD'S WILL

"This is the confidence we have in approaching God; that if we ask anything according to His will, He hears us."
1 JOHN 5:14 NIV

Do you have this confidence when you approach God?

"It is better, if it is God's will, to suffer for doing good than for doing evil."
1 PETER 3:17 NIV

Do you consider God's will best even if it includes suffering?

The Power of Praise

date:

He was a poor wretch of a little boy who didn't seem to have a chance. His dad was in debtor's prison, he'd only gotten to go to school for four years, and he was often hungry. As a young man he went to work in a rat-infested warehouse putting labels on bottles. He found lodging in a drafty attic room with two other boys from the slums of London.

But he wanted to write. He mailed his first manuscript in the middle of the night so no one would laugh at him, and story after story came back to him, rejected. Finally, when his first story got accepted, he was paid nothing. But the editor praised his work. The young man was so overjoyed he wept. That one bit of encouragement changed his whole life. He wrote with even greater desire and enthusiasm.

Without that editor's few words of praise the young man might have stayed in the dark factories, and the world would have been much poorer for lack of his writing. The boy's name was Charles Dickens. —Cheri Fuller, *The Fragrance of Kindness*

Who could you give some encouraging words to today?

"But encourage one another daily. . . ."
HEBREWS 3:13 NIV

Flexibility

Luke's Gospel tells the story of a religious man's encounter with the Messiah—a man named Jairus, a ruler of the synagogue. Jairus's 12-year-old daughter was dying, and he came to the Master to ask for help. But as Jesus was on his way to Jairus's house to heal the little girl, he was delayed by a woman. The poor woman had been hemorrhaging for 12 years.

date:

If I had been Jairus, seeking Christ for the life of my child, I probably would have fought for my place in line. But the Gospel gives no indication of impatience from Jairus, or from Jesus either, for that matter. Christ was flexible—willing to delay his mission in order to offer grace and love to a woman who needed him. And Jairus, too, demonstrated a remarkable level of compliance—waiting, trusting, even when his servants came to tell him that because of the delay, his little girl was dead.

Sometimes we need to bend. We need to let go of our preconceived notions of what we believe and how God is supposed to work in our lives. We need to open ourselves to the possibility that delay, too, might be part of God's plan, that the Lord is not bound by our time restrictions or our self-imposed limitations.

Jairus's daughter died. But then—an even more astounding miracle than the promised healing—Jesus brought her back to life again!

When our dreams die, when storms threaten to shatter our resolve, when our faith wavers in the face of unanticipated difficulty, we needn't panic. Flexibility, too, is a virtue, a reflection of the nature of God being formed in us.

You can't stop the wind from blowing. But you can let the Lord teach you how to bend. —Penelope J. Stokes, *Simple Words of Wisdom: 52 Virtues for Every Woman*

In what areas will you let the Lord teach you to bend?

"Be joyful in hope, patient in affliction, faithful in prayer."
Romans 12:12 NIV

There Are No Mistakes in Art

date:

"There's no such thing as a mistake in drawing," Melissa's elementary art teacher told the class. "So don't try to erase all your blunders. Every squiggly line, every misplaced circle, or splotch of color can be made into something creative and new." Then with a few skillful strokes of her paintbrush, she showed the kids how to change what looked like a messed-up painting into a work of art.

Since then, there have been lots of botched and squiggled canvases in Melissa's life: mistakes and messes of her own making or hurtful things she's experienced because of the mistakes of others. Sometimes she's tempted to sink into regret and think, *If only I could erase that, if only it hadn't happened, my life would be so much better.*

But in those times, she hears God whisper that although He doesn't erase history, He can use even our mistakes and the mistakes of others to create something beautiful—if we bring all the squiggled lines and broken pieces of our lives to Him, admit our mistakes, and ask Him for His help.

If an earthly artist can save a botched drawing and turn it into something lovely, how much more can God's love and power redeem every mistake in our lives. Hurts and losses become bridges for us to reach out and comfort others. Dreams that died are brought to new life. Weaknesses become blessings because they draw us closer to Him.

Can God create beauty out of mistakes? He specializes in that kind of art! —Cheri Fuller, *Quiet Whispers from God's Heart for Women*

What "botched drawing" do you need to ask God to help you salvage?

"Therefore, if anyone is in Christ, he is a new creation; the old has gone, the new has come!"
2 Corinthians 5:17 NIV

Focus on the Son

hen we hung our first bird feeder on the fence, I didn't stop to consider that the birds would help me plant the flowerbeds below. I had carefully planted these beds myself in a soft pallette of whites, pinks, and purples. So I cringed when I saw the little sunflower seedlings popping up everywhere!

date:

Though uninvited, I did not have the heart to pull them out. Later, I was so glad I had let them grow, because they added a wonderful whimsy to our garden.

As they grew, they seemed to be reaching with outstretched arms to the heavens. Their cheerful faces greeted the morning sun with a smile, and their uplifted heads followed its path of light throughout the day.

Oh, that we would do the same. Let's greet the Son in the morning with a smile and keep our eyes focused on Him every moment of the day. —Karla Dornacher, *Down a Garden Path To Places of Love and Joy*

How do you greet the Son, Jesus Christ, each morning? Are you focused on Him throughout your day? If not, what are you focusing on?

"Let the light of your face shine upon us, O Lord."
PSALM 4:6 NIV

The Greatest Gift Giver

date:

God is the greatest gift giver of all! He gives us food to eat and water to drink and offers us unconditional love, comfort, encouragement, and wisdom. Most of all, He gives us the gift of eternal life through His only Son, Jesus Christ.

Have you accepted God's gift of salvation? Have you received any encouragement from His Word? Have you found any peace or comfort or joy in His love?

The Bible says a generous person will prosper and be blessed! If you desire friendships that will bless your life, then be a friend who gives herself away generously!

Be willing to listen when your friend is burdened. Offer to make meals or clean the house for a friend in need. Write notes of encouragment to a working friend who needs a lift. Babysit for a friend so she can use the free time as she chooses. Send a handmade gift or craft as an anonymous gift of blessing. Take her flowers for absolutely no reason at all! And the list goes on. Whatever you give, give it generously as unto the Lord, and give it with a smile!

—Karla Dornacher, *The Blessing of Friendship: A Gift from the Heart*

What gift could you give someone today?

"God loves a cheerful giver."
2 CORINTHIANS 9:7 NIV

Discipline

"No discipline seems pleasant at the time, but painful. Later on, however, it produces a harvest of righteousness and peace for those who have been trained by it."
HEBREWS 12:11 NIV

How have you been trained by discipline?

"Whoever loves discipline loves knowledge, but he who hates correction is stupid."
PROVERBS 12:1 NIV

Do you allow others, and God, to correct you when you're wrong?

FRIENDSHIP

date:

The movie *Beaches* wasn't billed as a love story. C. C. Bloom and Hillary meet as preteens and see each other through three decades of turmoil. Through it all, the two forge an unlikely friendship that stabilizes them and gives them hope. At the end, as Hillary is dying, she is tempted to give up. Finally C. C. decides to stop coddling her, and tells her, "You're not dead yet. But you might as well be, the way you're acting." Hillary rises to the challenge, rallies, and is able to spend her last days close to the people she loves most—thanks to the honesty and faithfulness of her friend.

But *Beaches* is a love story. The kind of love that perseveres despite terrible odds; the kind of love that speaks truth even when it hurts. In our society, we don't call it love. We call it friendship. A friend is one who knows the truth about you, the whole truth, and still loves you.

Jesus said that there was no greater love than the kind of friendship that would lay down its life for a friend. And perhaps there is no greater virtue for a woman or man to possess than the ability to be a true friend. Friendship is an undervalued relationship in modern society. We have lots of acquaintances—people we socialize with, work with, invite to dinner, greet warmly on Sunday morning. But how many of them are true friends?

True friends are rare, and if we recognize their worth, we will cultivate those relationships with honesty and openness, with encouragement, affirmation, and acceptance. We will value them and give them priority in our lives. We will be there for them and allow them to be there for us as well.

Friendship mirrors the love God has for us, calling us not servants but "friends." —Penelope J. Stokes, *Simple Words of Wisdom: 52 Virtues for Every Woman*

Are you a good friend?

"Greater love has no one than this, that he lay down his life for his friends."
JOHN 15:13 NIV

The Gift of Time

Since love is spelled T-I-M-E, giving the gift of time is perhaps one of the kindest gifts of all. When a mom spends uninterrupted time snuggling with her child and reading a book or a teacher listens to her student, love fills the heart of the child. When a wife puts down her work to welcome her husband with a big hug as he comes in the door, he's encouraged and affirmed. When friends meet for lunch and hear what's going on in each other's lives, their hearts are refreshed. When we set aside time to volunteer, visit a shut-in, or offer hospitality to a new family on the block, the angels must surely applaud our encouragement-in-action! In this hurry-up world where time is measured in nanoseconds, making time for people is a challenge—but it's worth the effort. Giving a pocketful of time always encourages, lifts up the heart, and renews the spirit. And in the process of blessing others, we find ourselves refreshed. —Cheri Fuller, *The Fragrance of Kindness*

How could you spend time with someone to show them love?

date:

"Each of you should look not only to your own interests, but also to the interests of others."
PHILIPPIANS 2:4 NIV

Living with Purpose

date:

If we truly want to reflect the image of God in our personal lives and our relationships with others, we have to be clear about our purpose. Discovering what God has called us to will shape who we become and what we do with our lives.

But sometimes we get confused about the Lord's calling. We look around for a burning bush telling us to set the captives free; we wait through a long night of prayer expecting to hear the voice of God sending us to be a missionary or to preach the gospel in the inner city.

Yet what we do, as important as it may be, is secondary to our larger purpose for living. Romans 8:28–29 tells us: "those who love God . . . are called according to his purpose . . . to be conformed to the image of his Son." This is the higher calling and purpose of God—to be conformed to the likeness of Christ. To allow the Holy Spirit to work in us to purify and clarify the Divine Image that was imprinted upon human life at creation. Whatever we do grows out of that image, a response to the transforming power of God within us.

At the most fundamental level, Jesus was a person who lived in communion with God. A person who gave priority to internal matters like forgiveness and love and acceptance and self-awareness. The things he *did*—feeding the hungry, healing the sick, forgiving sin, defending the disenfranchised, speaking the truth—reflected character traits of love, justice, honesty, peace, and a mind in sync with God.

Jesus knew what mattered. He lived with purpose—and you can, too.

Look first to your purpose for living, and everything else will fall into place. —Penelope J. Stokes, *Beside a Quiet Stream: Words of Hope for Weary Hearts*

What is your purpose for living?

"And we know that in all things God works for the good of those who love him, who have been called according to his purpose."
ROMANS 8:28 NIV

A Love Affair in the Night

I will forever hold close to my heart an encounter I had with the night sky and the Comet of 1996. That's when the Hyakutake Comet whizzed by Earth and lit up the bottom half of the Big Dipper for six glorious nights.

date:

The moon made a thin smile on the horizon, and the stars were dusted like powdered sugar on black velvet. In the cold desert air, everything was crisp and clear. No haze, no city lights, no smog, and definitely no noise. Just the wispy sound of air moving through the pine trees—no, I take that back, we did catch the hooting of a couple of owls.

The heavy silence of the desert made the sparkling night sky all the more dramatic. How could something so big be so quiet? And there, after our eyes adjusted to the dark, just below the Big Dipper, was the comet. A fuzzy ball of light 9.5 million miles away.

And could it be? Yes, it was! After almost 30 minutes we saw the long, thin tail of the comet—cutting like a laser through the Big Dipper and touching the edge of a distant constellation.

The Hyakatuke Comet won't pass by again for another 10 millenia. It was a once-in-a-lifetime event. Little wonder as Ken and I got ready for bed, we found ourselves humming, "Sun, moon, and stars in their courses above, join with all nature in manifold witness, to God's great faithfulness, mercy and love."

Try it tonight. Go outside and look for your moon shadow. Take a star chart and spot a few constellations. Read Psalm 8:3 and pray. It's a great way to start a love affair with the sky.

—Joni Eareckson Tada, *Holiness in Hidden Places*

How do you see God's glory in nature?

"When I consider your heavens, the work of your fingers, the moon and the stars, which you have set in place, what is man that you are mindful of him? . . ."

Psalm 8:3 NIV

Complete Surrender

date:

Following her release from a German concentration camp at the end of World War II, Corrie ten Boom began traveling around the world to share a message of God's love and faithfulness in spite of the horrors of the war. Corrie's busy schedule of speaking engagements and meetings was exhausting. Many times she felt overwhelmed with ministry obligations. There was so much to be done, and she was elderly. She wasn't as strong as she'd been years before. She felt weighed down with responsibility.

Feeling especially burdened one afternoon, she poured out her heart to God, sharing her frustrations, worries, and concerns. Quietly, through the middle of her desperate pleas, He whispered, *"Corrie, have you surrendered completely to Me?"*

"Of course," she answered, "I have surrendered myself 100 percent to You."

"Then you don't possess anything anymore, Corrie." He reminded her. *"You are only a steward of what I give you. You aren't responsible for all of this, I am. Obey Me and follow Me, and I will be your victory, your strength, your all."* Corrie understood what God meant. His words carried her thoughts back to the concentration camp, where she had owned nothing but the clothes on her back—where she had no responsibility, where she was totally dependent on His care. That had not been her choice, of course; it wasn't a voluntary surrender. But God was reminding her now of a different surrender, a happy, blessed surrender of her life and all she had into His loving hands.

She didn't have to feel overwhelmed and burdened by responsibility. God's ability, wisdom, and love, working through her, would accomplish the work. His assurance filled her with incredible rest and peace. She smiled to herself, What a relief to depend on God's power and ability instead of my own!

—Cheri Fuller, *Quiet Whispers from God's Heart for Women*

What burden do you need to surrender to God?

"Praise be to the Lord, to God our Savior, who daily bears our burdens."
Psalm 68:19 NIV

GENEROSITY

"A generous man will prosper; he who refreshes others will himself be refreshed."
PROVERBS 11:25 NIV

Do you refresh others with your generosity?

....

....

....

....

....

....

....

....

....

"Command them to do good, to be rich in good deeds, and to be generous and willing to share. In this way they will lay up treasure for themselves as a firm foundation for the coming age, so that they may take hold of the life that is truly life."
1 TIMOTHY 6:18–19 NIV

How does generosity towards others help you lay up treasure for yourself?

....

....

....

....

....

....

....

....

....

Endurance

date:

You don't have to train for the Olympics to have the virtue of endurance. Other kinds of endurance are equally valuable, although perhaps not so publicly acclaimed: the stamina to hang in there with a rebellious teenager and help him turn his life around; the fortitude to weather a difficult storm in your marriage without giving up; the determination to finish your college degree even if you're the oldest person at graduation; the ability to hold onto your faith during a long dark night of the soul.

Whether you're expending the effort for the gold medal, your relationships, your education, or your spiritual life, the virtue of endurance is based on *love.* Love of the game. Love of your spouse or child. Love of learning. Love of God.

Athletes, who are experts in physical endurance, often talk about "pushing through the pain." You don't stop running because you're winded or exhausted or have a stitch in your side or a cramp in your calf. You keep going, knowing that somehow, at the end of the race, the pain will be worth the prize.

So it is in our spiritual lives. When adversities come, the person of endurance keeps going. When the relationship seems hopelessly bogged down in trivial matters, when the outcome just doesn't seem worth the effort, when God is silent and the night grows dark, we push beyond the pain and look ahead to the finish line. We hold on. We endure. We trust.

And we discover—perhaps not in the short run, but eventually—that God is still there, even when we do not hear the Divine Whisper in our ears. —Penelope J. Stokes, *Simple Words of Wisdom: 52 Virtues for Every Woman*

In which area of your life has God taught you endurance?

"Forgetting what is behind and straining toward what is ahead, I press on toward the goal to win the prize for which God has called me heavenward. . . ."
Philippians 3:13–14 niv

God's Provisions

Stephany was a brand-new Christian. Young and single, she enjoyed a great career working with commercial photographers. But the Monday morning after she gave her life to Christ, she walked into the studio and felt an overwhelming sense of "darkness." Now, all of a sudden, she heard God's voice. *"You need to get out of here. I'll provide something better for you."*

date: ....

His message was unmistakable. She left the job immediately, with no other prospects for work, and eventually found a position in sales for a fitness club. As the months went on, she desperately missed photography, but the only job she found was in a department store portrait studio.

In her prayer time, God spoke to her again. *"I want you to go to Mr. Graves (the vice-president of the fitness club) and ask him for money to start your own photography business."* She thought, "I must be thinking bizarre thoughts. I barely know Mr. Graves. How could I ask him for money?"

One morning soon after, the vice-president called and asked her out to breakfast. He had heard she was quitting and wanted to know why. Stephany explained that what she really wanted to do was photography. In the next breath, he offered to loan her enough money to get her business started and suggested she come by his office the next day—there might be some equipment she could use. With the equipment and the loan, she was ready to set up her business. She agreed to work for the health club another six months, so the loan was quickly paid off.

As her business grew, it was clear that God had done just what He said—provided something better, much better than she could ever have asked or dreamed. —Cheri Fuller, *Quiet Whispers from God's Heart for Women*

How has God exceeded your expectations?

"Now to Him who is able to do immeasurably more than all we ask or imagine, according to His power that is at work within us, to Him be glory in the church and in Christ Jesus throughout all generations, for ever and ever! Amen."

EPHESIANS 3:20–21 NIV

Be Still

date:

In C. S. Lewis's classic tale *The Lion, the Witch, and the Wardrobe,* the children—Peter, Susan, Edmund, and Lucy—enter through the door of a wardrobe and pass into a dense, snowbound forest, a wilderness of sorts. They don't know it quite yet, but they have entered Narnia—a magical land that ultimately becomes more real to them than their own world. In Narnia, they meet Aslan, the great Lion King, and in the process of relationship with him, discover their own inner capacities for good and evil. They grow and change, and ultimately come to rule the land in peace.

Our own solitary place with God can become a kind of "wardrobe door" for us, a portal that leads us into a new land of discovery—about God and ourselves. When we commit ourselves to times of solitude with the Lord, we cannot know what will happen, how we will change, in which directions we might grow. But we can be certain that time with God will result in something good, something beneficial for us and for those around us.

Sometimes our commitment to contemplation results in a conviction that God is calling us in new directions.

At other times, quietness before God simply results in a deeper level of personal peace and spiritual intimacy.

The problem is, we are not very adept at being quiet, at listening instead of talking. Our prayer times are often filled with requests but lacking in empty space, in silences that might, if we waited a little while, be filled with the presence and power of God.

Take a moment to listen. Be still, and you will discover that God is God. —Penelope J. Stokes, *Beside a Quiet Stream: Words of Hope for Weary Hearts*

When will you commit yourself to a time of solitude with the Lord?

"Be still, and know that I am God."
Psalm 46:10 NIV

Friendship Garden

The tending of a friendship garden is no small matter and is not to be taken lightly. Many a beautiful garden has gone to ruin for lack of proper care. Here are some tips that may prove helpful.

Prepare the soil by tilling it with God's unconditional love. Remove any rocks of judgment or critical attitudes. Pull out any roots of fear and jealousy. Destroy the seeds of gossip before they can even take root.

Seeds of friendship may be found most anywhere. Plant with care, using kind words and a listening ear. Germination is usually spontaneous, so be watchful. To ensure growth, water with kind deeds and a generous heart.

Make sure you give each friend plenty of room to grow. Be realistic—don't expect a marigold to smell like a rose. Fertilize generously with laughter and joy. Water deeply with tears of empathy and prayer to develop healthy roots and a stronger, more stable friendship.

Cultivating a friendship garden requires patience, perseverance, and time—but it's worth it! —Karla Dornacher, *The Blessing of Friendship: A Gift from the Heart*

Are you cultivating your friendships?

date: ....

"A friend loves at all times. . . ."
PROVERBS 17:17 NIV

The Spice of Life

date:

What a wonderful thing to consider that God uses your life to spread the aroma of His love to your family, neighborhood, church—even to the ends of the earth.

Think of simple kitchen symbols. The cooking pan represents your life, a mixture of your knowledge, love and personal dedication to God, stirred up with faith and heated by the fire of the Holy Spirit. And what does this delightful aroma smell like? It is the sweet and delicious smelling aroma of your ordinary life placed before God as an offering. It is an exquisite combination of kindness, tenderheartedness, forgiveness, righteousness, generosity, and good works!

In the Bible we are called the "salt of the earth," for as salt is a preservative for food, so our lives and words can have a preserving effect on the lives of others.

Sweet words are the words of life and health that we speak. Choose to lift up others with words of kindness, truth, encouragement, hope—even correction, seasoned with grace.

God has labeled your words of praise as the fruit of your lips, so be willing to give away jar after jar of peachy praise to the glory of God.

The greatest witness of God's love is a life generously given to bless the Lord and to minister to others.

Give away your life, your love, and your forgiveness, for with the same measure you use to give yourself away, blessing will be measured back to you.

—Karla Dornacher, *Love in Every Room*

Do you generously season those around you with the sweet words you speak?

"Let your conversation be always full of grace, seasoned with salt, so that you may know how to answer everyone."

COLOSSIANS 4:6 NIV

Grace

"For sin shall not be your master, because you are not under law, but under grace."
Romans 6:14 NIV

Do you live as though you're under grace?

"For it is by grace you have been saved, through faith—and this not from yourselves, it is the gift of God—not by works, so that no one can boast."
Ephesians 2:8–9 NIV

How thankful are you for God's saving grace?

Bouquets of Kindness

date:

Plant a garden of wildflowers or others flowers ideal for cutting—daisies, bachelor buttons, buttercups, hollyhocks, and corn flowers or sweetbriar. Don't just fill your own vases with blooms but grow enough to share with a friend or neighbor. Arrange any spring or summer blooms in a simple bouquet. Wrap a bright ribbon around the stems, include a gift card that says, "If God cares so wonderfully for flowers that are here today and gone tomorrow, won't He more surely care for you" (Matt. 6:30), and watch the smiles grow!

—Cheri Fuller, *The Fragrance of Kindness*

What kind gesture could you perform for someone—to demonstrate God's love for them?

"Consider how the lilies grow. . . . If that is how God clothes the grass of the field, which is here today, and tomorrow is thrown into the fire, how much more will he clothe you, O you of little faith!"
Luke 12:27–28 NIV

In the Image of God

In the modern world, we think a lot about image. About projecting the right impression to get a better job or a promotion. About presenting ourselves in the best light so that others will like us or respect us—or even fear us. Image, people say, is power.

date: ....

But for us as Christians, image is more than just wearing clothes designed to hide our flaws, finding the right hair color or the best make-up artist. Image goes to the very core of our being. For we are made in the image of Almighty God.

The story of creation tells us, "God created humankind in his image. . . ." (Gen. 1:27). What a wonderful legacy! You and I, despite our human weaknesses and frailties, bear in our deepest souls the indelible imprint of God's hand.

It should be—and can be—a truth that shapes our hearts and directs our lives. We are God's people, lovingly fashioned in the likeness of the One who called us to follow. With every step we become increasingly a reflection of the Lord who stamped us with the Divine Image.

Sometimes we forget who we are and where we are going. We focus on the failures of the past instead of the possibilities for the future. We do not travel on this journey alone.

Sit for a moment beside the quiet stream. Gaze into a still pool. The reflection you see is the face of one who has been touched by the Creator, set free by the Redeemer, empowered by the Spirit.

It is more than you. It is God within you, transforming you, working through you to reach the world with grace.

—Penelope J. Stokes, *Beside a Quiet Stream: Words of Hope for Weary Hearts*

What is your "image"? How is God transforming you into His likeness?

"So God created man in his own image, in the image of God he created him; male and female he created them."
GENESIS 1:27 NIV

A Quiet Witness

date:

"What's my purpose?" Not many people say it out loud, but lots of us think it. Sometimes the purpose is hard to pin down in this culture. Everything's so external. Disposable. Even people who seem to have no purpose in living.

Case in point—Cody. He was born totally paralyzed and unable to speak. He is deaf and blind. He needs a ventilator in order to breathe and a feeding tube in order to eat. All this baggage attached to a little 17-month-old boy.

I met Cody at one of our recent Joni And Friends Ministries' Family Retreats. I prayed silently, asking God to comfort and console Cody, to speak, "not in words taught us by human wisdom but in words taught by the Spirit" (1 Cor. 2:13).

I thought of those who would say, "His life has no meaning, no purpose." But 2 Corinthians 5:16 warns us to "regard no one from a worldly point of view." Elsewhere we are reminded that "inwardly we are being renewed day by day. So we fix our eyes not on what is seen, but on what is unseen" (2 Cor. 4:16-18).

God's Word is as true for Cody as it is for anyone. The Spirit expresses truth to him—not in audible words, but in spiritual words. Inwardly he is being renewed. His value is "not on what is seen, but on what is unseen."

The Spirit is active and powerful, and although we can't see the spiritual activity happening in Cody's life, it's there. And spiritual activity gives life value, no matter how humble a person's situation. Cody isn't doing much more than being. But God is an intentional God with motive and mission. His design for that little boy is to simply live, breathe, and encourage others. It's enough to give life meaning and purpose.

—Joni Eareckson Tada, *Holiness in Hidden Places*

Do you see life value in every person?

"For who among men knows the thoughts of a man except the man's spirit within him?"
1 CORINTHIANS 2:11 NIV

The Power of Playing

A few years ago when my 18-year-old daughter came home from a weekend visit with my mother, I asked what they'd done.

"Tried on wedding dresses," she said as if that were the most common pastime for 18-year-olds and their grandmothers. With a little probing, I discovered that her cousin Leanne had spent the weekend also, and they had talked their grandmother into driving them all around the Dallas-Fort Worth metroplex just to try on dresses and dream.

The older my mother gets, the more she plays. She plays "Battleship" with Courtney and "I-Spy" with Mason. Her 8-year-old and 10-year-old granddaughters are usually up for movies and pizza. She keeps a cache of dress-up clothes and old jewelry in the hall closet for drama demands. A few months back, she accompanied her 20-year-old grandson to shop for a new computer.

Even as adults, few things gain higher priority than play with those you love. Play patches hearts together for eternity. —Dianna Booher, *Mother's Gifts to Me*

How has playing with those you love brought your hearts closer together?

date:

"Is anyone happy? Let him sing songs of praise."
James 5:13 NIV

PURITY

date:

The Boy in the Plastic Bubble is the story of a young man who, because of a rare disorder in his immune system, is forced to live his entire life cut off from the world. His plastic bubble, free from germs, protects him. He is protected, but he is also imprisoned.

When religious people talk about purity, they leave their listeners with the impression that the Lord's followers are *The Christians In the Plastic Bubble*. Wanting to be unstained and uninfluenced by the world, we cut ourselves off, fearing contact with those "on the outside." We send our kids to Christian schools. We socialize exclusively with other Christians. We play the Christian "Trivial Pursuit."

But purity, according to biblical standards, is not based on externals. Jesus claims, contrary to Jewish tradition, that it is not what goes *into* people that defiles them, but what comes *out* of them (Matt.15:17-19).

Why are we so afraid of contaminating ourselves? Jesus wasn't. He rubbed shoulders with the sinful masses, welcomed lepers, had dinner parties with prostitutes and tax collectors, and ate with "unclean hands."

We don't purify our minds and souls by imprisoning ourselves in a bubble of righteousness and refusing to be desecrated by the world around us.

Love makes us pure. Love creates in us a habit of Christlikeness and a willingness to risk. Love gives us the vision to see Jesus in those around us, and the compassion to get involved. Love frees us from the fear of spiritual infection and strengthens our soul's immune system.

Jesus is the only fortress you will ever need.

—Penelope J. Stokes, *Simple Words of Wisdom: 52 Virtues for Every Woman.*

How can you reach out to those on the outside of your Christian "bubble"?

"To the pure, all things are pure, but to those who are corrupted and do not believe, nothing is pure."
TITUS 1:15 NIV

Self-Control

"For the grace of God that brings salvation has appeared to all men. It teaches us to say 'No' to ungodliness and worldly passions, and to live self-controlled, upright and godly lives in this present age."

Titus 2:11–12 NIV

How do you resist the ungodly passions you face each day?

"The end of all things is near. Therefore be clear minded and self-controlled so that you can pray."

1 Peter 4:7 NIV

Why is it important to be clear minded and self-controlled while you pray?

God's Perspective

date:

Caylon's husband, Bob, lay in the hospital because of internal bleeding. The doctor gave them the diagnosis: ulcerative colitis. "Colitis is often triggered by stress," he said. "I don't know what stressors you have in your life, but you need to eliminate them."

Caylon began to lecture Bob about what she thought should be done. "The cows, chickens, pig, and other animals are just pets that have to be taken care of. They've got to go!" She was sure the animals were the source of Bob's stress.

She continued, "They do nothing but sap your energy when you've already put in a full day of work."

Too weak to argue, Bob responded, "Okay, whatever."

Caylon was sure he would get rid of the animals, and she became frustrated when he didn't. One day she walked past the bay window and spotted Bob surrounded by a menagerie of animals eating out of his hand. God froze the scene before her and whispered, *"Does that look stressful?"*

Caylon saw her husband through God's eyes—this was how Bob enjoyed unwinding after a hard day of work. No, the animals weren't the stress in his life—perhaps her attitude was. Caylon realized that she had been drawing conclusions based on her perspective rather than God's. But God saw Bob's heart and had provided what satisfied him.

With her heart and eyes open, Caylon began to ask God for His perspective on other matters about her husband and found her marriage slowly transformed.

God speaks to us through His creation. Through nature, through song. He reaches one person one way, and another in other ways. He reached Caylon through some chickens and a cow. —Cheri Fuller, *Quiet Whispers from God's Heart for Women*

What circumstances are you viewing from your own perspective rather than God's?

"A fool finds no pleasure in understanding but delights in airing his own opinions."
Proverbs 18:2 NIV

From Caterpillar to Butterfly

Butterflies are delightful reminders of the power of God's love to transform our lives. Watching a butterfly dance in the air, it is hard to believe that it was once a common caterpillar.

Within the protective covering of the chrysalis, the lowly earthbound caterpillar is slowly transformed into a remarkable creature of freedom and beauty.

A similar process of transformation takes place in our lives as we allow God's Holy Spirit to soften our hearts and change our pattern of thinking. Only God's love and truth can bring genuine freedom and beauty into our lives by changing us from the inside out.

As you live in obedience to God's Word each day, your life will be transformed—you will become more and more like Jesus. —Karla Dornacher, *Down a Garden Path To Places of Love and Joy.*

In what ways has God's Holy Spirit transformed you from the inside out?

date: ....

"The Lord Jesus Christ, who, by the power that enables him to bring everything under his control, will transform our lowly bodies so that they will be like his glorious body."
PHILIPPIANS 3:21 NIV

Cocreators with God

date:

When a baby is born, there is, perhaps, a little window of time when God has everybody's attention. It is important, then, for us all to stop things down and gather to consider what is going on here. All through the Bible, God forbids us to usurp His position by "playing God," but there is one exception. He has made it possible for two human beings to come together in love, to be joined as one flesh and, at that moment, to become cocreators with God of an eternal soul. No wonder such strict religious laws govern our sexual behavior and permit intercourse only in the confines of a faithful marriage union. Something so eternal must be considered sacred and protected against desecration.

But whether human beings have played by the rules or not, there is something holy about a baby. Birth is one of the most sacred passages human beings can experience. So sacred that Jesus Himself used it as a metaphor for the experience of coming to know God—the birth of our spirits—the "second birth."

No baby should come into this world without someone making a moment. This entrance is sacred. All of us who accept the responsibility for handling this new creation should give our blessing to this child, so full of potential. And we should sanctify ourselves as we commit long-term to this new, eternal soul entrusted to our care.

—Gloria Gaither, *Bless This Child*

How do you nurture the "eternal souls" entrusted to your care?

"Sons are a heritage from the Lord, children a reward from Him. Like arrows in the hands of a warrior are sons born in one's youth. Blessed is the man whose quiver is full of them."
Psalm 127:3–5 NIV

The Exhausted Spirit

It's true. Jesus didn't directly command us to "love ourselves." But inherent in the second of the "greatest commandments" is the implication that we as human beings do love ourselves, and that as an extension of our love for God and ourselves, we are called to love and care for others.

date:

Sometimes we interpret "loving others" as denying our own needs and being enslaved to the expectations of those around us. We teach our children to sing, "J-O-Y—Jesus, then others, then you—what a wonderful way to spell J-O-Y."

Not always. Sometimes putting yourself last spells frustration, depression, fatigue.

But we're afraid of being perceived as selfish. So, we work hard, trying to prove our selflessness and to demonstrate our commitment to God. But our *work* doesn't always result in joy. We get worn out and resentful.

We make a grave mistake when we assume that what we *do* can substitute for who we *are*. Sometimes our Christian activity is less a reflection of love for God than love for the praise of others.

We need to remind ourselves that we are loved just as we are. Christ, who died for us when we had done nothing to deserve such a sacrifice, lives within us according to the same standard.

If we don't take time and space for ourselves, to nurture our personal relationship with God, our "works of love" become "dead works," motivated by fear or the need for performance rather than by love for God or for our neighbor.

It's not a sin to care for your own soul. It's a spiritual prerequisite for a deep relationship with God.

—Penelope J. Stokes, *Beside a Quiet Stream: Words of Hope for Weary Hearts*

What motivates your sacrifices and love for others?

"We love because he first loved us."
1 John 4:19 NIV

Gratitude

date:

Gratitude is a virtue we would do well to nurture. Life, after all, doesn't owe us happiness or contentment or personal fulfillment. These are not the *source* of gratitude, but its *results*. We become happy, spiritually prosperous people not because we receive what we want, but because we appreciate what we have.

What does it mean to cultivate a heart of gratitude? It means looking at the blessings that fill our lives. It means recognizing our family and friends, as aqueducts through which God's great love flows out to us. It means rejoicing in all we've been given rather than resenting what we lack.

"God's divine power," Peter reminds us, "has given us everything we need for life and godliness" (2 Pet. 1:3). We have only to keep our hearts and eyes open, and we will be overwhelmed with the multitude of God's blessings.

But gratitude doesn't end with our private thanks to God. We need to show gratitude as well to those who touch our lives, who love us, minister to us, and make the world we live in a warmer, safer, kinder place.

As we express our gratefulness to the people who have given themselves to us, we minister to them and honor them for their faithfulness to God. But we also minister to ourselves. Gratitude tenderizes our hearts and makes us quicker to see and appreciate the daily gifts that come our way.

It's easy to take the gifts of life for granted, to accept them casually, as if we deserved God's generosity. But when we get a glimpse—just the tiniest glimmer—of the blessings that have been bestowed upon us, our hearts will overflow with gratitude, and our joy and contentment will spill over to those around us. —Penelope J. Stokes, *Simple Words of Wisdom: 52 Virtues for Every Woman*

How can you thank God and others for the blessings in your life?

"And be thankful. Let the word of Christ dwell in you richly as you teach and admonish one another with all wisdom, and as you sing psalms, hymns and spiritual songs with gratitude in your hearts to God."
Colossians 3:15–16 NIV

Sharing with Others

"And do not forget to do good and to share with others, for such sacrifices God is pleased."
Hebrews 13:16 niv

How do you sacrifice to give others what they need?

"We who are strong ought to bear with the failings of the weak and not to please ourselves."
Romans 15:1 niv

When have you helped to bear someone's failure or difficult circumstance? When has someone shared with you during a time of need in your life?

ACCOUNTABILITY AND COUNTING

date:

I never had a curfew. Mother saw curfews as permissive. She preferred accountability. When I left the house with a new boy for a new activity, the conversation always began, "What time will you be home?"

"I don't know," I would respond.

"Well, let's figure it out," she'd say. "What time does the movie start? Then how long will it take you to drive to Jamie's party?" and so on we reasoned until we came to the same reasonable conclusion, given the night's agenda.

When I was tempted to deviate from the plan, I knew I faced questions that would not stop until she had the full picture.

Being fully accountable was restricting at the time, yet liberating for a lifetime of decisions. —Dianna Booher, *Mother's Gifts to Me*

How has accountability for your actions—whether as a child or as an adult—benefited you in the long run? What means does God use to hold you accountable?

"So then, each of us will give an account of himself to God."
ROMANS 14:12 NIV

Encouraging Words Give Confidence

Maya walked down the San Francisco hill to take a streetcar to the train station, where she would begin her journey home across the country. Her mother, whom she'd been visiting, accompanied her to the trolley stop.

date:

At 20 years old, Maya was struggling to find her way in life but kept running into obstacles and trials. For the past several days, mother and daughter had enjoyed a cherished visit, but now it was time for Maya to return to the fray of everyday life. After kissing her goodbye, Maya's mother said, "You know, baby, I think you're the greatest woman I've ever met."

Her mom turned and slowly made her way up the hill. Maya stood alone, waiting for the streetcar. Suppose Mom's right, she thought to herself. Suppose I really am somebody. It was a turning point, one of those incredible moments when the heavens roll back and the earth seems to hold its breath. It filled her heart with confidence and hope.

Maya Angelou eventually became a best-selling poet and novelist. She delivered her most famous poem at President Clinton's inauguration.

—Cheri Fuller, *The Fragrance of Kindness*

How have encouraging words from someone given you renewed confidence? Who can you encourage today?

"I have great confidence in you; I take great pride in you. I am greatly encouraged; in all our troubles my joy knows no bounds."
2 Corinthians 7:4 NIV

SAIL ON!

date: ....

Catherine and John live across Puget Sound from Seattle. John, a retired Navy officer, loves to go sailing. Catherine is a little nervous about getting into the sailboat unless the wind is calm. The problem is, calm winds make sailing very dull.

In our spiritual lives, too, we don't get anywhere without taking a bit of a risk. We need a bit of wind and a few waves to move us toward our destination.

We want to grow, to change, to be challenged in our faith, but when the challenges become a bit more dangerous than we had counted on, our courage fails us. We cry out for calm waters and still winds.

The Lord calls us to stretch our souls, to reach a little further than we have before, to go the distance, to square our sails and tack into the wind.

We fuss and argue and try to go our own way. But when we finally relent, when we come through the test, we discover that we are stronger than we thought we were. We no longer need to hang onto our preconceived notions of who the Lord is and what the Spirit might call us to do. We've gone through the wind and waves and come out changed.

The waters are not always calm, but God is in control. And when we trust that truth, we find ourselves brought to a new place, a place that strengthens our hearts, nurtures our souls, and feeds our faith.

So don't panic when the winds kick up and waves grow strong. Hoist your sail, prepare for adventure. The One who created, redeemed, and loves you is at the helm. Sail on!

—Penelope J. Stokes, *Beside a Quiet Stream: Words of Hope for Weary Hearts*

What circumstance in your life right now requires much courage—the squaring of your sail?

"Be strong and courageous. Do not be terrified; do not be discouraged, for the Lord your God will be with you wherever you go."
JOSHUA 1:9 NIV

Self-Awareness

Most of us have a secret garden inside, a neglected, walled-off part of our souls. Maybe we've just spent too much of our time and energy making a living, raising children, caring for infirm parents, or acquiring the external trappings of the good life. Maybe we're a little afraid to find out what's inside.

date:

But God makes it very clear that the important stuff is inside of us, not on the outside. Jesus said, "The kingdom of God is within you" (Luke 17:21).

We might expect Christ's words to be addressed to the disciples, those who already believed and followed faithfully. Yet he was speaking to the Pharisees—those religious leaders who were convinced that access to the kingdom of God lay in adherence to regulation and laws. "Look to your heart," Jesus was saying, "not to your rules."

But we're suspicious of our hearts. It's easier to follow regulations than to listen for the still small voice inside. It's more comfortable to keep to the well-worn paths, rather than take the risk of opening the secret garden and cutting away the dead branches.

Self-awareness is a scary prospect. We are likely to find dark places where the sunlight of God's renewing love has never penetrated. We may dig up hidden motivations we don't want to admit, shadowed corners of selfishness and greed, tangled branches of deceit—secrets we'd like to keep locked away. But we'll also uncover fragrant roses about to bud, long-buried bulbs pushing their blooms toward the light.

The Lord already knows the state of our inner garden. There is no risk of losing God's love. The transformation may be painful at first, but the miracle is worth it.

—Penelope J. Stokes, *Simple Words of Wisdom: 52 Virtues for Every Woman*

What might you find if you uncovered the innermost part of your soul?

"The kingdom of God does not come with your careful observation, nor will people say, 'Here it is,' or 'There it is,' because the kingdom of God is within you."
Luke 17:20–21 NIV

A Lesson from the Trees

date:

After the birth of her daughter, Lynn felt God leading her to leave a 20-year career. She fretted over this wrenching decision, clinging desperately to a respectable income, friends, and lots of recognition. Lynn worried that she would sink into depression in the isolation of her home, deprived of interaction with colleagues and meaningful work.

Patiently, God began to pry loose her grip. One weekend as she walked in the autumn woods, she watched the colorful leaves cling to branches, struggling to hold on. With each gust of wind, as if by God's command, they simply let go. They pirouetted with abandon in the breeze.

At that moment God whispered, *"Lynn, let go!"*

She gave her employer notice and committed to enter whatever "dance" God was choreographing for her.

Soon, depression, doubt, and loneliness ensued as she struggled to adjust to life without her career. Yet again God spoke to her through nature. Like a winter tree, she was stripped of the lush foliage of professional purpose and friendships. Though the winter tree looks dead, it is alive; the leaves are gone but life remains in the roots. Likewise, as she rooted herself in God's Word, her life would be fruitful.

Trees don't fret. They bloom in season, and in times of barrenness raise their leafless limbs in praise to their Maker. Stripped of foliage, they behold the stars shining like brilliant jewels between their branches.

Lynn took a lesson from the trees. She decided to stop fretting, to look instead for the stars twinkling between the branches of her life. And each day she discovered a host of luminaries and blazing constellations of joy.

—Cheri Fuller, *Quiet Whispers from God's Heart for Women*

What do you need to let go of in your life in order to follow God's plans for you?

"Look at the birds of the air; they do not sow or reap . . . and yet your heavenly Father feeds them. Are you not much more valuable than they? Who of you by worrying can add a single hour to his life?"
MATTHEW 6:26–27 NIV

Persistence

"To those who by persistence in doing good seek glory, honor, and immortality, he will give eternal life."
Romans 2:7 NIV

What motivates you as a Christian to persist in doing good and seeking God?

"We also rejoice in our sufferings, because we know that suffering produces perseverance; perseverance, character; and character, hope."
Romans 5:3–4 NIV

How have your persistance and perseverance through sufferings produced a deeper character and hope in Christ?

A Time to Rest

date:

Sometimes my life is so busy the only thing I am able to do in my garden is work. The tasks I normally enjoy become chores and, worst of all, I do not take the time to simply rest and delight in the garden's beauty.

There is a time for tilling, a time for planting, a time for weeding, and a time for resting.

Jesus calls to us in the midst of our busyness. He invites us to spend time with Him.

Take time to be still. Lay aside your tools, your seed packets, your garden gloves, and sit with Him. Delight in His beauty and the glory of His creation.

Look into His Word and see the depth of His love for you. Be refreshed with His peace and strengthened by His promises. Let Him restore to you the joy of the simple tasks of life.

As you leave your quiet place, the world will know you have been in the presence of the Master Gardener.

—Karla Dornacher, *Down a Garden Path To Places of Love and Joy*

When was the last moment you took time away from the busyness of life to be still with God? When is a good time each day for you to seek God's presence?

"Sow for yourself righteousness, reap the fruit of unfailing love, and break up your unplowed ground; for it is time to seek the Lord, until he comes and showers righteousness on you."

Hosea 10:12 NIV

Passion

My father taught me an important lesson about having passion for life. "Never make major life decisions based solely on money," he said. "Do what you love, and love what you do."

date:

Sad to say, we live in a society that doesn't value passion as my father did. People drag themselves to work every day, hating what they do but needing to hang onto the security of the paycheck. They lead a routine existence, finding little joy even in the company of those they love most.

As Christians, however, our perspective on the ordinariness of life is radically altered by the cross, and by our participation in the work of God.

Christlike passion views everything in our lives—every action, every interaction—through the lens of God's love and grace. The smallest act of love takes on eternal significance; the greatest opportunity leaves us humbled and breathless in the presence of the Spirit's power.

My father's advice to me is good counsel for all who would serve God wholeheartedly: Follow your passion.

Does your soul weep for the homeless, the hungry, the outcast? Use your energy to work for change, to show compassion, to touch those who need to see Jesus through human love.

Ministry is not just for the preachers, the seminarians, the ordained. The Spirit calls all of us to reconcile the world to God, to give ourselves in an outpouring of love. It doesn't matter if you're a doctor, a teacher, or a stay-at-home mom—all of us can embrace the call of God with zeal and joy.

Follow your passion. It will lead you to your heart's true home. —Penelope J. Stokes, *Simple Words of Wisdom: 52 Virtues for Every Woman*

What is your passion in life? How can you follow your passion?

"Whatever you do, work at it with all your heart, as working for the Lord, not for men. . . . It is the Lord Christ you are serving."
COLOSSIANS 3:23–24 NIV

Hopefulness

date:

Hope. The promise of spring. Christians, of all people, should be people of hope. We have every reason to be optimistic, to set aside our cynicism and believe in good things to come. After all, God has promised that "hope does not disappoint us" (Rom. 5:5).

But hopefulness is by definition a future-oriented virtue. And sometimes we get so caught up in our present condition that we can't see beyond the current difficulties. The dreariness of spiritual winter has us convinced that the sun will never come out again.

If we truly desire to be hopeful people, we need to understand that faith, which is the basis for our hope, is not dependent upon *circumstances,* but upon the *character* of God. When we focus on circumstances, we question the character of God. When we focus on the character of God, however, we put circumstances into their proper perspective.

God has given us the assurance that our lives—present, past, and future—are in more capable hands than our own. " 'I know the plans I have for you,' declares the Lord, 'plans to prosper you and not to harm you, plans to give you hope and a future' " (Jer. 29:11).

Our parents called it optimism. Self-help groups call it positive thinking. God calls it *hope,* and tells us that when nothing else remains, this virtue, along with faith and love, will still be standing strong. —Penelope J. Stokes, *Simple Words of Wisdom: 52 Virtues for Every Woman*

Why does focusing on your circumstances instead of focusing on the character of God squelch your hope?

"But hope that is seen is no hope at all."
Romans 8:24 NIV

A Welcoming Basket

Moving is not only exhausting, it's often a lonely experience, especially for those who move into a community where they have no friends.

When you see a new family unpacking the moving van, why not put together a welcome basket of healthy snacks and finger foods.

Add a tag that says, "Welcome to Our Neighborhood!" and perhaps a map of the area or other helpful information.

You'll start off on the right foot, encouraging your new neighbors when they need it the most—in the midst of putting down new roots. —Cheri Fuller, *The Fragrance of Kindness*

Who is new in your neighborhood or church that you could welcome with a basket of treats? How has someone encouraged you when you've been in a new situation?

date: ....

"Love your neighbor as yourself."
MATTHEW 19:19 NIV

Shipwreck

date:

A few years ago, my parents booked a cruise to Alaska from Vancouver. On the way in to dock at the first Alaskan port, they heard the sound of impact and felt the deck shudder beneath them. The giant ocean liner had run aground on the rocks.

Shipwreck. The very word evokes images that chill us to the bone. Images of danger, even death. Fortunately, in my parents' case, no one was seriously hurt.

But what about our spiritual life? How do we recover when our faith begins to sink? We learn from Paul's experience of shipwreck.

In Acts 27–28, Paul set sail for Rome. He was in chains; even so, he knew he was being sent by the Spirit to bring the good news of Jesus Christ to the Romans. Then, the ship hit a reef and ran aground, and Paul and his companions washed up on Malta, an island unknown to them. And as if the near-death experience of the shipwreck wasn't enough, a viper came out of a bundle of wood and bit Paul.

Imprisonment. Shipwreck. And just when you think things can't get any worse, a snake in the woodpile. Where is God in all this? What about the promises of protection and provision and abundant life?

Paul didn't die from the snakebite. The imprisonment, the shipwreck, the viper—all of those adverse experiences gave Paul the opportunity to minister to the people of the island. Paul didn't know where Malta was. But God knew.

And God knows where you are, too. Right in the middle of your storm, even if it feels as if you're all alone, hanging onto the wreckage of your faith in the middle of the sea. Don't let go. Hold on. The Lord will bring you safely to the shore. —Penelope J. Stokes, *Beside a Quiet Stream: Words of Hope for Weary Hearts*

Does your life feel like a shipwreck? In what ways can you hold on and trust God?

"Commit your way to the Lord; trust in him and he will do this: He will make your righteousness shine like the dawn. . . ."

Psalm 37:5–6 NIV

Confession

"Therefore confess your sins to each other and pray for each other so that you may be healed."

James 5:16 NIV

What secret sins do you need to confess to a prayerful person in order that you might be healed and overcome?

"If we confess our sins, he is faithful and just and will forgive us our sins and purify us from all unrighteousness."

1 John 1:9 NIV

How has God been faithful to purify you and to deliver you when you've confessed your sins?

Encouraging Words Fill the Heart

date:

Hyacinth Morgan, a Jamaican-born woman who had only an elementary school education, was working as a nanny to support her two children. She was a most unlikely candidate for medical school. But one day her employer asked her if she had a dream, a goal for her life. "Yes," Hyacinth answered, "I'd like to go to college. And then to medical school."

The employer could have told her the dream was impossible because of her lack of education, but instead he encouraged her and explained how she could get a GED.

Hyacinth worked hard and accomplished that goal. Later, her straight A's at community college brought her to the attention of the college counselor, who helped her apply to Johns Hopkins University. A full-scholarship student, Hyacinth earned a degree in math and biology and graduated with honors.

Now that her own children are in college, Hyacinth is in medical school pursuing the degree she dreamed of long ago.

Like Hyacinth, most of us have had significant moments when a compliment, a word of encouragement, or praise gave us the assurance we needed that the future could be brighter. It gave us the courage to pursue our dreams. Yet so often the people who gave the encouragement don't even know the positive impact they had on our lives.

—Cheri Fuller, *The Fragrance of Kindness*

Who has had a positive impact on your life through their words? Have you ever told them how much they encouraged you? Who can you encourage today through a simple word of advice?

"The way of a fool seems right to him, but a wise man listens to advice."
PROVERBS 12:15 NIV

Treat Family Like Company

Mother goes all out for kids and grandkids. During each holiday season (July 4th and Valentine's Day included), she hauls out the appropriate decorations and recipes and prepares as if the Pope were coming to visit. Never mind that no one but the family will see it all. Every time we sit down to her dining table as a family with whatever placemats, napkins, and dishes she has chosen for the occasion, we feel special. We count.

On the other hand, I've walked into the kitchen to find company sitting at a table of dirty dishes. A friend had called to say she was running late leaving work and needed to be at the school by 6:30 for a parent-teacher conference. Because we lived a couple of blocks from the school, mother invited her to drop by for a drive-off bologna sandwich and a paper towel full of chips on the way.

And many times a pastor of ours, single at the time, made it a point to drop by our house unexpectedly at dinner time. If we were eating leftovers, he forked into his share just like the rest of us.

In short, Mother treats her family like company and her company like family. —Dianna Booher, *Mother's Gifts to Me*

How do you treat your family? How do you treat your company?

date:

"A kindhearted woman gains respect. . . ."
PROVERBS 11:16 NIV

Joyful Noises

date: ....

Giggle, laugh, and make joyful noises! God gave us such a wonderful gift when He gave us the capacity to laugh! And how much greater is that gift when shared with a friend. The Bible encourages us to develop a cheerful heart, not only for our own well-being, but also for encouraging and uplifting others.

My friend Fern calls me once in a while to ask if I have anything to donate to a charity organization. Whether I say "yes" or "no," she always makes me chuckle by sharing a simple silly joke. She is a friend who cultivates humor and reaps a smile from me every time.

I want to be that kind of friend, don't you?

Struggles and challenges will always be a part of life, but they don't have to consume us. Jesus came to give us abundant life, and He wants us to enjoy it.

Take time to play, to be silly, to have fun! Cut out a comic. Write down a joke.

Look for humor in the everyday "stuff" and share it with friend! —Karla Dornacher, *The Blessing of Friendship: A Gift from the Heart*

Who can you laugh with and encourage today? Who reaps a smile from you every time?

"I know that there is nothing better for men than to be happy and do good while they live."
Ecclesiastes 3:12 NIV

Giving Away Your Best

Christmas was rapidly approaching. My daughter, Alison, and I were cuddled on her bed reading the Bible story of the rich man who gained wealth and food and amassed so much hay and grain that he had to build bigger barns for it all. The story said he loved all of his things more than he loved God.

date: ....

"You see," I explained to Ali, "God can always tell if we love our things more than we love Him. Because if we do, we won't share the things He has given us."

That made sense to Alison, and she reminded me of one of her favorite Christmas traditions—picking out one or two of her favorite toys to give to a child who might not receive a present at Christmas. "I want to give someone a doll this year, Mom. I guess I could give Shelley (her beautiful German doll) or Newborn (her soft, most precious baby doll) to a girl at the orphanage."

I found the words coming out of my mouth before I could stop to think. "Oh, Alison, not Shelley or Newborn! How about Baby Beth or one of the Cabbage Patch dolls?" (The German doll had taken quite a bit of saving on my part, and Newborn had been part of the family since Alison was a baby. I guess those dolls were my favorites, too.)

"But, Mom, doesn't the Bible say that when we give, we ought to give our best?" Alison asked.

I felt as though God had asked me the question Himself. I was humbled and faced with my own selfishness.

Later that night I prayed: *God, work in my heart so that I will love You far more than all the things of life that seem so important. Help me to find joy like Ali does in giving away my best.* —Cheri Fuller, *Quiet Whispers from God's Heart for Women*

How do you love your things more than you love God? Will to give away your best things to others in need?

"Do not store up for yourselves treasures on earth, where moth and rust destroy. . . . But store up for yourselves treasures in heaven. . . . For where your treasure is, there your heart will be also."
Matthew 6:19–21 NIV

Seasons of Life

date:

Summer is the most fun season of life, as well as the most work! The garden is filled with the beauty of flowers in full bloom, the celebration of friendships, and the laughter of life! It is also the time of weeding, battling garden pests and disease, fertilizing, and watering.

Be careful during this season to stop and pick a bouquet of God's goodness in the midst of your busy day!

As the summer sun yields to the harvest moon and the bright summer colors give way to the beauty of autumn leaves, let your heart be filled with thanksgiving.

Fall is the time for reaping the rewards of your labor of faith, the abundance of God's provision. It is the season for storing within your heart the memories of all He has done for you—memories of all He has done for you—memories to carry with you through the cold days of winter.

Though the garden plot appears to be barren and bleak, winter is a necessary season of rest and regeneration. In the cold stillness the Master Gardener is at work, revealing His design and purpose for your life.

This is a time, not only of reflecting on the past, but also of looking forward, with expectation, to what lies ahead. Winter always gives way to spring.

Buds bursting with promise, the song of the sparrow as it builds its nest, the freshly tilled soil ready for seed—these signs of spring bring a joyful celebration of new life.

The Master Gardener specializes in new beginnings! He sows His seeds of mercy new every morning in the garden of your heart. This is a season of rejoicing!

—Karla Dornacher, *Down a Garden Path To Places of Love and Joy*

Are you rejoicing in the season you're experiencing?

"He has made everything beautiful in its time."
Ecclesiastes 3:11 NIV

Holding Your Tongue

"When words are many, sin is not absent, but he who holds his tongue is wise."
Proverbs 10:19 NIV

When has holding your tongue in a situation been the wisest choice? Why?

"The tongue that brings healing is a tree of life, but a deceitful tongue crushes the spirit."
Proverbs 15:4 NIV

How has a deceitful tongue crushed your spirit? What kind of words bring healing?

Go Fly a Kite

date:

Have you ever responded "Later!" to a child's discovery of a spotted, green crawly creature? Perhaps on your way to adulthood your sense of wonder and awe faded and was replaced by busyness and practicality, or work and worries.

Mine did. With the addition of each of our children, my schedule got more hectic. I was missing the small miracles God placed along my path. I wanted to share in my children's joy and sense of discovery, but there was so much to do!

Finally, quite frustrated, I asked God, "What do I do?"

Quietly He seemed to whisper, *"Go fly a kite!"*

"Oh, Lord," I replied, "that seems so silly and impractical."

"That's the point!" He responded.

So I went to the toy store and bought a kite to fly at our next family outing in the park. Chris and Justin enjoyed the challenge of getting the kite up to catch the breeze, and Alison loved having her turn to fly it, but eventually they all got bored and ran off to play. I was left holding the string.

As the bright red and blue kite swept up and flew almost out of sight, my spirits soared. The breeze blew my hair, and a fresh sense of wonder blew over my heart. I forgot all the things I needed to accomplish and reveled in the blue sky, the huge cascade of clouds. Then, as I gazed up, there it was! A spectacular double rainbow! A double promise, a double blessing.

Flying the kite not only refreshed my spirit but pointed me upward, toward God, who knew what would make my heart sing. —Cheri Fuller, *Quiet Whispers from God's Heart for Women*

What is God telling you in the midst of your busy schedule? How can you discover His small miracles and promises?

"The Lord is faithful to all his promises
and loving toward all he has made."
PSALM 145:13 NIV

Your Spiritual Closet

If you're like most of us, you've found yourself, more than once, searching frantically in the closet and declaring you have nothing at all to wear! What you see either doesn't fit, is not appropriate for the occasion, or needs to be laundered!

date:

Just as you would never think of wearing dirty clothes or even hanging them in your closet, God calls you as His child to take off the dirty rags you've been wearing—old attitudes and bad habits—and put on the clean clothing of godly attitudes and habits that He wants to develop in your life.

God has filled your spiritual closet with the most beautiful and well-made wardrobe you could ever imagine! He created these garments Himself. They are guaranteed to fit well and last long.

Open your closet and see: the garment of praise for the spirit of heaviness, the undergarments of tender mercies, humility, and forgiveness, the belt of truth, the vest of right living, well-fitting shoes of the Good News of peace, the protective head-covering of salvation and much more!

Most importantly . . . put on love!

As you learn to dress from your spiritual closet you will be able to teach your children and others how to do the same. —Karla Dornacher, *Love in Every Room*

What can you now find to wear from your spiritual closet that you've not worn in a while?

"Clothe yourself with the Lord Jesus Christ. . . ."
Romans 13:14 NIV

A Gift of a Picnic

date:

Maureen, a young mother with two little ones, and her husband were struggling financially. It seemed they were so busy scrimping and "getting by" that life was just passing them by. They often felt discouraged and depressed.

Then one Sunday someone in their church delivered the kindest gift they had ever received. An older couple called and told Maureen not to worry about fixing lunch on Sunday. She thought they were going to invite her little family over to eat or take them to a restaurant. Instead, after the final hymn was sung and the congregation dismissed, the elderly couple handed Maureen a colorful blanket, a full picnic basket, and a map with directions to an unknown destination.

Maureen and her family followed the map to a wildflower meadow ablaze with color: red poppies, yellow coreopsis, purple irises, wild daises, and all kinds of native flora. There, amidst the beauty of a spring meadow, they relaxed and enjoyed the delicious picnic lunch. The children dipped their feet in the clear pond as Maureen delighted in the butterflies and singing birds. Her heart was deeply touched by this kind act. Somehow her burdens felt lighter.

For many years after that Sunday, the family returned to the wildflower meadow—a fragrant reminder of the gift of kindness. —Cheri Fuller, *The Fragrance of Kindness*

What is the kindest gift you've ever received? What can you give to a family you know to lift their spirits?

"He who is kind to the poor lends to the Lord, and he will reward him for what he has done."
PROVERBS 19:17 NIV

Bitter Waters or Blessings?

In a recent election, our state held a bond issue for clean water—tax money to keep the streams and rivers unpolluted. The bond passed, but not without a fight. A lot of people didn't want to spend an extra dollar to protect our water sources.

date:

The Israelites in the wilderness faced a "bond issue" of their own. In Exodus 15, they had just come out of Egypt, just witnessed the Pharaoh's troops drowned in the Red Sea.

Then, three days in the wilderness, they came upon an oasis. The name of the place was Marah, which means "Bitterness." The waters were undrinkable.

The Israelites could invest a little of their faith and wait to see what God would do on their behalf, or they could give in to the bitterness. They chose the latter. They complained.

Bitterness is a habit that can seriously hinder our spiritual journey. When it doesn't seem as if God is providing for our needs, we have a decision to make. We can hold onto our faith and trust that God has an answer in mind, or we can complain and let our souls become embittered.

When we lose sight of the grace of God, bitterness takes root. But when we keep our eyes fixed on the character of God and on the ways our Provider cares for us, we're less likely to become disgruntled when an oasis turns out to be bitter.

At Marah, God showed Moses a tree, and when he threw a branch into the bitter waters, they became sweet (Exod. 15:25). An image, perhaps, of the cross, of the sacrificial love that sweetens even the bitterest experiences of life.

Expecting an oasis, but finding a bitter stream? Don't lose sight of the grace of God. Look to the cross, where the curse is turned into a blessing. —Penelope J. Stokes, *Beside a Quiet Stream: Words of Hope for Weary Hearts*

How has God rescued you from a bitter stream in life?

"See to it that no one misses the grace of God and that no bitter root grows up to cause trouble and defile many."
Hebrews 12:15 NIV

THE LITTLE GIRL AND THE GIFT

date:

Holiness is often hidden—no, I take that back—is often showcased in a child. Take the time I was in an airport drugstore in Hawaii. When I wheeled up to the cashier's counter, I learned that the total for my purchase was $17.89. I asked the clerk to reach into my handbag, get my wallet, and take out a $10-dollar bill and seven ones. "If you don't mind counting it out, I have enough change to make the 89 cents."

And so, while standing next to me and holding my wallet open so I could see, she proceeded to dig for pennies and count them out on the counter one-by-one.

Suddenly, a little girl darted up and—clink!—very delicately dropped a penny into my change purse.

The little girl must have been watching me the whole time. When she saw the clerk rummaging through my wallet to help me find change to pay my bill, she must have thought I was poor and didn't have enough money to pay my bill. *Should I tell her I didn't need her penny? How should I respond?*

I wheeled over to the child, smiled and said, "I want to thank you very much for helping me." I caught her dad's eye and added, "You have the wonderful quality of compassion, and if you don't know what that means, ask your daddy and he will tell you." Although I didn't need her gift, reinforcing her generosity was more important than rectifying her impressions.

God was surely looking down and smiling that day. A child's generous spirit was reinforced, and her compassion encouraged. A father was made proud. And God received the glory. —Joni Eareckson Tada, *Holiness in Hidden Places*

How can you display compassion and thoughtfulness today? How has someone's generosity touched your life?

"A gift opens the way for the giver and ushers him into the presence of the great."
PROVERBS 18:16 NIV

Grief

"He heals the brokenhearted and binds up their wounds."
Psalm 147:3 NIV

In the past, how has the Lord healed your wounds with his love?

"The Lord is close to the brokenhearted
and saves those who are crushed in spirit."
Psalm 34:18 NIV

When and how have you felt God's nearness during a time of heartache?

Water from the Rock

date:

With Moses, God began to lead the Children of Israel out of the bondage of Egypt, toward the Promised Land. But to get to the land flowing with milk and honey, they had to pass through the wilderness. No milk there. No honey. Not even water.

Unhappy with the situation and forgetting the promise, the people grumbled against God. So God sent Moses up to Horeb and told him: "Strike the rock, and water will come out of it, so that the people may drink" (Exod. 17:6). The water flowed out of the rock and the people were satisfied—for a little while. Even after the water, they still complained.

Did the Children of Israel need water? Sure they did. Did God intend to provide for their thirst in the wilderness? Apparently so. But I wonder what might have happened if they had trusted God's provision instead of just complaining about it. Perhaps they would have stumbled upon a different kind of miracle—an oasis or a well—something a little less obvious than water gushing from a stone in the desert. Would they, then, have asked the mocking question, "Is the Lord among us, or not?" (Exod. 17:7).

I wonder, too, about us modern Christians. In our private wildernesses, do we complain until we see water gushing from the rock, when the oasis is just over the hill? Do we find it hard to keep from griping when we're not given instant gratification of our spiritual or material needs?

The answer to the Israelites' question is a resounding YES. God is with us. God provides. We may get a spiritual spectacle—water from the rock—or we may get a rich land that will yield its produce when we ourselves do the sowing and harvesting. Either way, it's a touch of God. Either way, it's a miracle. —Penelope J. Stokes, *Beside a Quiet Stream: Words of Hope for Weary Hearts*

How has God provided for you with a miracle?

"I provide water in the desert and streams in the wasteland, to give drink to my people. . . ."
Isaiah 43:20 NIV

Obedience

The boy had been misbehaving. The mother whispered, "Sit down and behave yourself." The boy sat down. "I may be sittin' down on the outside," he muttered, "but I'm still standin' up on the inside." External restraint does not necessarily reflect internal obedience. We can do all the right things. But the Lord is interested in something a little less obvious. God wants not just our submission, but our hearts.

Keeping God's statutes is important, to be sure. But the motivation behind that obedience is the key to true godliness.

Biblical obedience is not a matter of outward appearance but of inward reality. If we obey God still "standing up on the inside," our obedience means nothing. "The multitude of your sacrifices—what are they to me?" God says. "Stop bringing meaningless offerings. They have become a burden to me; I am weary of bearing them" (Isa. 1:11, 13-14).

God wants not just outward obedience, but a heart softened to the Divine will. A spirit that acknowledges that God not only has the right to our obedience, but knows what is best for us and can lead us.

Obedience in the inner soul is based not on fear but on love. Because we love God, we seek to obey. Because we know God loves us, we can trust that what the Lord asks of us will not be too difficult for us, and will result in our good.

The secular world often mocks what it calls "blind obedience" in religious people. But obedience is not blind. Even when it cannot understand God's reasons, it trusts God's character. Obedience sees with the heart that God is good, and thus submits itself to One who is wiser, stronger, and more faithful. —Penelope J. Stokes, *Simple Words of Wisdom: 52 Virtues for Every Woman*

Why do you obey? Do you obey not only with your actions, but also with a submissive heart?

date:

"Blessed are they who keep his statutes
and seek Him with all their heart."
Psalm 119:2 NIV

Follow God to Your Dreams

date:

Louise had a deep concern for the homeless in her town of Portland, Maine. And she felt God guiding her to open a shelter. So although Louise and her husband, Claude, were both in their mid-seventies, they took their life savings of $50,000 and began searching Portland for a large house. "You'll never find a house for that money," real estate agents told them repeatedly.

But God said, *"Remember, I've given you this dream of what I want you to do."* God's voice won out, and find a house they did—a fourteen-room dilapidated structure. Restoring it was a huge project, but God directed them to the Cumberland County Jail. The city agreed to lend them the jail's manpower. With the inmates' help, Claude and Louise restored the entire three-story house.

As the completion date drew near they faced many obstacles, but God always provided. Even after the reconstruction, more funds were needed in order to open the shelter. So for weeks, Louise went to churches for contributions of blankets, furniture, food, and money.

Finally, the night before Christmas Eve, 1985, Friendship House opened its doors to serve the first of thousands of homeless with a graciousness and love their "guests" (they were never called clients) never dreamed of. God guided Louise and showed her the steps to take, but she did her part to follow His leading.

Sometimes God's whispers launch us into a dream much larger than ourselves. But when we listen for His voice, we can confidently look for His provision—He never leaves us on our own. —Cheri Fuller, *Quiet Whispers from God's Heart for Women*

What dream has God whispered to you? Will you let Him lead you to accomplish your dream?

"When Jesus spoke again to the people, he said, 'I am the light of the world. Whoever follows me will never walk in darkness, but will have the light of life.' "
John 8:12 NIV

The Vine and Its Branches

There is a story in the Bible about a vine and its branches. It tells us that Jesus is the true Vine and we, as believers, are His branches. We are part of Him and He is part of us, joined together as one. Each branch receives its life through the Vine. As you spend time with Jesus—reading your Bible and letting Him speak to your heart—His life will flow in and through you, bringing fruitfulness and fulfillment.

But there is one major difference between God's grapevine and those here on earth. As branches of the true Vine we have been given a will—we must choose either to meet with Him each day and enjoy the benefits of His love and wisdom or ignore Him and try to face the challenges of life in our own limited strength.

Are you wilting from the cares of the world? Do you feel dry and empty? Choose to set aside time to be with Jesus today and every day. Enjoy the life that is yours in Him! —Karla Dornacher, *Down a Garden Path To Places of Love and Joy*

Each day, do you choose to be connected to Jesus—the true Vine of life? Or do you choose to remain a dry and empty branch?

date: ....

"I am the true vine. . . . No branch can bear fruit by itself; it must remain in the vine."
John 15:1, 4 NIV

The Gift of Grace

date:

Have you ever disappointed a friend? Not lived up to her expectations? I have. In fact, I've lost friends because they were not able to forgive my shortcomings or, in some cases, accept me for who I am.

I remember the first time I disappointed my friend, Kathy. I had forgotten to do something I said I would do, and even though it was unintentional, she had every right to be upset. But instead of being angry, she said with a smile, "It's okay. I give you grace."

Hearing those words was like sweet music to my ears. I was forgiven and accepted, even though I had failed!

Grace is unmerited favor. It is God's gift of unconditional love, forgiveness, and acceptance—even when we don't deserve it! Like Kathy, when we accept this gift from God through faith in Jesus, we are able to share it with others.

Have any of your friends ever failed or disappointed you? Showed up late? Forgotten your birthday? Hurt your feelings? If they haven't, they will! We are all imperfect people, and we all make mistakes. We all need grace!

There is only one Friend who will never fail you and that's Jesus. For all your other friends, give them grace!

—Karla Dornacher, *The Blessing of Friendship: A Gift from the Heart*

To which friends do you need to give some grace—unmerited favor?

"I was shown mercy. . . . The grace of our Lord was poured out on me abundantly, along with the faith and love that are in Christ Jesus."
1 Timothy 1:13–14 NIV

Freedom from Sin

"To Him who loves us and has freed us from our sins by his blood, and has made us to be a kingdom and priests to serve his God and Father—to Him be glory and power for ever and ever! Amen."

Revelation 1:5–6 NIV

How did God free us from our sins by His blood? How do you respond to God's gift of freedom?

"But now that you have been set free from sin and have become slaves to God, the benefit you reap leads to holiness, and the result is eternal life. For the wages of sin is death, but the gift of God is eternal life in Christ Jesus our Lord."

Romans 6:22–23 NIV

What does it mean to you to no longer be a slave to sin, but instead to be a slave to God? What are the benefits of being a slave to God's love?

Know Thyself

date:

For the Christian, self-knowledge is essential—first to salvation, and then to the ongoing, ever-changing relationship with God. Initially, we must acknowledge our need in order to come to the Savior. And then, I think, we ought to pray for an honest, realistic view of our own capabilities—both in Christ and apart from God. For when we become aware of our capacity for both good and evil, we will be drawn continually to dependence upon the grace of God.

But spiritual awareness can be a pretty scary prospect. In Psalm 139, David gives us a glimpse into the process: "O Lord, you have searched me and known me . . . you discern my thoughts . . . you are acquainted with all my ways."

Only God can truly know our hearts, and thus only God can reveal our innermost selves to us.

When we stop trying to fill our lives with meaningless activity and turn inward for a moment, we discover something wonderful: By God's grace, we are who we are. By God's grace, we will become who we were meant to be.

It means that whatever we discover about ourselves—whatever our gifts or shortcomings, whatever our fears or desires—God already knows all about us.

There's a great liberty that comes with knowing ourselves. A freedom that enables us to take risks, to grow, to change, to set sail for horizons we've only seen in our dreams.

Who are we? We are people, made—lovingly, and with great care—in the image of our Creator. We don't have to prove ourselves. We don't have to be superspiritual or indispensable. We only have to be who we are.

—Penelope J. Stokes, *Beside a Quiet Stream: Words of Hope for Weary Hearts*

Who are you? What has God revealed to you about yourself?

"Search me, O God, and know my heart; test me and know my anxious thoughts. See if there is any offensive way in me, and lead me in the way everlasting."
Psalm 139:23–24

Gifts from the Kitchen

Homemade food is a gift from the heart. The fragrance of kindness that accompanies homemade bread, cinnamon rolls, or even a simple cocoa mix in a bright mug delivers much comfort and encouragement.

Whether you are rejoicing over a friend's new baby, giving relief to someone who is ill, or welcoming new neighbors, gracious giving from the kitchen doesn't have to be complicated.

When you bake muffins, fix an extra batch and freeze it for spontaneous giving. When you make a casserole, divide it in half and give some to a shut-in who would love a home-cooked meal.

You will leave someone feeling a little merrier and maybe make a new friend. —Cheri Fuller, *The Fragrance of Kindness*

When has someone shared kindness with you through a gift of food? How did their gift make you feel? Who in your life would appreciate a homemade gift from your kitchen?

date:

"He who despises his neighbor sins, but blessed is he who is kind to the needy."
PROVERBS 14:21 NIV

Fear Like a Flood

date:

In his first Inaugural Address, President Franklin D. Roosevelt gave the rallying cry through years of war, deprivation, and struggle: "The only thing we have to fear is fear itself." Roosevelt was right—fear paralyzes. Fear keeps us from moving forward.

But we fear a lot more than fear itself. We fear the unknown, the unanticipated, the unprepared-for conflicts of life. Even when things are good, we cling to Murphy's law: *If anything can go wrong, it will.*

But God doesn't want us to live in fear. Fear is the opposite of faith. It wreaks havoc with our ability to trust and undermines the peace that the Lord desires for us.

How do we deal with the riptides of fear that threaten to take us under? How do we keep our heads above water when the whirlpool sucks at us and pulls us down?

"Don't fight it," my teacher advised me when I was first learning to swim. "The water will bear you up if you just relax."

Just relax.

It was easier said than done, I'll have to admit. Terrified of drowning, I kept on flailing my arms and legs, trying with all my might to stay on the surface. But then, one day, I just got tired. Tired of struggling. Tired of gulping air and being sure my next breath would be my last. So I gave up.

And with the surrender, I floated to the surface, and the water that had been my enemy became my ally.

When fear overtakes you like a flood, don't let it paralyze you. Relax. Let God's trustworthiness bear you to the surface, to light and air and safety. —Penelope J. Stokes, *Beside a Quiet Stream: Words of Hope for Weary Hearts*

What are you afraid of? How can you relax in God's trustworthiness and shelter?

"He who dwells in the shelter of the Most High will rest in the shadow of the Almighty. You will not fear the terror of night, nor the arrow that flies by day."
Psalm 91:1, 5 NIV

First Things First

"What's the most important thing you do, Joni?" It was a press conference in Poland. My mind zipped through answers all significant to me. But what is most important to me? I smiled. Among all the options, I knew.

date:

"Being a good wife to my husband." The group of 20 reporters chuckled. I guessed their thoughts. *She can't be serious. Surely she's being gratuitous.*

When I stand before Jesus, I will be judged first for my faithfulness in marriage. My commitment to my marriage vows places me in a profoundly significant relationship with the most important human being on earth—my spouse. And if I can't be faithful in loving my husband, how can I be faithful in a ministry to millions?

Being faithful to Ken means saying "no" to speaking at a crusade because the date conflicts with Ken's speech at his school's baccalaureate. It means scheduling overseas travel so I can always be in town to help him chaperon the prom. It means calling him every night when I'm away and occasionally bringing home an unexpected gift.

Most of all, it means praying for Ken daily and in a specific way. Nothing bonds me closer to my husband than interceding for him. If I sense my passion waning or my emotions sagging, if I find myself pulling back from the demands of marriage, I pray—for Ken. Nothing ignites love for my husband faster.

Your circumstances may be different, but you can do the same. Just remember who is the most important person on earth. Your spouse—that one in a million.

—Joni Eareckson Tada, *Holiness in Hidden Places*

What is the most important thing you do? Do you treat your spouse like he is the most important person on earth?

"Wives, submit to your husbands as to the Lord. For the husband is the head of the wife as Christ is the head of the church. . . . Husbands, love your wives, just as Christ loved the church. . . ."

Ephesians 5:22–25 NIV

Raising the Bar

date:

One Saturday morning I finished my chores in record time so I could go out with my friends. When mother noticed I was getting ready to leave, she questioned me, "Did you finish dusting already? In 10 minutes?"

"I did."

"Everywhere? Did you do it well?

"I did."

She made a quick inspection; the dusting work didn't pass. Neither did the ironing. "These shirts aren't ironed well either. Look at those wrinkles. You have to give the steam enough time to penetrate. You don't just swipe the iron over them and run." She said it as if I should know—after all, it wasn't the first time I'd heard it.

High standards surface two feelings: a feeling of not being able to measure up and a sense of great accomplishment when you do. Focusing on the latter builds self-confidence and makes future bosses proud.

—Dianna Booher, *Mother's Gifts to Me*

What high standards have you accomplished, giving you increased self-confidence?

"I press on toward the goal to win the prize for which God has called me heavenward in Christ Jesus."
PHILIPPIANS 3:14 NIV

INTERCESSION

"Christ Jesus, who died—more than that, who was raised to life—is at the right hand of God and is also interceding for us."
ROMANS 8:34 NIV

How does it make you feel to know that Jesus is at the right hand of God praying and pleading for you?

"If anyone sees his brother commit a sin that does not lead to death, he should pray and God will give him life."
1 JOHN 5:16 NIV

Why is it important for you to intercede and pray on others' behalf, especially when they are immersed in sinful behavior?

INTEGRITY

date:

The Most Absurd Television Commercial: "I'm not a doctor, but I play one on TV." We are supposed to take the word of the actor when he declares the healing properties of his product. After all, he plays a doctor on television; surely he knows all about medicine.

Children call this game of pretense "play like." But when adults "play like," God calls it something else. Hypocrisy. Deception. Lack of integrity.

Integrity is the state of truly being on the inside what we seem to be on the outside.

Integrity shields us from the exhausting practice of trying to convince others that we are something they want or expect us to be. There is liberty in integrity. We can be ourselves—human, flawed, fallible people, ever striving toward greater spiritual understanding.

But we must first learn to be honest with ourselves—and with God. To be people of integrity, we have to face our inadequacies and limitations candidly, give ourselves permission not to be perfect.

God knows we're not perfect. We are no less spiritual for owning up to our faults and weaknesses—in fact, God honors such frankness. In the admission of our weaknesses, the power of Christ has opportunity to work.

God calls us to be people of integrity. To allow the truth of what is inside to be revealed outwardly. For then we can place our trust in God rather than in the appearance of spiritual maturity.

And rather than being a spokesperson for a product we know nothing about, we can speak the truth because we have lived it. —Penelope J. Stokes, *Simple Words of Wisdom: 52 Virtues for Every Woman*

When is the last time you were frank with God—and yourself—about your weaknesses and limitations?

"May integrity and uprightness protect me, because my hope is in you."

PSALM 25:21 NIV

WHO NEEDS TO CHANGE?

During a time of concern about our 10-year-old son, I became overly critical of his attitudes and actions. Chris was irritated with my reminders to clean his room and stop bugging his sister. I wanted him to talk and he clammed up. I wanted him to change, and he wouldn't. I wanted him to know how much I loved him, and yet irritations pushed us farther apart.

So I began to pray. And the more I prayed for him, the more I heard God whisper, *"You're the one who needs to change. You need to accept Chris just as he is. Don't merely tolerate him but enjoy and appreciate him. There is a time for correction, but this is a time for acceptance."*

Over the weeks ahead, I prayed, "Lord, change me! Help me to be a loving and understanding mom. Help me to see Chris through Your eyes."

As God answered that prayer, He worked in both of us. Chris and I started taking time after he got home from school to throw a baseball in the backyard or shoot hoops. My usually quiet son began to share his thoughts with me. He talked about what he was worried about and what frustrated him, what he loved about baseball, what his hopes and dreams were.

As we played and chatted together one day, I remembered the saying "Kids need love the most when they are the most unlovable" and thought that's how God treats us. Long before we loved Him, He loved us. Over the next few weeks God gave us great fun together and brought an acceptance and closeness where there had been criticism and separation. I'm so glad God restored our relationship through a divine "whisper" and didn't let us drift apart.

—Cheri Fuller, *Quiet Whispers from God's Heart for Women*

Who have you wanted to change, when God showed you that it was really yourself who needed to be changed?

date:

"I will give them an undivided heart and put a new spirit in them; I will remove from them their heart of stone and give them a heart of flesh."
EZEKIEL 11:19 NIV

The Garden of Your Life

date:

I saw an ad in the paper for a class on how to become a "master gardener." I love to garden, but if you came to visit my garden you would find that I am much more of a dabbler than a "master"! In fact, God is the only *true* Master Gardener.

He not only created the first garden, He also created you and the spiritual "garden of your heart." His desire is for you to be a strong, healthy, well-watered garden—even in the midst of the "weeds, thistles, and thorns" of daily life.

He longs for you to be firmly rooted and established in His love and to be able to recognize the touch of His hand as He labors in the spiritual garden of your life: tilling, planting, watering, and weeding.

Is there an area of your life that needs the special touch of the Master's hand? Call to Him today. Ask Him to make a beautiful, bountiful garden of your life, for it is His pleasure and delight to watch you grow, blossom, and bear much fruit! —Karla Dornacher, *Down a Garden Path To Places of Love and Joy*

What area of your life needs the special touch of the Lord—the Master Gardener?

"He cuts off every branch in me that bears no fruit, while every branch that does bear fruit he prunes so that it will be even more fruitful."
John 15:2 NIV

Loneliness

We all have moments when we feel insignificant and alone. Maybe you're feeling that way right now. Everywhere you look, other people are busy with their own lives. They don't seem to even see you. You want to reach out, but your cup is empty. And you feel as though you have nothing to offer.

Dear friend, we can become so discouraged when we're alone. The more we look to others, the more parched and empty we can become until we think we might die of thirst.

We can choose to be hurt or angry. We can even try to fill our own cup. But being alone may very well be God's design to draw you closer to Himself. He longs to be your very best friend. He loves you more than you'll ever comprehend, and He alone is able to meet the deepest needs of your heart.

As you make Jesus the center of your life, He fills your emptiness to overflowing, with plenty left over to share.

When you reach out with this cool, refreshing drink of God's love—one of acceptance, compassion, mercy, and encouragement—you may soon find another drinking from the same cup, and you both will be refreshed.

—Karla Dornacher, *The Blessing of Friendship: A Gift from the Heart*

Who do you look to when you are feeling alone and empty? Do you seek others or Jesus? Will you make Jesus the center of your life and receive His overflowing love and comfort?

date:

"The Lord is my shepherd, I shall not be in want. He makes me lie down in green pastures, he leads me beside quiet waters, he restores my soul. . . . You anoint my head with oil; my cup overflows."

Psalm 23:1–3, 5

Knock, Knock

date:

You stand at the door, hesitant to knock. You have a list of challenges you're facing as keeper of your home, but you don't know what to do.

God does not want you to stay outside on the porch and face your struggles alone. His welcome mat is always out and His door unlocked. He invites you to come in and share your heart with Him. He has promised to help if you will just ask; He will care for you as a shepherd cares for the sheep.

Knock and the door of God's love and blessing will be opened to you.

Enter into His presence for there you will find refreshment and rest for your soul, and the light of Christ to guide you through your day.

And what about those who are knocking at your front door? As the keeper of your home, you have been called by God to be hospitable. Take time to put out your welcome mat and open your heart to those who knock at your door: family, friends, neighbors, even those you do not know.

Invite them in to share in your life and the blessings you have been given. —Karla Dornacher, *Love in Every Room*

Have you knocked at the door of God's love? Will you enter into His presence to find refreshment and guidance? Who can you welcome into your life?

"Ask and it will be given to you; seek and you will find; knock and the door will be opened to you."
Matthew 7:7

Servant's Spirit

"Live as free men, but do not use your freedom as a cover-up for evil; live as servants of God. Show proper respect to everyone: Love the brotherhood of believers, fear God, honor the king."
1 Peter 2:16–17 NIV

How do you live as a servant of God?
Do you love others, fear God, and honor Him?

"Serve wholeheartedly, as if you were serving the Lord, not men, because you know that the Lord will reward everyone for whatever good he does, whether he is slave or free."
Ephesians 6:7–8 NIV

Do you live your life as if you are serving the Lord? Who or what does your heart serve most often?

GIFTS GIVEN IN LOVE

date:

Whether the gift is handmade or thoughtfully chosen at a store, from your garden or kitchen, quilted or painted, from across the world or right from your own backyard, gifts given in a spirit of love and kindness can deliver buckets of encouragement to the recipient. The time and care it takes to give a gracious, personal gift speaks volumes and gives pleasure both to the giver and receiver. A steaming pot of chicken soup delivered to a friend's door when she's had surgery encourages her to "Get well soon!" A gift of fragrant flowers can say "I love you" or "I'm sorry" or "You did a great job!" Handmade quilts and crafts convey friendship; gift baskets can be personalized to meet the needs of someone we love.

There are expected gifts given at holidays or birthdays, but the spontaneous, unexpected gift from the heart is perhaps best of all. To give gracious gifts, we can think, "What would make this person happy or lighten her load?" "What does she need today?" or "What would bring delight?" Whatever the answer to that question, in the process of giving and receiving gracious gifts, kindness blossoms! —Cheri Fuller, *The Fragrance of Kindness*

What gift could you give with love to someone today?

"If you, then, though you are evil, know how to give good gifts to your children, how much more will your Father in heaven give good gifts to those who ask Him?"
MATTHEW 7:11 NIV

Wade in the Water

I attended a concert of an a capella quartet, and one song in particular reverberated in my soul. It was the old spiritual, "Wade in the Water"—a song I had heard many times. But this time it struck me with fresh truth. "You gotta step out in faith," one of the women said as the song began. "You gotta get your feet a little wet; gotta put your foot in the river before the Lord will open the way."

date:

Didn't God push back the waters so that the Israelites could cross over on *dry ground*? Wasn't that the pattern of redemption? No doubt that's what the Israelites thought when they finally came to the River Jordan and were about to cross into Canaan. They had already seen God open the waters of the Red Sea; they knew how it was supposed to work. And now here was Joshua, telling them that this time the priests carrying the Ark of the Covenant would have to step *into* the river—at flood stage, no less—before the water would part for them to cross over. (Josh. 3:12–13)

That wasn't the way God did it before. This time the miracle happened only when Joshua and the priests were willing to take a risk.

But we don't want to get our feet wet, do we? We don't want to take the chance of stepping into the flood. We might get swept away by the current. We want the Lord to give us the kind of miracle we're accustomed to.

It's an issue of walking by faith. And faith is the evidence of things not seen. We step out, trusting that the dry ground will be there, even if all we see is water.

So go ahead. Wade in the water. Get your feet wet. And keep your faith-eyes open. You'll see God work in unexpected ways. —Penelope J. Stokes, *Beside a Quiet Stream: Words of Hope for Weary Hearts*

When have you had to "wade in the water" before God blessed you?

"So we fix our eyes not on what is seen, but on what is unseen. For what is seen is temporary, but what is unseen is eternal."

2 Corinthians 4:18 NIV

God's Quiet Whispers

date:

Elaine and her husband decided to sell a large house in the city and refurbish a ramshackle 1920s farm house. Elaine vacillated between the excitement of decorating a new place from scratch to stark panic at the thought of moving into such a small house and all they'd have to do to make it livable.

Elaine began the task enthusiastically, but 11-hour days in the Texas summer heat soon put a damper on the excitement.

One afternoon, when construction workers had failed to show up all week and a string of crushing time pressures had reduced her to tears, she broke down and sobbed, "God, I can't take this anymore! We need a carpenter, we need an electrician to fix the old wiring so the house won't burn down, we need a painter and someone to fix the holes in the roof, we need someone to fix the floor . . ."

Through all the panic, turmoil and frustration, she heard God's quiet whisper: *"You don't need any of that. You need Me. Don't you think I will take care of you? Just keep doing what you can and let Me do the rest."* She started going over her list of needs again with God when suddenly she realized He didn't want her to focus on her list of requirements and people—He wanted her to focus on Him.

God's whisper didn't change one splinter or remove one rotten board in the house, but it did take away the panic and fear. It also helped Elaine to clarify her heart's desire that their "new" home might glorify God. If she was ever tempted to ask "Why God? Why do we have to leave our beautiful house for this tiny one?" she simply looked across the green fields and rolling hills at all the beauty God had provided and her heart was at rest.

—Cheri Fuller, *Quiet Whispers from God's Heart for Women*

Are you ever still enough to hear God whisper?

"Love the Lord your God, listen to His voice, and hold fast to Him."
DEUTERONOMY 30:20 NIV

Nearness and Distance

Mother laid the groundwork for a close-knit family. And close has little to do with distance. Our family now lives close enough to allow all 18 of us to routinely gather together as one big family in times of need or celebration. But that's not always been the case. The intimacy has more to do with the head than the highway.

Mother loves us all individually, but treats us all equally.

She never repeats one child's secrets, business, or dreams to another without their permission.

She never "wonders" aloud why a certain family member acts, or says, or does a peculiar thing.

She has no favorites, yet she makes each one of our clan feel individually special by cooking their favorite food on a holiday or remembering to ask about their difficult project on hold.

Close-knit families serve to insulate members from the chill of isolation in a technologically wired world. Nearness and distance are conditions of the heart.

—Dianna Booher, *Mother's Gifts to Me*

How intimate are you with your family? What would you want to improve about your relationship with your family members?

date:

"He tends his flock like a shepherd; he gathers the lambs in his arms and carries them close to his heart; he gently leads those that have young."

Isaiah 40:11 NIV

HUMOR

date:

Some Christians might raise an eyebrow at the idea that humor is a spiritual virtue. Mark Twain said "There is no humor in heaven." I sincerely hope he has found out differently by now. Still, a lot of us Christians seem to think that humor is a sacrilege, that laughter somehow undermines God's public image. Spirituality is serious business, after all.

Abraham's wife, Sarah, apparently adhered to that perspective. In Genesis 18, when the Lord came to bring her husband the news that she would give birth to a son, Sarah laughed. I'm not sure why she laughed. Maybe she didn't believe it—she was in her nineties, and well past her childbearing years. Or maybe the final fulfillment of the promise was just too wonderful for words. Whatever the reason, when the Lord asked why she had laughed, she denied that she had done so. Obviously, Sarah didn't think laughter was very spiritual.

But God evidently changed her mind. When the long-awaited son finally arrived, she named him Isaac, which means "he laughs"—rather like naming your firstborn after Chuckles the Clown. And she said, "God has brought me laughter, and everyone who hears about this will laugh with me" (Gen. 21:6).

We need to be able to laugh at ourselves, to diffuse stress, to give the gift of lightheartedness to those around us.

And we have plenty of reason to smile. We are recipients of the lavish grace of God; the heavy burden of sin has been lifted from our shoulders. Like the Virtuous Woman in Proverbs 31, we can "laugh at the days to come" because we know our security lies not in ourselves but in our Redeemer. —Penelope J. Stokes, *Simple Words of Wisdom: 52 Virtues for Every Woman*

How often do you "laugh at the days to come"?

"Our mouths were filled with laughter, our tongues with songs of joy."
PSALM 126:2 NIV

ETERNITY

"The world and its desires pass away, but the man who does the will of God lives forever."
1 JOHN 2:17 NIV

Are you clinging too tightly to the world and its desires?

"For my Father's will is that everyone who looks to the Son and believes in him shall have eternal life, and I will raise him up at the last day."
JOHN 6:40 NIV

Do you believe in Jesus, the Son of God?
How can you thank God for this amazing gift?

Memorizing God's Word

date:

Cynthia had recently been hired by an organization that required its staff to memorize Scripture. She rebelled at the idea. She finally tackled her first verse, Isaiah 48:17. "Thus says the Lord, your Redeemer, the Holy One of Israel: I am the Lord your God, who teaches you to profit, who leads you by the way you should go."

About the same time, Cynthia decided to apply for a summer mission program in Russia, and the application needed to be postmarked by a certain day. When the deadline arrived, she headed for the post office on her way to work. With everything necessary for the application—check, application, and envelope—she ran into a shop to copy the application. When she ran back to the car, however, she suddenly realized she'd left the keys in the car!

Immediately God spoke the recent memory verse to her heart, *"I am the Lord your God, who teaches you to profit, who leads you by the way you should go."* So she said, "Okay, God, I chose to trust that You're directing me. Either You've got a way to get my car unlocked, or they'll accept my application even if it's late, or maybe I'm not supposed to go."

She walked calmly to her job, leaving her car at the copy shop. A short while later her sister happened to drop by at work—something she had never done—and produced another set of keys for Cynthia's car. Cynthia mailed the application and was accepted for the mission in Russia.

Many times God has brought that verse back to Cynthia's mind and reminded her that He is leading her and teaching her—and how valuable it is to hide His Word in her heart. —Cheri Fuller, *Quiet Whispers from God's Heart for Women*

Are you committed to memorizing scripture?

"I have hidden your word in my heart that I might not sin against you."
Psalm 119:11 NIV

Encouraging Words Lift Up the Weary

During World War II, China Inland missionary Gladys Aylward was making a harrowing and dangerous journey over the mountains out of war-torn Yangcheng toward free China with more than a hundred orphans in tow. During the desperate days and nights she struggled with despair as never before in her life. After one sleepless night, when she saw utterly no hope of reaching safety and totally felt like giving up, a 13-year-old girl in the group reminded her of their beloved story of Moses and the Israelites crossing the Red Sea.

"But I am not Moses!" Gladys cried in desperation.

"Of course you aren't," the young girl said, "but Jehovah is still God!"

Those few hope-filled words from a child infused Gladys with the extra courage she needed to persevere. She and the orphans did make it safely through the mountains to a refuge, proving again God's faithfulness and the power of a person's—even a young person's—words of encouragement and hope. —Cheri Fuller, *The Fragrance of Kindness*

What are you facing now that will take courage from God?

date:

"God is our refuge and strength, an ever-present help in trouble. Therefore we will not fear, though the earth give way and the mountains fall into the heart of the sea. . . ."
PSALM 46:1–2 NIV

Following Jesus

date:

Follow the leader! It's a game most of us know from our childhood. The leader would feel so special—hopping and skipping and twirling around—while the rest of us, the followers, would giggle and laugh, trying to imitate her every move.

When I first met Sandi, she was the new leader of the women's ministry, and I was new in the church. As I watched her, I knew she was a woman I wanted to imitate. In fact, I met several women that year who not only became my good friends, but also greatly influenced my life as they led me, by their example, into a deeper love for the Lord, His Word, and His people.

Whether we realize it or not, we are all leaders—and followers! We are all in a position to influence and be influenced by those around us. I thank God for those friends who have had such a godly influence on my life, and I pray that I might be that kind of friend to others.

We are called to be like Jesus, to live a life characterized by humility and unconditional love; to serve and not be served; and to love God and people more than things or experiences. Follow Jesus and let love lead!

—Karla Dornacher, *The Blessing of Friendship: A Gift from the Heart*

How do you positively influence those around you? Who influences you the most? How?

"Be imitators of God, therefore, as dearly loved children, and live a life of love, just as Christ loved us and gave Himself up for us as a fragrant offering and sacrifice to God."

Ephesians 5:1–2 NIV

Spread Christ's Love

You are a vessel designed to pour out God's love and encouragement to those around you. He says your words hold the power of life and death. Through words alone you can bless and build up or wound and destroy.

date: ....

The world is full of hurting people. Make it a habit to pour out life, building up others and strengthening them through positive and encouraging words.

There is no greater need for encouraging others than in your own home. Your husband and your children need to know how much you love them and how special they really are!

Ask God to show you practical ways to express His love to others today. It might be a vase of flowers or a quiet embrace. It might be a phone call filled with bright and cheery words of hope or it might be a note of gentle encouragement. Whether your note is penned on beautiful stationery or on a sticky note in a child's lunchbox, you are the scented ink God uses to spread the fragrance of Christ's love. —Karla Dornacher, *Love in Every Room*

Will you ask God to show you ways to show His love to others today?

"We loved you so much that we were delighted to share with you not only the gospel of God but our lives as well, because you had become so dear to us."

1 Thessalonians 2:8 NIV

Keepsake Notes

date:

During the nine months of pregnancy, there are so many special moments to remember. Why not write your loving thoughts in letters to your unborn child? You might want to put all the letters in a journal to give to your child someday as a source of encouragement and a lifelong treasure.

If you want to extend the life of the journal, you can continue to write keepsake notes as your child grows. Write about things you're proud of, family history you want to pass on, and your gratefulness for all the chances your child gives you to go to the park, make sandcastles at the beach, make birthday cakes, and give fun parties!

(sample note for baby's journal)

April 26, eight weeks in utero

Dear Baby,

Your daddy and I were totally amazed when we saw your first picture on the ultrasound. We could also hear your heart beating so fast! It was incredible! Daddy carries your "picture" with him all the time, and mine is on the refrigerator. Friends and family who have seen your first picture have fallen in love with you just as we have. Your daddy thinks you're going to be very smart since your head is so big!

Totally in awe, Mommy

—Cheri Fuller, *The Fragrance of Kindness*

What words would you write to your unborn child?

"For you created my inmost being;
you knit me together in my mother's womb."
Psalm 139:13 NIV

Word of God

"For the word of God is living and active. Sharper than any double-edged sword, it penetrates even to dividing soul and spirit, joints and marrow; it judges the thoughts and attitudes of the heart."
Hebrews 4:12 NIV

Do you see God's word as living and active?

"As for God, his way is perfect; the word of the Lord is flawless. He is a shield for all who take refuge in him."
2 Samuel 22:31 NIV

Have you thanked God for giving us this flawless word so we can know more about Him?

Dead Ends

date:

In our spiritual lives, we sometimes come to dead ends. We're so certain we've heard the voice of God and are following the Lord's direction. And then, without warning, a barrier. No more road. Not so much as a detour. Not even an alternate route.

That's the kind of dead end the Israelites came to when they followed Moses out of Egypt. Everything had looked so perfect. Moses had performed miracles not even the Pharaoh's magicians could reproduce. The Pharaoh had relented and let them go with all their livestock and possessions and even some of the treasures of Egypt. A new life awaited them in a land of milk and honey.

Or so they thought—until they looked up and saw a terrifying sight. The Red Sea stretched out before them, and behind them the Egyptian army was closing in. They were going to die, all of them, right there on the banks of the sea.

And they did what most of us do when we come to a dead end. They lifted up their voices and howled.

What they didn't know was that there are no dead ends with God, no barriers that can't be overcome.

We all know what happened at the Red Sea that day—a wildly dramatic miracle. The waters parted, the Israelites crossed over on dry ground, and the enemy troops who pursued them were destroyed.

Don't let your dead ends get the best of you. The same God who delivered the Israelites stands beside you. The Lord will open an unexpected way, a way you've never thought of before. You can be part of the miracle. Just stand firm. —Penelope J. Stokes, *Beside a Quiet Stream: Words of Hope for Weary Hearts*

How do you prevent dead ends from getting the best of you?

"Moses answered the people, 'Do not be afraid. Stand firm and you will see the deliverance the Lord will bring you today.' "

EXODUS 14:13 NIV

Meeting God in Stillness

After my diving injury, I lay still for three months waiting to be moved from the intensive care unit into a regular hospital room. After more months of lying still, I was finally moved to a rehabilitation center. While in rehab, I stayed put in my wheelchair for hours outside of physical therapy, waiting my turn to go in. And in the evenings, my manufactured stillness would madden me as I sat by the door waiting for friends or family to come for a visit.

It was more frightening when I laid down at night. In bed, gravity became my enemy—I was terrified of being paralyzed. In bed, I couldn't move at all except to turn my head on my pillow.

But time, prayer, and study in God's Word have a way of changing many things. And somewhere in the ensuing years, I discovered that the weakness of those claustrophobic hours was the key to God's peace and power. My enforced stillness was God's way of conforming the inside to what had happened on the outside.

Now, many years later, my bed is an altar of praise. It's the one spot on this harried planet where I always meet God in relaxed stillness.

When you find yourself in forced stillness—waiting in line, sitting by a hospital bed, or stuck in traffic—instead of fidgeting and fuming, use such moments to practice stillness before God.

You can be still and know that He is God. And you don't have to break your neck to find out.

—Joni Eareckson Tada, *Holiness in Hidden Places*

How will you respond the next time you find yourself in forced stillness?

date:

"Be still before the Lord and wait patiently for Him. . . ."
Psalm 37:7 NIV

God's Timetable

date:

Six months after Steve's accident, he came out of a coma and was able to recognize people. But his progress slowed again; he had a blood clot in his lungs and had trouble communicating.

After a trip to see him at the hospital, Cindy was vacuuming and praying through her tears. "God, I don't get this; I don't understand. You have the power to do something about the condition he's in. I don't understand why you aren't acting now."

Just then her six-year-old son Tate ran into the house yelling, "Mom! Mom! The big boys are playing basketball, and they won't let me play."

"Tate, they're in the middle of a game right now," she explained. "When they finish, I'm sure they'll let you play."

Cindy realized that Tate didn't have a clue why she wouldn't go out there and get him into his brother's game. It seemed cruel and unloving. He couldn't understand that it wouldn't be in his best interest for her to intervene.

Did God have a perspective on Steve's situation that she couldn't understand? Did God's apparent inaction have a higher purpose than she knew?

Cindy felt His presence and heard Him whisper, *"Trust My ways even though this looks senseless and wasteful. I love Steve more than you, and you've got to trust Me even though you don't see the whole picture."*

Cindy quit trying to figure out everything and released her timetable to a loving God who had her best interests—and her husband's—at heart. While Steve continued to make tremendous gains, it was a slow and painful process. After nearly two years of surgeries and rehabilitation, their family experienced the most joyful homecoming of their lives.

—Cheri Fuller, *Quiet Whispers from God's Heart for Women*

How could you release your timetable to God?

" 'For my thoughts are not your thoughts, neither are your ways my ways,' declares the Lord."
Isaiah 55:8 NIV

Sincerity

During the Italian Renaissance, it became a practice among inferior artists to "wax" their works. A thin layer of clear wax smoothed across the marble disguised the minute pits, cracks, and imperfections and gave the appearance of an undamaged surface. The finest sculptors, however, created their models without resorting to the deception of wax. That flawless satiny finish of the polished marble was, in Latin, *sine cera*—without wax—and from that image we derive the English word, sincerity.

You'd think in this well-waxed world, Christianity would stand out as the exception. Surely in the realm of faith, what you see is what you get. Christians wouldn't gloss over the surface to give the impression of flawlessness, would we?

But Christ, the reflection of Divine Perfection, doesn't need our human attempts at making faith appear more attractive. God values sincerity—the unwaxed, unvarnished truth of who we are.

And the world, too, is looking for that kind of veracity. People are drawn not to perfection, but to reality. They need to witness—from us, with all our faults and failings—how God's power can work in real people whose conflicts and adversities mirror their own. They need to know, because they see it in us, that our Lord is genuinely compassionate, truly gracious, authentically loving.

With all its struggles and difficulties, faith is a masterpiece, a finely sculpted testimony to the majesty of the Creator. No camouflage is needed, no apologies required. We don't have to put on a wax job to make the Lord look good. All we need is sincerity. —Penelope J. Stokes, *Simple Words of Wisdom: 52 Virtues for Every Woman*

date: ....

How are you sincere as you describe your relationship with Christ to others?

"But the wisdom that comes from heaven is first of all pure; then peace-loving, considerate, submissive, full of mercy and good fruit, impartial and sincere."
James 3:17 NIV

God's Comfort in Hard Times

date:

Jane had never been quite so afraid in her entire life. Her parents had just experienced a financial reversal; they lost their home and were left with little but the clothes on their backs and a few salvaged possessions. Six months later, she discovered that her husband was involved in an alternate lifestyle.

Life became a twisted reality. Soon she found herself with no job and no energy to interview for a new one. Her parents had no means to help, and her husband was leaving her. Jane couldn't understand why her life had taken such a horrible plunge.

Yet the darker her surroundings became, the more she was aware that God was with her. Quietly but distinctly, little holes were punched in the darkness and strong streams of light flowed in. With each one God seemed to whisper, *"You're not alone. I'm with you."*

The first stream of light came when she received a call from a college acquaintance who had purchased a historic home and needed help decorating it. When they toured the house, the friend handed Jane $1,500 to get her started. The woman just remembered that Jane had a flair for decorating and decided to call. Other streams of light came when an aunt opened her home, a part-time job became available, and Jane's brother moved halfway across the country to be near her and offer unlimited love and support.

Jane had never felt such tangible and direct answers to prayer. It was as if God Himself had handed her these gifts right from heaven. It was as if He had wrapped His arms around her—which was exactly what He had promised to do. —Cheri Fuller, *Quiet Whispers from God's Heart for Women*

How has God comforted you when your life seemed to fall apart?

"Cast all your anxiety on him because he cares for you."
1 Peter 5:7 NIV

Mercy

"Judgment without mercy will be shown to anyone who has not been merciful. Mercy triumphs over judgment!"
James 2:13 NIV

Do you show others mercy over judgment?

"It does not, therefore, depend on man's desire or effort, but on God's mercy."
Romans 9:16 NIV

Are you counting on your desire or effort for salvation or on God's mercy?

Partnering with the Master Gardener

date:

There are vegetable gardens and perennial gardens, gardens to attract butterflies, and some designed for their perfume. As you pore over the seed catalogs and garden books, you must ask yourself, what is the purpose of your garden. What do you want to reap from your garden plot? This will determine the seed that you sow. You can then choose the perfect seeds to produce the bounty you desire.

The Bible is the book of inspiration for gardeners of the heart. There you will come to know and love the Master Gardener and delight in His wisdom. Its pages are filled with seeds of promise and hope. As you open your heart, He will plant in you the perfect seeds to produce a rich and fulfilling garden life. And while you are there you will also be inspired by stories of other gardeners who planted seeds of faith and patience and reaped abundant harvests of God's grace and goodness.

As God's Word takes root and grows in your heart it will naturally begin to blossom and bear fruit. It is through the fruit of your words, attitudes, and deeds that you become a partner with the Master Gardener, scattering the seeds of His love in the lives of others. —Karla Dornacher, *Down a Garden Path To Places of Love and Joy*

What kind of fruit is growing in your heart?

"The grass withers and the flowers fall,
but the word of our God stands forever."
ISAIAH 40:8 NIV

Dressing Up

Did you ever play "dress up" with a friend when you were a little girl? A friend once told me that she and her girlfriends took themselves very seriously as they wiggled into her mom's old dresses and high-heeled shoes.

date: ....

As adults, we need to be aware that we can still help "dress" each other in godly garments by the way we relate and interact as friends.

The Bible says we are to put on "the garment of praise for the spirit of heaviness" (Isaiah 61:3). When you call a friend who you know is struggling and help her find joy in the midst of her trying circumstances, you are showing her how to put on that garment of praise. When you confide in a friend and ask her to pray for you, you're giving her the opporunity to put on love and compassion and reflect the character of Christ.

But we must be careful: We can pick up and put on filthy rags by mistake. Gossip, grumbling, covetousness, and complaining are not pretty, and they can feel uncomfortable and heavy.

So get serious: Call your girlfriends and help them wiggle into some of God's glorious garments. —Karla Dornacher, *The Blessing of Friendship: A Gift from the Heart*

How can you help dress your friends in godly garments? What are some godly garments?

"Charm is deceptive, and beauty is fleeting;
but a woman who fears the Lord is to be praised."
Proverbs 31:30 NIV

Your Value

date:

How appropriate that a dressing table with a large mirror should be called a "vanity." It beckons us to come, sit a spell, and find a sense of satisfaction, perhaps even a bit of pride, in our reflection. But God is pleased when you look in the mirror and find an inner peace and contentment, knowing that He created your features and, in fact, has numbered each hair on your head.

Don't spend your time worrying about your outward appearance—how you style your hair, the jewelry you wear, the cost of your perfume or the name brand of your clothes—rather let the beauty shine forth from within. Let the hidden person of your heart reflect a gentle and quiet spirit. This is precious in the sight of God.

Your value is not determined by your outward beauty. It is based on the truth of who God says you are: His dearly beloved child, formed in His image, created with a purpose and a calling.

As a godly woman and a representative of Jesus Christ, a clean and attractive appearance is an important example to your children and to the world, but more important is the care and nurture of a kind and loving heart.

—Karla Dornacher, *Love in Every Room*

How do you determine your value as a woman?

"Your beauty should not come from outward adornment such as braided hair and the wearing of gold jewelry and fine clothes. Instead, it should be that of your inner self, the unfading beauty of a gentle and quiet spirit, which is of great worth in God's sight."

1 Peter 3:3–4 NIV

An Anniversary Poem

For nearly every anniversary of our 30-year marriage, I have written a poem to my husband, Holmes, and presented it to him as a gift. It serves as a reminder of how our relationship has grown and how grateful I am for him, along with my hopes for our future. Each year as he reads the poem, whether by candlelight or in the harsh glare of a MacDonald's restaurant (once when we were moving back to Oklahoma from Maine), his heart is encouraged and warmed.

"We married on an autumn Saturday 26 years ago, but it was the spring of our marriage. Texas weather was sunny, our outlook as bright as the yellow mums blooming all around the church. We drove away in a white Chevy Nova as family and friends smiled and cheered to an overnight stay, then back to Waco where our jobs and reality awaited. As we joined our lives and hearts, our destinies, God's grace was always near the third strand of our relationship. So in seasons to come, during the winters of our marriage—some more joyful and painful than we'd ever dreamed—we would stand and stand together. May our hearts keep dancing always, celebrating the gift of life all our days. Much love, Cheri"

—Cheri Fuller, *The Fragrance of Kindness*

What words would you include in a poem to your husband?

date:

"If we love one another, God lives in us and his love is made complete in us."
1 John 4:12 NIV

Journey of Faith

date:

The tale of Moses begins with a slave baby, marked for death, hidden by his mother until he was three months old. The mother did something completely incomprehensible. She fashioned a basket and set the child adrift on the river (Exod. 2:1–4).

In modern times the woman's actions would be unthinkable—abandoning a helpless infant to the elements, leaving him to float into an uncertain future. We know, of course, what happened to the baby. It was all part of God's plan to set the Israelites free from Egyptian bondage. But his mother didn't know. She simply responded to the situation out of faith, and trusted God to take care of her son.

In our own journey of faith, we sometimes feel as if we are floating, too—caught in the whirlpool of circumstance, unable to control our destination, subject to the currents and eddies of the river that bears us along.

The Lord knew exactly where Moses was headed when he floated down the river. He was moving toward his future in God—first as an adopted Prince of Egypt; then as an exile from his own kind; and finally, after years of resistance, as the great Liberator who faced down the Pharaoh.

We can never know, when we're floating out of control on the current, just where God is taking us. But we can trust. We can remember how the Lord has led us in the past, and be at peace.

Do you feel as if you're up the river without a paddle? Don't panic. The water is not your doom, but your salvation. The current will bring you to the place you need to be. And maybe, it will be the first leg of a journey that will change your life forever. —Penelope J. Stokes, *Beside a Quiet Stream: Words of Hope for Weary Hearts*

Which areas in your life do you feel are floating out of control on the current?

"The Lord is good, a refuge in times of trouble.
He cares for those who trust in him."
NAHUM 1:7 NIV

ENVY

"A heart at peace gives life to the body, but envy rots the bones."
PROVERBS 14:30 NIV

How can you prevent envy from seeping into your life?

"Therefore, rid yourselves of all malice and all deceit, hypocrisy, envy, and slander of every kind."
1 PETER 2:1 NIV

Do you consider envy as devastating or as sinful as malice, deceit, hypocrisy, and slander? Does this verse change your thinking?

Potential Blessings

date:

When Cathy and Robert moved as college students to Oklahoma, the transition was difficult. But the elderly residents in their apartment complex rushed to their aid, making them feel part of the family. God used another neighbor to teach Cathy a valuable lesson that changed her life—and her spiritual viewpoint.

Sonia, a woman in her late thirties, left an abusive home at 17 to seek a career in nursing. At first Cathy and Robert found her difficult to get to know, but over time she slowly warmed up to them.

Robert and Cathy didn't have much money or food—yet on days when they planned to open a can of beans until the next paycheck, Sonia would suddenly appear at the door with a platter of roast chicken and wild rice!

Once their studies were finished, Cathy and Robert made plans to move to Massachusetts. Before they moved, Cathy said to Sonia, "You give and give, and I don't have much to give you. But I'd like to pay you back in some way for all the kindness you've shown us."

Sonia smiled at Cathy and answered, "You can pay me back by helping your new neighbors in Massachusetts."

God often brought Sonia's request to Cathy's mind. When she saw a new single mom, He whispered, *"There's someone you can help"* and nudged her to provide a meal.

Then just as Cathy felt she had paid back Sonia's kindness, she turned to Romans 12:1. "Present your bodies a living sacrifice, holy, acceptable to God, which is your reasonable service." Suddenly she realized that every opportunity to serve was another opportunity to worship God. The needs of her neighbors were not intrusions, but potential blessings! —Cheri Fuller, *Quiet Whispers from God's Heart for Women*

How can you worship God by serving others?

"This service that you perform is not only supplying the needs of God's people but is also overflowing in many expressions of thanks to God."
2 Corinthians 9:12 NIV

From an Adult's Perspective

All children love their mothers and see them larger than life. But it's through the eyes of an adult that we examine our own upbringing and begin to get a more balanced view. Happily, in my case, that childlike assessment of my mother hasn't changed through the years. As she approaches her sunset years and I follow her through the cycle of mothering and grandmothering, my appreciation of her work and wisdom grows. Even through the filter of adulthood, she still looms larger than life.

Only if my own children still give their upbringing high marks when they arrive at middle age will I have a true measure of my contributions to their life. Mothering stripped of its sentiment matters most. —Dianna Booher, *Mother's Gifts to Me*

How do you view your mother now that you're an adult? Will you share your views with her someday?

date:

"Listen, my son, to your father's instruction and do not forsake your mother's teaching. They will be a garland to grace your head and a chain to adorn your neck."

Proverbs 1:8–9 NIV

Self-Discipline

date:

Self-discipline is a private, secret virtue. It's not a practice that brings us external rewards, the accolades of others, or public recognition. And, to tell the truth, it's not the kind of virtue that most of us get a lot of pleasure out of pursuing.

Each of us has an individual calling to self-discipline. It may be the habit of setting aside regular time for prayer and Bible study. It may be curtailing the tendency toward workaholism in order to spend more time with the family. It may mean living on a budget, or finding the energy to do volunteer work, or tithing, or the rigorous commencement of a healthy diet and exercise program.

And we might as well admit it, self-discipline doesn't come easy. Hebrews 12:11 gives us a realistic picture: "No discipline seems pleasant at the time, but painful. Later on, however, it produces a harvest of righteousness and peace for those who have been trained by it."

Self-discipline is personal training—training in spiritual growth, in physical strength and health, in mental awareness. We work through the pain, through the discomfort and inconvenience, with our eyes fixed on the goal.

And we need to remember that our call to self-discipline is just that: our call. God may challenge others to a different kind of discipline, one we do not understand or cannot recognize.

Whatever God is asking you to do, whatever self-discipline is required, do it. The rewards will be greater than the cost. —Penelope J. Stokes, *Simple Words of Wisdom: 52 Virtues for Every Woman*

What kinds of self-discipline has God called you to practice?

"For God did not give us a spirit of timidity, but a spirit of power, of love and of self-discipline."
2 Timothy 1:7 NIV

Christian Marriage

"It is not good that a man should be alone." And God Himself solved this problem by creating, unique in all creation, a partner for man—not of the dust of the earth, as was every other creature including man, but from an eternal being.

date:

Weddings in Scripture were occasions of rich gifts, sumptuous feasting, and exquisite clothing. The bride's name was changed and the blessing of the parents and those who were committed to being "community" for the couple was seriously and joyfully bestowed.

It is my deep and passionate desire that weddings find their way once again to the place of sacred importance that reflects the significance, permanence, and deep joy that marriage can and must possess if the human race is to survive physically, spiritually, and psychologically.

This significance must be recaptured by us, who make up the community of faith. We must train our children to value virtues and treasure true character so that they will be and look for marriage partners of quality. We, ourselves, must keep our promises and fulfill our commitments to give our children a model of what marriage and home can look and feel like.

And we must be there for couples who marry, not just at the wedding, but all along their journey, to lift, support, encourage, nurture, and at times comfort, reminding them of their vows and our belief that problems should and can be solved. May we never forget that God Himself has pronounced marriage honorable (Heb. 13:5), intimate (Matt. 19:5), and permanent (Matt. 19:6). —Gloria Gaither, *Bless This Marriage*

In what ways could you encourage married couples you know?

"The Lord God said, 'It is not good for the man to be alone. I will make a helper suitable for him.' "
Genesis 2:18 NIV

Heart Soil

date:

Beautiful blooms and a bountiful harvest require good soil. In the Bible, Jesus uses a word picture of garden dirt to help us understand how the beauty and the bounty of our character, our life, and our deeds are dependent upon the condition of our heart soil. The seed of God's Word requires good soil to germinate, take root, grow deep, and bear abundant fruit.

Good heart soil is an ongoing, never-ending process. As you open your heart to the tender hand of the Master Gardener, He is able to till the hard places, remove the rocks, and pull up the weeds of the world that would entangle and choke out the life of His love.

Take time to cultivate your relationship with the Master Gardener. Ask Him to show you any areas of your heart soil where you need to let go and let Him work. Seek to be the beautiful and bountiful garden He designed you to be.

—Karla Dornacher, *Down a Garden Path To Places of Love and Joy*

What are some areas in your heart and in your soul that you need to let go to God's hands?

"But the one who received the seed that fell on good soil is the man who hears the word and understands it. He produces a crop, yielding a hundred, sixty or thirty times what was sown."

Matthew 13:23 NIV

OBEDIENCE

"If anyone loves me, he will obey my teaching. My Father will love him, and we will come to him and make our home with him."
JOHN 14:23 NIV

Do you obey Christ's teachings out of love for him?

"But if anyone obeys his word, God's love is truly made complete in him. This is how we know we are in him."
1 JOHN 2:5 NIV

Have you experienced God's complete love through obedience to His Word?

Prayer Partners

date:

"Oh Peggy, I can't do this!" I sobbed, as I anxiously poured out my heart over the telephone from 2,000 miles away. I was supposed to speak before a group of people in less than an hour, and fear had overcome me. All I could do was cry!

I thank God for praying friends like Peggy! When I call her, I'm confident that she will not feel sorry for me or try to "fix" me but she will lead me to Jesus, the only One who can truly meet my needs.

We all have struggles in life, moments when we want to run and hide, fears that overcome us, circumstances we don't know how to handle. I know how difficult it can be to share these struggles with others, to be vulnerable and express our need or sin or failure. But we need to look for and be the kind of friend Peggy is, one who will use times of weakness to point us to Jesus.

A power is released into our lives through prayer, one that is not available through any other activity on earth. It is a power that breaks down walls, unites our hearts, and leads us to look to and depend on Jesus and not ourselves.

—Karla Dornacher, *The Blessing of Friendship: A Gift from the Heart*

Do you have friends who will lead you to Jesus in a time of need?

"Do your best to present yourself to God as one approved, a workman who does not need to be ashamed and who correctly handles the word of truth."
2 Timothy 2:15 NIV

Spiritual Mothers

When I was processing the loss I felt when my mother died of cancer, I found that not only did I miss Mom, but I missed the nurturing influence of an older woman—someone who was farther along on the journey and could share her wisdom.

date:

As the reality of her passing sank in, God quietly whispered to me. *There are other mothers, spiritual moms I have provided along your path.*

There was Flo, an elderly widow from church. She told me that shortly after meeting us, God had instructed her to bring our family into her circle of prayer and intercede for us daily, as she did for her own children and grandchildren. When I visited Flo, she wanted to hear all about our three kids and never got bored with the details of Chris's college plans, Alison's mission trip, or my writing projects.

There was Billie, a shut-in I visited, who always gave me encouragement, prayer, wisdom, and tea. There was Patty, a friend in her sixties who celebrated each day in a colorful and zany way. Once when I was overwhelmed with the task of packing our belongings to move, Patty appeared at my door with boxes, sturdy tape, and white paper. She talked enthusiastically about new beginnings and the positive aspects of changing residences and prayed with me about our move. Her motherly encouragement made all the difference in my attitude.

When I think how these and other women have touched my life, God seems to whisper to me. *Look around you. What younger woman needs a motherly touch?* God has many mothers, grandmothers, and daughters in the Body of Christ. Perhaps you need one. Perhaps you can *be* one.

—Cheri Fuller, *Quiet Whispers from God's Heart for Women*

How have older women influenced your life?

"Teach the older women to be reverent in the way they live, not to be slanderers or addicted to much wine, but to teach what is good. Then they can train the younger women to love their husbands and children."

Titus 2:3–4 NIV

Love Letters

date:

Marriage Encounter weekends have helped thousands of couples recover the lost art of writing love letters, communicating with each other, and learning to share personal feelings in a heart-to-heart encounter.

Here's how you can incorporate this idea in your marriage. First determine a question you both want to answer such as, "What qualities do I love most about you?" (or a question related to children, work, or anything else). Spend 5 to 10 minutes writing an answer to the question and expressing your feelings in loving detail.

After exchanging letters, talk about your responses. Reach out to understand your spouse's feelings. Write these "love letters" weekly or more often and watch your relationship grow.

—Cheri Fuller, *The Fragrance of Kindness*

What question would you most like to answer with your husband?

"Each one of you also must love his wife as he loves himself, and the wife must respect her husband."
Ephesians 5:33 NIV

Miracles of Grace

God gave Jonah the mission of bringing the truth—and perhaps repentance—to the wicked city of Nineveh. It could have been a great adventure, a wonderful opportunity to see the grace of God at work. But Jonah didn't like the call. The people of Nineveh didn't deserve the Lord's mercy, Jonah had decided. Rather than responding in faith, he ran the other direction. It took being thrown overboard and swallowed by an enormous fish to bring him around to saying yes to God—and even then he did it reluctantly with an attitude.

When life gets difficult, when God calls us to outrageous obedience, rebellion can be a whirlpool that drags us under. And no matter how much effort we put into redecorating the interior of that fish's belly, it's still a place of darkness. It's still a place of separation from the One who has chosen and sent us.

We may not always understand why God works in such unconventional ways—why we need to be in a particular place at a particular time, or what the outcome of our obedience will be. Even after the fact, we may scratch our heads in confusion and wonder, "What was *that* all about?" We may sacrifice a great deal to obey God, only to see no visible results from our efforts. The people of our Nineveh may not repent at all.

But the *outcome* is not the issue. Our *attitude* is what matters to the Lord. Our willingness to respond affirmatively when the Spirit nudges us, even when we don't know why.

Who knows what miracles of grace may be wrought when you say yes to God. —Penelope J. Stokes, *Beside a Quiet Stream: Words of Hope for Weary Hearts*

date: ....

When have you seen the "miracles of grace" after you've obeyed the Spirit's nudges?

"This is love for God: to obey his commands.
And his commands are not burdensome. . . ."
1 John 5:3 NIV

A Life of Devotion

date:

Most of us, as Christians, have a pretty good idea of what "devotion to God" means. It means setting aside regular time for prayer and meditation, for Bible study. It means making a plan, having an agenda, putting it on our calendars—whatever we have to do to make sure that we spend time with God.

But if we're not careful, we can turn valid spiritual disciplines into a frantic effort to "get it done"—to fill the necessary quota of prayer time, Bible reading, or a dozen other "necessary" activities for maturity. God does not want our meaningless rituals. God wants our hearts.

Our intentions may be well placed, but a lot of our frenzied religious activity falls into the category of burdensome "burnt offerings"—or in the case of the modern Christian, "burnt-out offerings."

We cannot become deep, silent pools when our riverbeds are filled with the boulders of self-imposed—or church-imposed—expectations.

God, however, imposes no such artificial boundaries or regulations upon our spiritual intimacy with the Lord who loves us. There is a vast difference between having a prayer time and praying, between attending worship and worshiping.

God is more concerned with our life of devotion than with our devotional life.

We do not have to follow an approved format to come into the presence of the Lord, to find a place of deepening, and of peace. Our times of quietness, our moments of contemplation with God, do not have to conform to some artificial standard or rule. The important thing is that we have them. —Penelope J. Stokes, *Beside a Quiet Stream: Words of Hope for Weary Hearts*

Describe your times of quietness before the Lord—are they artificial or real?

"Your word is a lamp to my feet and a light for my path."
Psalm 119:105 NIV

Sacrifice

"The sacrifices of God are a broken spirit; a broken and contrite heart, O God, you will not despise."
Psalm 51:17 NIV

How can you give your broken spirit and heart to God?

"Therefore, I urge you, brothers, in view of God's mercy, to offer your bodies as living sacrifices, holy and pleasing to God—this is your spiritual act of worship."
Romans 12:1 NIV

Have you offered your body as a living sacrifice to God?
What do you think this entails?

Haven't I Heard That Somewhere?

date:

Experts tell us we have more than 177 messages coming to us each day by phone, E-mail, paper, or media ads. Obviously, repetition is what counts—in selling, in supervising, or in sharing our lives with our kids.

Truisms from the mouths of mothers have shaped the lives of children from generation to generation. Here are some of my mother's favorites:

- Mothers have eyes in the backs of their heads.
- A little bird told me.
- Pretty is as pretty does.
- If you don't have time to do it right the first time, how will you ever have time to do it over?
- If anything's worth doing, it's worth doing well.
- Just do your best—that's all anybody can expect of you.
- The early bird gets the worm.
- Elbow grease works well.
- Early to bed, early to rise, makes a person healthy, wealthy, and wise.
- Honesty is the best policy.
- What no one else sees, God always does.

—Dianna Booher, *Mother's Gifts to Me*

What are some sayings your mother said to you when you were a child? And how did her words influence you?

"My son, do not forget my teaching, but keep my commands in your heart, for they will prolong your life many years and bring you prosperity."
PROVERBS 3:1–2 NIV

PERSEVERANCE

In the movie *Titanic*, Rose—a woman trapped in a social structure she despises—stands on the ledge of the ocean liner about to commit suicide. Then Jack Dawson, a penniless artist, talks her from the edge. He grabs her hand and promises, "I won't let go."

date:

As the ship goes down, he holds her and says once more, "I won't let go." Rose survives, hanging onto floating debris. And Jack, bobbing in the frigid water, dies still holding her hand. He was true to his promise. He didn't let go.

It's a picture of the power of perseverance that holds on, in the face of insurmountable odds, to faith and hope and—for the Christian—to the conviction that God "won't let go."

The writer of Hebrews gives an extraordinary illustration of perseverance. Hebrews 11 cites examples of the great warriors of the faith, those who "kept the Passover, . . . passed through the Red Sea, . . . and received back their dead, raised to life again" (Heb. 11:28-35, NIV).

But it's not success that demonstrates the power of God, but perseverance. There were "others," who were put to death. "These were commended for their faith, yet none of them received what had been promised" (Heb. 11:39).

Real life doesn't always give us a conquest. We may never live to see the fulfillment of the promises, yet the promises are true, and our perseverance is not in vain.

And so we hold onto our faith when we can't see the way ahead. We wait, when we have no direction. Sometimes our perseverance seems like a frantic grasping at something to buoy us up in the cold water. But we hold on. Because God is present, reaching out to us, promising, "I won't let go."

—Penelope J. Stokes, *Simple Words of Wisdom: 52 Virtues for Every Woman*

When have you shown perseverance? How has God encouraged you to keep holding on?

"Consider it pure joy, my brothers, whenever you face trials of many kinds, because you know that the testing of your faith develops perseverance . . . so that you may be mature and complete, not lacking anything."
JAMES 1:2–4 NIV

Are You Willing?

date:

Hannah Hurnard was a withdrawn and fearful girl who dreaded people. But when she surrendered her heart to Christ at 20, He began to transform her life. She joined the Evangelistic Band and traveled around the countryside holding open-air meetings in the villages of England. She felt that some day she would be a missionary, but she had no idea where she would go.

After four years with the Evangelistic Band, Hannah spent some time in Ireland. One afternoon, she was invited to go on an outing to Ireland's Eye. When Hannah found herself alone, she sat on a grassy knoll and took out her Bible. God whispered to her, *"Hannah, would you be willing to identify yourself with the Jewish people in the same way Daniel identified with the Israelites?"*

Hannah was upset by the question, for she didn't have any particular liking for the Jews. "How could I be a missionary to people I don't even like?" she asked.

"If you are willing to go, I will help you love the Jews and identify with them. It all depends on your will," God replied.

Hannah knelt on the hillside and told God she would obey. Her doctor advised that her health would never withstand working abroad, and after writing to the only mission she knew of in Palestine, she was rejected.

But Hannah persevered and eventually did go to Israel. She had to pay her own expenses to travel and minister to the Jewish people, but because of her obedience that day at Ireland's Eye, God launched Hannah Hurnard into a lifelong ministry of evangelism, speaking, and writing that touched millions of people around the world for Christ.

—Cheri Fuller, *Quiet Whispers from God's Heart for Women*

What has God asked you to do for Him that at first you didn't want to obey?

"The world and its desires pass away,
but the man who does the will of God lives forever."
1 John 2:17 NIV

Open the Gate

There are many "gates" along life's way that open to fields of thorny thistles, tangled weeds, and briar woods. But there is only one gate that opens into the presence of the Master Gardener—and Jesus is that Gate!

If you are feeling overgrown with the challenges of daily life, weary of pulling out the weeds of the world, or tired of the path you are walking, open the Gate! Invite God to come into the garden of your heart through faith in Jesus Christ. Ask Him to be the Master Gardener of your life.

He wants to meet with you there in the quiet places and walk with you as your closest friend. He wants to plant roses where there are weeds, remove the rocks that cause you to stumble, and water the dry and barren places of your life with His love and blessings. —Karla Dornacher, *Down a Garden Path To Places of Love and Joy*

Is anything keeping you from opening the gate and inviting Jesus into the garden of your heart?

date: ....

"Ask and it will be given to you; seek and you will find; knock and the door will be opened to you. For everyone who asks receives; he who seeks finds; and to him who knocks, the door will be opened."
Matthew 7:7–8 NIV

An Overflowing Cup

date:

Even though I'm a coffee-by-choice woman, I delight in cup of hot tea served in a beautiful floral teacup and savored in the company of dear friends.

My friend Sandi collects teacups and teapots—not just because they're so pretty, but because she truly enjoys tea, much like I enjoy coffee. Whenever I visit her, she always has the teakettle whistling, ready to fill my cup with some fragrant herbal brew. This friend graciously serves me not only a cup of tea, but also the cup of total acceptance and love—a drink of blessing that overflows my heart.

I first met Sandi during a very difficult time of my life. I was emotionally wounded and lonely. She somehow saw through the "bandages" I had applied to my heart, not bandages for healing, but for protection. She reached out with the love of Christ and encouraged me as I loosened the thick wrappings and allowed myself to once again experience the true friendship of other women.

Dear Jesus, help me to have a servant heart—to be a woman who pours a drink more refreshing than tea. May the cup I offer to the women you have placed in my life always overflow with your love and acceptance.

—Karla Dornacher, *The Blessing of Friendship: A Gift from the Heart*

What fills the "cup" you offer to those God has placed in your life? To whom can you offer a cup of kindness?

"May the Lord make your love increase and overflow for each other and for everyone else, just as ours does for you."
1 Thessalonians 3:12 NIV

Heirs of God

"So you are no longer a slave, but a son; and since you are a son, God has made you also an heir."
Galatians 4:7 NIV

Have you ever thought of yourself as an heir of God?

"Now if we are children, then we are heirs—heirs of God and coheirs with Christ, if indeed we share in his sufferings in order that we may also share in his glory."
Romans 8:17 NIV

As an heir of God, what do you hope to inherit?

Praise Him

date:

Like true love, praise is not based on an emotion but a decision. Your feelings may say there is nothing to be thankful for, but by choosing to focus on what is true, good, and worthy of praise, you can change your thoughts and your attitude. And when you praise God with your mind, your heart is soon to follow.

If you are not in the habit of praising God, begin today. Celebrate all He has done for you and the wonder of who He is.

And remember, children learn best from example. The importance of passing on the habit of praise to your children cannot be overemphasized!

If you need inspiration, read the Word of God, especially the book of Psalms.

God gave you your voice, so why not lift it up to Him in praise? Don't wait until Sunday, turn on the music and praise Him today!

Worshipping at God's footstool has a way of putting things on this earth into proper perspective.

—Karla Dornacher, *Love in Every Room*

Will you praise God today?

"From the rising of the sun to the place where it sets, the name of the Lord is to be praised."
PSALM 113:3 NIV

WRITE IT ACROSS THE SKY

After former President Richard Nixon resigned from the presidency in shame and humiliation, he had to undergo major surgery. Overwhelmed with so much disappointment and physical pain, Nixon became severely depressed. Lying in the hospital room day after day, he began to lose hope and even the will to live. He told his wife, Pat, that he wanted to die. But at his lowest moment, a nurse came into the room, opened the curtains, and pointed to a small plane flying back and forth in front of his window. It was pulling a sign that read: "GOD LOVES YOU AND SO DO WE!"

Seeing that letter written across the sky, and sensing the loving prayers behind it gave Nixon the courage to recover. Later, he found out that Ruth Bell Graham had personally arranged for the plane to fly around the hospital. The former president not only survived, but went on to serve both his family and country with dignity and grace for several years.

What strength comes with positive words of encouragement—whether spoken or written across the sky!

—Cheri Fuller, *The Fragrance of Kindness*

Who needs to hear an encouraging word from you today?

date:

"An anxious heart weighs a man down, but a kind word cheers him up."
PROVERBS 12:25 NIV

Outrageous Directions

date: ....

What do you do when God's will doesn't make sense? It's a question that troubles us all, from time to time. Logic seems to direct us one way; our best reasoning, our "pros and cons" list all point in the same direction. But something else—others call it instinct, a gut feeling; I call it the Spirit's leading—tells us no.

We're okay with the Spirit's leading as long as the outcome seems reasonable. But to step out in faith, without the finances or the spiritual resources or the emotional strength to do what we're being called to do? Then we balk, second-guess ourselves, and rationalize: "God couldn't possibly be directing me to do something so completely outrageous."

Abraham was told to leave his home and travel to a land he'd never seen. Moses heard a voice from a burning bush instructing him to go back to Egypt to set the captives free. Noah was given plans to build a floating zoo. Mary, unwed, frightened, and little more than a child herself, received the announcement that she'd been chosen to bear the incarnate Immanuel.

When God seems to be leading us in outrageous directions, the experience can be a challenge to our faith—a whirlpool that sucks us into confusion and fear, a riptide that seems to pull the bottom out from under us. "I can't do that!" we protest. "I'm not equipped for the job."

Is God asking you to do something outrageous? To risk your comfort, or your security, or your reputation for the sake of obedience? Have faith, the faith of those who have gone before you into dangerous waters. Faith is stronger than any riptide. —Penelope J. Stokes, *Beside a Quiet Stream: Words of Hope for Weary Hearts*

Are you willing to trust God even if His will doesn't make sense?

"Now go; I will help you speak and will teach you what to say."
Exodus 4:12 NIV

Christ in Us

We parked overlooking the Sea of Galilee and wandered through a field to a natural amphitheater tucked on the side of the hill. It was late in the day. All the tour buses were gone, and the hillside was quiet. A breeze rustled a tree nearby. Ken drew a deep breath, stretched his arms wide and said, "Oh, to be where Jesus was!" Looking up at him, I smiled in reply.

date:

The sky was large and wide, ablaze from the setting sun. With a dry wind whipping his hair, he faced the glowing sky and began to recite Jesus' words: "Blessed are the poor in spirit, for theirs is the kingdom of heaven. Blessed are those who mourn, for they will be comforted . . ."

The wind carried Ken's words, caressing the land with the same beatitudes Christ once pronounced over the hill. "Blessed are those who hunger and thirst for righteousness, for they will be filled. Blessed are the peacemakers, for they will be called sons of God."

As Ken slowly recited the sermon, picking up speed as he went, I was gripped. Not so much by the thought of being where Jesus was but where He is, right now, shining through the eyes of my husband, resonating through every fiber of Ken's being, filling his life with virtue and courage. He's living now as Ken gives voice to His words.

Yes, to be where Jesus was is heartwarming. That He's coming back is heart pumping. But the most powerful reality is that Jesus is. He is the great I AM living in the present tense, sustaining everything by the power of His word.

The present reality of Christ pulsing and breathing life and vitality into our souls is matchless. The past and the present can't touch it. I know. I saw it that day on a hill above the Sea of Galilee. —Joni Eareckson Tada, *Holiness in Hidden Places*

How is the reality of Christ evident in you each day?

"I have been crucified with Christ and I no longer live, but Christ lives in me."
Galatians 2:20 NIV

Self-Acceptance

date:

Self-acceptance is a virtue often challenged by the religious community. Suspicious of pop psychology and self-help programs, it claims that self-acceptance is not nearly as important to the Christian's life as God's acceptance. What really matters, they say, is what God thinks of me; never mind what I think of myself.

God's acceptance of us in Christ Jesus is the fundamental truth upon which we build our lives. But if we ignore the necessity of self-acceptance, we render ourselves unable to take full advantage of the abundant life offered to us in our Redeemer.

Yes, we need to acknowledge our limitations, to face our weaknesses, to confess our sins. But if we want to be active, productive participants in the realm of God, we also need to recognize our gifts, to appreciate our strengths, to build on the abilities God has given us. We need to balance humility with confidence.

Flannery O'Connor, a brilliant writer and devout believer, was once asked why she became a writer. "Because I'm good at it," she replied. It was a statement of fact, not a declaration of arrogance. Self-acceptance is not pride. It is the proportional "sober judgment" (Rom. 12:3) that allows us to see ourselves as we truly are, as God sees us.

Almighty God created us, redeemed us, called us, endowed us with gifts and abilities and perceptions. To demean the gift is to insult the Giver. —Penelope J. Stokes, *Simple Words of Wisdom: 52 Virtues for Every Woman*

Which strengths, gifts, and talents has God given you? How can you glorify Him with them?

"For by the grace given me I say to every one of you: Do not think of yourself more highly than you ought, but rather think of yourself with sober judgment, in accordance with the measure of faith God has given you."
Romans 12:3 NIV

Trials

"Blessed is the man who perseveres under trial, because when he has stood the test, he will receive the crown of life that God has promised to those who love him."
James 1:12 NIV

During which trials have you persevered?

....

....

....

....

....

....

....

....

....

"Dear friends, do not be surprised at the painful trial you are suffering, as though something strange were happening to you. But rejoice that you participate in the sufferings of Christ, so that you may be overjoyed when his glory is revealed."
1 Peter 4:12–13 NIV

Are you able to rejoice as you suffer through trials?

....

....

....

....

....

....

....

ENCOURAGING TRUTH

date:

Sometimes God whispers to us during the noise of everyday life through familiar voices. Jennifer had such an experience one spring day when she and her eight-year-old son were playing a marble game. Because of diminishing eyesight due to a chronic disease, she had to cut the game short.

"Clayton, Mama needs to play a different game. I just can't see to do this anymore." As her son put up the game it was obvious he was in deep thought.

Finally he said, "Mom, I don't think God will heal you here on earth."

Immediately, Jennifer heard the quiet voice of her Heavenly Father say, *"Listen, listen to My heart."* She reflected on what Clayton had said and asked him, "Why don't you think God will heal me on earth?"

He answered, "Because I think God wants you to love heaven more, and if He healed you on earth, you might like earth more—and heaven is best!"

Jennifer knew that God's voice had swept truth through her spirit in the words of her child. Truth she would never forget. Truth that would encourage her in weariness and sustain her through heartache. —Cheri Fuller, *Quiet Whispers from God's Heart for Women*

When has God spoken an encouraging truth to you through the familiar voice of a family member or friend?

"Therefore we do not lose heart. Though outwardly we are wasting away, yet inwardly we are being renewed day by day. For our light and momentary troubles are achieving for us an eternal glory that far outweighs them all."
2 CORINTHIANS 4:16–17

Children of Light

My husband and I live in the Great Northwest, and we love it here. Though the climate is mild, we have more than our share of rainy days. For many, this lack of sunlight can be depressing, but when the sky turns blue and the sun decides to shine, folks begin to smile, and joy fills the air. There is a sense of celebration everywhere you go!

Jesus is called the "light of the world." Walk with Him as your closest Friend, and you cannot help but soak up the glorious streams of His love and blessing. As the light of His goodness flows into the dark and dreary places of your heart, despair gives way to hope, and there truly is a sense of celebration and joy in His presence!

God call us "children of light." As we walk through life, we are like stars in the darkness, shining God's love and blessing into the lives of those around us. The more we reflect the character of the Son, the brighter we shine. It's the warm rays of love, generosity, integrity, honesty, and caring that bring life to the heart of true friendship.

—Karla Dornacher, *The Blessing of Friendship: A Gift from the Heart*

As a child of light, are you shining brightly today?

date:

"In the same way, let your light shine before men, that they may see your good deeds and praise your Father in heaven."
Matthew 5:16 NIV

Rest for Your Soul

date: ....

Keeping a home, nurturing others, and facing life's daily challenges can easily leave you tired, weary, and burdened. Jesus is waiting to give you rest for your soul.

Jesus has sent you a personal invitation. "Come to me all you who are weary and burdened, and I will give you rest." Accept His invitation today!

Let your heavenly Father wrap you in His quilt of love and tenderness so you will know how special you are to Him. You are the apple of His eye!

The Holy Spirit comes to you as your comforter, to speak peace to your heart and to guide you. As you spend time with Him, you will see the beauty and the majesty of His loving care even in the midst of your circumstances. Use this quiet time to reflect and meditate on God's Word.

Come, worship at God's footstool, for His Word says that as we humble ourselves before Him, He will lift us up.

—Karla Dornacher, *Love in Every Room*

Will you come to God today for rest and peace?

"My soul finds rest in God alone; my salvation comes from him. He alone is my rock and my salvation; he is my fortress, I will never be shaken."
PSALM 62:1–2 NIV

WAYS TO ENCOURAGE

Creative ways to encourage your family:

•Tuck notes of encouragement in lunch boxes or brown bags.

•Slip notes in tennis shoes or leave on a pillow to be found at bedtime.

•Make a family mailbox and put in pieces of paper that family members can use to write notes of encouragement and appreciation to each other.

•Create a writing basket for each child, complete with bright notepaper and envelopes, sticky notes, pen or pencil, stickers, and stamps. Encourage your children to write to teachers, cousins, and friends they meet at camp.

•Slide notes under the bedroom door: When your child becomes a teenager, you'll be glad if you've already established a custom of writing notes to one another.

•Slip notes, such as "Don't forget to take out the garbage," under the door. They will probably be better received than nagging. And "I'll be cheering for you in tomorrow's soccer game" inspires confidence.

•Write notes such as "I'm sorry I lost my cool last night. Please forgive the spillover of my stress on you, honey!" They're great for apologies and can smooth relationships between parents and teens.

—Cheri Fuller, *The Fragrance of Kindness*

How could you encourage your family today?

date: ....

"Pleasant words are a honeycomb, sweet to the soul and healing to the bones."
PROVERBS 16:24 NIV

Sorrows Like Sea Billows

date: ....

We'd like to think that our lives as Christians would be free from disaster. But difficult times do come. Relationships hit the rocks, faith is overwhelmed by the flood. Confusion besets us, and we're left with one of the huge unanswered questions of the universe: Where is God when the clouds roll in?

Job, that great biblical example of faith in the midst of despair, expresses for us all our feelings during stormy times: "Truly the thing that I fear comes upon me, and what I dread befalls me. I am not at ease, nor am I quiet; I have no rest, but trouble comes" (Job 3:25–26).

Many of us, however, have difficulty being as honest with God as Job was. Instead of understanding that rough waters are an inevitable part of our spiritual journey, we take the role of Job's "comforters." We question our own integrity. We confess imaginary sins. We figure that somehow we must be at fault when our lives seem to fall apart.

And certainly, sin sometimes does play a part in the difficulties we encounter. On occasion we bring trouble upon ourselves by the choices we make, and when that happens we need to turn back to our Savior. But we also need to understand that the whirlpools and riptides we encounter as we travel through life may simply be part of the process, the ways we learn and grow and strengthen our trust.

Don't be afraid to express your fears and questions. Job did, and in the end God spoke to him and revealed treasured truths about the Divine Nature that he couldn't have gained any other way.

Sorrows may roll over you like the billows of the sea, but as long as you hold onto God, you can say from the depths of faith: "It is well with my soul." —Penelope J. Stokes, *Beside a Quiet Stream: Words of Hope for Weary Hearts*

When have you been strengthened through a storm?

"In my anguish I cried to the Lord, and he answered by setting me free. The Lord is with me; I will not be afraid."
Psalm 118:5–6 NIV

Truth

"I, the Lord, speak the truth; I declare what is right."
Isaiah 45:19 NIV

How has the Lord spoken the truth to you? Do you recognize that His ways are what is right for you?

"Jesus said, 'If you hold to my teaching, you are really my disciples. Then you will know the truth, and the truth will set you free.' "
John 8:31–32 NIV

How does knowing, believing, and holding to the truth set you free? What are some of Christ's truths that you know and follow?

Reverence

date:

In a quiet sanctuary, people kneel praying. Priests or monks. Holy people. People set apart for service to God. It's an image of reverence that pervades religious consciousness. But there was another kind of monk—one who discovered a deep relationship with God in a monastery kitchen.

His name was Brother Lawrence, and his book, *The Practice of the Presence of God*, gives us a different perspective of reverence. "Lord of all pots and pans and things," he prayed, "make me a saint by getting meals and washing up the plates!" Now, here is an image of reverence we can identify with.

Most of us have to discover God in the midst of a harried schedule. We rarely find time for meditation. We don't have the luxury—or the discipline, perhaps—of hours of solitude with God.

But reverence is more a state of the heart than a matter of silence. We revel in those times of quiet meditation, certainly. We long for them, and welcome them when they come. But we can, like Brother Lawrence, learn to give ourselves to a spirit of reverence no matter what we're doing.

The prophet Jeremiah reminds us of our motivation for approaching God with reverence: "No one is like you, O, Lord. . . . Who should not revere you?" (Jer. 10:6–7).

And that truth is all we need to live in a spirit of awe and worship before the Lord. No matter what we're doing, we can live in a state of reverence toward God.

O Lord, let me hear your voice above the clamor of my daily life, for "there is no one like you." —Penelope J. Stokes, *Simple Words of Wisdom: 52 Virtues for Every Woman*

How can you live in a state of reverence toward God during the clamor of your daily schedule?

"No one is like you, O Lord; you are great, and your name is mighty in power. Who should not revere you, O King of the nations? . . . there is no one like you."
Jeremiah 10: 6–7 NIV

God Will Help

A missionary wife and mother, Paula and her family were on their way to the airport with her mom and dad. Their furlough was over. The recurring sadness of leaving parents, siblings, friends, and homeland to serve for four more years in Thailand was overwhelming. And the sight of her four backpack-laden children, a small mountain of carry-on luggage, and nineteen suitcases was almost more than Paula could handle.

Quickly and efficiently her dad pulled the car up to the curb and gave the family orders on what to do. Within seconds they were all outside the airport entrance saying good-bye. Then she watched her parents' car speed off. Paula stood on the curb feeling totally alone. Her parents were gone, her husband had run into the airport for check-in, and she was left with the sole responsibility of four excited kids. Paula's eyes swung around for one more head count, every nerve in her body strung taught with emotion.

Just then, it was as though Someone stood next to her and quietly whispered, *"Fear not, for I am with you; be not dismayed, for I am your God. I will strengthen you, yes, I will help you, I will uphold you with My righteous right hand"* (Isaiah 41:10).

Those words of assurance were just what Paula needed. Suddenly she knew without a doubt that God, who had called her to this unique lifestyle, was with her and would give her strength for the journey ahead.

Two days later they arrived safely in Bangkok, weary but smiling—a dad, a mom, four kids, and all 19 pieces of luggage! —Cheri Fuller, *Quiet Whispers from God's Heart for Women*

How has God whispered calming words of reassurance and encouragement to you during an overwhelming time in your life?

date: ....

"We wait in hope for the Lord; he is our help and our shield."
Psalm 33:20 NIV

THE GIFT OF FRIENDS

date:

Have you ever tried to find the "perfect" gift to give a special friend? You want her to know how much you care, so you're willing to shop 'til you drop to find it!

To give the perfect gift you must first know the heart of your friend. It needs to fit who she is—her personality, her style, her season of life!

Because God already knows your heart, your friends are His perfect gift to you. He knows the need for a proper fit! Consider for a moment the friendships you've enjoyed. Every one has been unique, no two alike. Each one was chosen with great care, by God, especially for you!

We may sometimes even wonder at God's choice, but He knows us and our needs better than we know ourselves. He gives us friends, not only for our own blessing, but to teach us to be better blessing-givers.

May we rejoice in the goodness of the greatest Gift-Giver of all and the gifts of friendship we've been given.

—Karla Dornacher, *The Blessing of Friendship: A Gift from the Heart*

Who are the friends God has blessed you with? How have your friendships taught you to be a better blessing-giver?

"He who did not spare his own Son, but gave him up for us all—how will he not also, along with him, graciously give us all things?"

ROMANS 8:32 NIV

The Boat Will Float

In recent times not one but two television networks have produced movies about Noah and his enormous boat. It's a story of audacious obedience to God, who knows what the future holds.

date:

Noah, the Bible tells us, was a righteous person in an unrighteous world. When the Lord gave him the command, he built the ark, rounded up the animals and his family, and waited. And then it happened. "The rain fell on the earth forty days and forty nights" (Gen. 7:12).

Noah had faith. He had no outward sign the flood was coming. He didn't really understand what the future would bring, but he responded to God. He built the ark, and then entrusted his life and the lives of those he loved to the boat. He didn't steer or try to figure out where they were going. He just watched and waited as the ark was borne up on the waters and set down again on the mountain.

My dad taught me a similar lesson when I fished with him as a young girl. "Trust the boat," he told me. "If something happens and we capsize, the boat will float. Hang onto it—don't strike out on your own."

Our lives, even as Christians, are fraught with uncertainty. Storm clouds gather. The rains begin to fall. Lightning and thunder strike fear into our hearts. God doesn't reveal the future to us, doesn't tell us what is going to happen or how things will turn out. But the Lord does give us assurance that when the floods come, we will be borne up and brought to a new place in our relationship with God.

Resist the temptation to strike out on your own. Have faith. Wait. Sooner than you expect, the waters will subside.

—Penelope J. Stokes, *Beside a Quiet Stream: Words of Hope for Weary Hearts*

How can you have faith in God in the midst of the rising waters of your life?

"Then they cried out to the Lord in their trouble, and he brought them out of their distress. He stilled the storm to a whisper; the waves of the sea were hushed."
Psalm 107:28–29 NIV

A Teacher's Encouragement

date:

People often ask me, "Who encouraged you to be a writer?" When I began writing, there was little career counseling for girls. We were told we could be nurses, teachers, or secretaries, but no one included being a writer.

Yet my high school English teacher Miss Carpenter wrote "lucid writing" on my *Anna Karenina* critical essay and "insightful, articulate thoughts" on my research paper. Her sprinkling of encouraging words on these and other compositions planted seeds of possibility in me, for which I'll always be grateful.

When I began teaching right out of college, I wrote up a list of "99 Ways to Say 'Very Good!' " and kept it right in my grade book, as a reminder to find something positive in every composition or essay I graded for my ninth grade students. It helped me to encourage them—and thus pass on the kindness I had received. —Cheri Fuller, *The Fragrance of Kindness*

Who motivated you to do what you're doing now? How did they encourage you? How does God encourage us and tell us "very good"?

"May our Lord Jesus Christ himself and God our Father, who loved us and by his grace gave us eternal encouragement and good hope, encourage your hearts and strengthen you in every good deed and word."
2 Thessalonians 2:16–17 NIV

REWARDS

"You know that the Lord will reward everyone for whatever good he does, whether he is slave or free."
EPHESIANS 6:8 NIV

How have you been rewarded for doing good in the Lord's name?

"And without faith it is impossible to please God, because anyone who comes to him must believe that he exists and that he rewards those who earnestly seek him."
HEBREWS 11:6 NIV

Do you seek God really believing that He will reward you? What kind of rewards do you receive when you seek God with faith and believe in Him?

JOY FROM THE WELL

date:

We used to sing it in Sunday school—a rousing little song that never failed to evoke clapping and laughter:

I've got the joy, joy, joy, joy down in my heart.
Down in my heart.
Down in my heart . . .
Down in my heart to stay.

But I wondered as I grew older—*Why was the joy down in my heart to stay?* Shouldn't it be flowing out, spilling over to affect my life and the lives of those around me?

People say that joy and happiness are not the same thing. Happiness is external, based on circumstances. Joy is like a deep current, unaffected by what's happening on the surface.

But shouldn't the deep joy in our hearts have an effect on how we view our circumstances, how we deal with stormy weather and disappointment? Joy isn't something we cling to the way a drowning person clings to a life raft. Joy is the inner conviction that something is fundamentally right in our lives, in our relationships with God and others.

The well of salvation is deep and pure and clear. Drawing from it changes everything—not just our eternal destiny, but our daily lives. Salvation transforms our everlasting souls, to be sure, but it also alters our hearts and minds, our relationships, our attitudes and actions.

Let down your bucket into the well of salvation and draw up the water of life with joy. Shout out loud.

You've got the joy down in your heart—don't let it stay hidden there. —Penelope J. Stokes: *Beside a Quiet Stream: Words of Hope for Weary Hearts*

How can you outwardly display the joy in Christ that's deep in your heart?

"With joy you will draw water from the wells of salvation. In that day you will say: 'Give thanks to the Lord, call on his name; make known among the nations what he has done, and proclaim that his name is exalted.' "

ISAIAH 12:3–4 NIV

God's Feast

You have been invited to a banquet prepared by the Lord Himself! He wants to set before you foods that are guaranteed to delight your palate and nourish your soul. Come, taste and see for yourself just how wonderful and good He is.

date:

This is a come-as-you-are dinner. You don't have to dress up. You don't have to hide your scars, weaknesses, or failures, for He sees you through the eyes of unconditional love. And to Him you are beautiful. He wants you to come just as you are to His table of goodness and grace.

Just as He fed the multitudes with the loaves and fishes, Jesus has promised to supply your needs as well.

Accept His invitation. Take time to sit at His table.

Open your Bible and allow Him to fill your empty plate. "Chew" the Word thoroughly, meditate on it and think about how it applies to your life. Then allow it to become part of who you are, nourishing, refreshing, and energizing your very being.

As you look upon this table, let the bread remind you that Jesus is the Bread of Life, the source of all you need. He has promised to bring you to a land of milk and honey, a place of spiritual abundance. The herbs and vinegar are reminders of the variety of flavors—both sweet and bitter—that God uses to season our days.

When you partake of the Lord's feast, trusting and believing in His provision for every area of your life, you will be able to lead others, especially your children, to the table of the King. —Karla Dornacher, *Love in Every Room*

Will you accept God's invitation, take time at His table, and allow Him to fill your empty plate with the Bread of Life?

"Then Jesus declared, 'I am the bread of life. He who comes to me will never go hungry, and he who believes in me will never be thirsty.' "

John 6:35 NIV

Watching over You

date:

At a speaker's training seminar, Lael and the other participants were invited to share prayer requests. Lael asked for wisdom for her writing and speaking ministry. The seminar leader spoke up, "I'd like to pray for you, Lael, that because of your rheumatoid arthritis and difficulties in getting around, God would raise up someone to travel with you and assist you."

I appreciate her thoughtfulness, Lael thought, but I certainly can't afford someone to travel with me.

Before flying back home to Houston, Lael checked in her rental car and the attendant asked, "Why don't you leave your bags in the car and I'll just drive you up to the gate?"

At the gate, Lael was fumbling with her coat, carry-on bag, and briefcase when the skycap offered, "Why don't you let me put all that in a box for you?" With only her briefcase, Lael looked at the stairs to the Cleveland commuter plane. How was she going to manage the stairs? Before she had time to wonder, a skycap whisked her in a wheelchair through the airport and out to where she boarded the plane.

In Cleveland, Lael waited for her flight to Houston. The clerk handed Lael a new ticket and said, "We bumped you up to first class. We thought you'd be more comfortable there."

Lael could hardly believe her good fortune. She could almost hear God saying *"Isn't this fun? I'm smiling on you and enjoying watching over you today!"*

She thought of the seminar leader's prayer request. Lael giggled, realizing that God—or one of His angels—had been her flight partner all the way home! —Cheri Fuller, *Quiet Whispers from God's Heart for Women*

Lately, how has God smiled on you and watched over you during challenging circumstances?

"You discern my going out and my lying down; you are familiar with all my ways. You hem me in—behind and before; you have laid your hand upon me."
Psalm 139:3, 5 NIV

Repentance

"Like a spider dangling over the pit of hell by a single thread . . ." Jonathan Edwards's simile is one of the most memorable images ever devised to convey the necessity of repentance. That sermon, "Sinners in the Hands of an Angry God" may have been what modern folks would call "fire-and-brimstone preaching," but it worked.

In terms of initial salvation, Edwards's illustration is certainly an apt one. We often have to come to the end of our spiritual rope, to the exhaustion of our own resources, before we see the need to repent and turn to the Lord.

But repentance is not a one-time act, a moment in which we see the enormity of sin and call out to God for redemption. For the believer, repentance is a state of mind and heart, a willingness to keep turning away from anything that threatens to separate us from the Lord we love and serve.

If repentance means "to turn around, to change your mind, and go in the other direction," then our daily lives are filled with repentance decisions. Choosing to obey rather than resist. Deciding to forgive rather than seek revenge. Determining to love rather than nurture resentment.

We need repentance of sin for salvation. But we also need repentance of "self." We need to have hearts tuned to hear the voice of God's Spirit within that tells us to turn around.

We need a change of mind.

In the world's view, changing your mind is a sign of instability. Once you make a decision, you stand by it. But God wants to move us, to change us, to conform us to the image of Jesus Christ. And repentance is the first step in that change.

So let your heart reach toward God in repentance. It's okay to change your mind. —Penelope J. Stokes, *Simple Words of Wisdom: 52 Virtues for Every Woman*

date: ....

How do you need to change your mind and repent?

"This is what the Sovereign Lord, the Holy One of Israel, says: 'In repentance and rest is your salvation, in quietness and trust is your strength. . . .' "
Isaiah 30:15 NIV

A Letter of Blessing

date: ....

Steve Lynn is a business executive in Nashville. At each milestone in his children's lives, he writes them a letter of blessing such as the one below. It's a precious tradition, and the letters will certainly be treasures for his children to keep forever.

A letter of blessing for Laura Whitney Lynn as she begins middle school:

My dear Whitney,

Our chosen little baby, tomorrow is another major passage as you become a beautiful, unique young lady. Your Mother and I are grateful for you. We are proud of your external and internal beauty, your bright exploring mind, mothering instincts, loving heart, and creativity.

Through Christ our Lord, I bless you and pray God's blessings upon this step and throughout your life journey. I pray for self-discipline, focus, and commitment to excellence; for balance and enjoyment of the journey; for lots of good friends; and for a focus on relationships rather than things. I encourage you to understand that true freedom comes only from a call to personal responsibility to our fellow man and to our creator.

You have already experienced some of life's hurts. I praise you for how you have overcome them, and I continue to pray daily that you will be surrounded by God's protective angels. You are God's child given to Mom and me for a time until, in a few short years, you are fully ready to be a responsible adult. We are so thankful that you and God chose us. May our Lord bless and keep you.

Love, Dad

—Cheri Fuller, *The Fragrance of Kindness*

How have your parents' words guided you at a milestone in your life?

"Train a child in the way he should go,
and when he is old he will not turn from it."
PROVERBS 22:6 NIV

Trusting God

"Those who trust in the Lord are like Mount Zion, which cannot be shaken but endures forever."
Psalm 125:1 NIV

In the past, how has your trust in the Lord allowed you to not be shaken by troubles?

"In that day they will say, 'Surely this is our God; we trusted in him, and he saved us. This is the Lord, we trusted in him; let us rejoice and be glad in his salvation.' "
Isaiah 25:9 NIV

Have you rejoiced and praised God for His trustworthiness and salvation?

SATISFACTION

date: ....

Years ago it was the "All You Can Eat Buffet." The advertisement conjured up images of truck drivers sitting at a table with food and stuffing themselves until they could barely stagger to the door. Now we've renamed the ritual "All You Care to Eat." Either way, it's a picture of complete gustatory satisfaction—or excess.

In the sixties, the Rolling Stones sang, "I Can't Get No Satisfaction." The song became a byword for a generation. We're never satisfied. We're always looking toward the future—a higher paying job, a bigger house, more toys, more elaborate vacations. Sometimes, even a younger and better-looking spouse.

But that's not the kind of satisfaction the Lord guarantees.

God's promise for prosperity and fulfillment isn't about what we own or what designer labels we wear or which kind of car we drive. Certainly, the Lord is concerned with our physical lives—food and shelter, clothing and love. But the all-you-can-eat buffet isn't high on the divine priority list.

Satisfaction in God has a different focus. "Hungry and thirsty, their soul fainted within them." the Psalmist tells us. "Then they cried to the Lord . . . and he delivered them from their distress . . . He satisfies the thirsty, and the hungry he fills with good things" (Ps. 107:5–9).

When we get discontented—reaching out for something more, longing for better things, restless for change—perhaps our souls are fainting within us, calling out to be delivered from our distress. We can charge the maximum on our credit cards, or we can turn to God, whose steadfast love feeds us in ways our dissatisfied world cannot understand.

—Penelope J. Stokes, *Beside a Quiet Stream: Words of Hope for Weary Hearts*

What are you seeking to satisfy the hunger in your soul?

"They asked, and he brought them quail and satisfied them with the bread of heaven."
PSALM 105:40 NIV

Compassion

An old Hasidic rabbi shared his wisdom with a young student. Overcome by his mentor's teachings, the young man cried out, "I love you, my Master!" The old man turned to the student with a sad expression on his face. "How can you claim to love me," he responded, "when you do not know what makes me weep?"

date: ....

In Christian circles we talk a lot about compassion—empathizing with others and ministering to the needy. But God requires more of us than random acts of charity. God calls us to "love our neighbor as ourselves."

It's a challenge. We know what makes us weep. But do we know the hidden anguish in the hearts of those around us? Do we know what makes God weep?

Matthew gives us a clue. "When [Jesus] saw the crowds, he had compassion upon them, because they were harassed and helpless, like sheep without a shepherd" (Matt. 9:36).

People today, even members of our families and churches, citizens of our own hometowns—our literal neighbors—are harassed and helpless, wandering sheep. But it's not enough simply to herd them into church and tell them spiritual stories about the Good Shepherd. Jesus did more than teach them. He lived among the lost sheep, healing them and feeding them, listening to their stories of brokenness, shattered dreams, and unmet needs.

A lot of shepherdless sheep roam among us. They are waiting. We can bring hope and healing, direction and protection. But we dare not go to them with superficial piety. We must go as Jesus did. He loved them. He knew what made them weep. And he wept with them.

—Penelope J. Stokes, *Simple Words of Wisdom: 52 Virtues for Every Woman*

Do you know the hearts of those around you—what makes them weep?

"Jesus had compassion on them [two blind men] and touched their eyes. Immediately they received their sight and followed him."
Matthew 20:34 NIV

Perfect Timing

date:

I pulled out of the parking lot at Children's Hospital after spending the morning writing with the children in the cancer center. I'd helped Chandler—between getting her blood count and receiving chemotherapy—write a story about her cat, Bruno.

As I pondered the events of the morning, I heard God whisper, *"This is the time for you to be here. You wanted to be here earlier, but your time doesn't always line up with My time."*

My mind went back six years when I first had the idea to use my experience as a writer to work with cancer patients at the hospital. When I shared my ideas with the volunteer coordinator, I was appointed to serve coffee in the surgery waiting room. The coordinator said they didn't need me to work with the children; they already had enough people doing that. So I served coffee for a number of months and, eventually, stopped volunteering.

Recently I had begun to paint ceramics with an old friend, Marcia, and she described the art projects she was doing with cancer patients at the hospital. She asked if I'd help one of the teenagers write a book about his experiences, and I agreed. I shared my ideas with the new volunteer coordinator.

Her enthusiastic response took me by surprise. "You're just what we need!" The ideas were the same ones God had given me six years before, but somehow, in His divine plan, that was not the right time to put them into practice.

It caused me to think how we often get frustrated when things don't happen according to our timetables. As I headed home I whispered a prayer, *"Lord, help us to realize there's a right time for everything, and help us to wait for your perfect time."* —Cheri Fuller, *Quiet Whispers from God's Heart for Women*

How have you had to wait on God's perfect timing?

"Wait for the Lord; be strong and take heart and wait for the Lord."
Psalm 27:14 NIV

The Pavilion of Care

No one is exempt from times of trouble. But as you face the storms of life, you can always stand confident that Jesus wants you to come to Him. He wants to shelter you in the pavilion of His tender care.

There are not two chairs in this pavilion, but a loveseat where Jesus wants to sit with you and embrace you with the strength of His love and protection.

When you come into His presence and share your deepest burdens with Him, He will lift them from you and give you rest and peace.

The Holy Spirit, as a dove, comes to bring comfort, encouragement, and hope.

Let this pavilion be a place to draw away with God, to worship Him, to hear His voice, to trust Him as your best friend. —Karla Dornacher, *Down a Garden Path To Places of Love and Joy*

Do you need to draw away with God and allow Him to shelter you with tender care?

date:

"He will cover you with his feathers, and under his wings you will find refuge; his faithfulness will be your shield and rampart."
Psalm 91:4 NIV

The Spring of Faithfulness

date:

Faithfulness seems to be a scarce commodity in our world. We make promises—to ourselves, to those we love, even to God—only to break them. Half of all marriages end in divorce. Friends betray one another. To succeed, we have to swim with the sharks.

Or do we?

Judging from the amount of scripture devoted to the subject, faithfulness is pretty important to God. But sometimes we think that to be faithful, we have to dredge up from within ourselves some kind of superhuman resolve, to exert all our determination to be true to the promises we've made.

Faithfulness goes deeper than what we *do*. It cuts at the heart of who we *are* in God, and what is happening in our spiritual lives. The Psalmist describes faithfulness not as effort, but as the inevitable outflowing of a soul right with God: "Faithfulness will spring up from the ground, and righteousness will look down from the sky" (Ps. 85:11).

Faithfulness will spring up . . .

A spring is a natural water source, bubbling to the surface of its own accord. To get water from a spring, you don't have to work. You just have to hold out your hands and let the water flow.

Sure, relationships demand diligence. We have to devote effort to nurturing them. But if we have given our heart and mind and soul to the One who created us and redeemed us, faithfulness becomes a way of life, not a difficult task.

If we depend upon God's steadfast love in our lives, upon the righteousness that only comes from the Almighty, then faithfulness will flow from us like a spring of fresh water. —Penelope J. Stokes, *Beside a Quiet Stream: Words of Hope for Weary Hearts*

Is faithfulness a way of life for you—flowing like a spring of fresh water?

"Let love and faithfulness never leave you; bind them around your neck, write them on the tablet of your heart."
PROVERBS 3:3 NIV

FULLNESS

"That the body of Christ may be built up until we all reach unity in the faith and in the knowledge of the Son of God and become mature, attaining to the whole measure of the fullness of Christ."
EPHESIANS 4:12–13 NIV

Do you strive and pray to attain the whole measure of the fullness of Christ? Do you understand all that Christ, in Himself, has to freely offer you?

"For in Christ all the fullness of the Deity lives in bodily form, and you have been given fullness in Christ, who is the head over every power and authority."
COLOSSIANS 2:9–10 NIV

How is Christ both fully God and fully man? How does it make you feel to know that through Christ, you have been given His same fullness and status?

Acceptance

date:

Recently I watched a television program entitled "Difficult Daughters." It was about the tenuous relationships between mothers and daughters. The host cut to the heart of the matter. "You have to *accept*," she said. "Accept the fact that your daughter *is* different—different from you. Accept the reality that life doesn't always go the way we'd like. Accept what is, and move on from there."

It's wise advice for us Christians. Life doesn't always deal us the perfect hand. If we want to have peace in our lives, we need to begin with acceptance.

Acceptance is a matter of trust. Trust not in ourselves, or in our ability to convert those around us to our way of perceiving things, but trust in God, who alone can see the heart. There are things in our lives that we *can* change, of course. If we're physically and mentally able, we can work to pay the bills. We can spend more time with our families and set aside opportunities to get to know God better.

But we can't change other people. That's God's job, and we need to leave it in the Lord's capable hands.

The heart that accepts is a heart at peace. Rather than constantly striving to re-create our lives and the people we love, let's learn to be content through the grace given to us in Jesus Christ.

The well-known prayer of Reinhold Niebuhr reminds us: "Serenity accepts the things we cannot change. Courage changes the things we can. May God grant us wisdom to know the difference."

—Penelope J. Stokes, *Simple Words of Wisdom: 52 Virtues for Every Woman*

Have you accepted the things in your life that you cannot change? What do you need to relinquish into God's hands?

"I have learned the secret of being content in any and every situation, whether well fed or hungry, whether living in plenty or in want. I can do everything through him [Christ] who gives me strength."

PHILIPPIANS 4:12–13 NIV

The Long, Straight Stretch

At the beginning of our journey I glanced out the window and remarked, "Look at that beautiful cornfield, Ken . . . why, it stretches for as far as the eye can see." After a hundred miles of endless cornfields, I exclaimed, "We've been on this road for ages. Look around us, who in the world eats all this corn?"

date:

Instead of thinking, isn't it wonderful that our country can feed itself and so many others on such plenty, I thought, how boring—this long road and all this corn.

Someone once said that the challenge of living is to develop *a long obedience in the same direction.* When it's demanded, we can rise on occasion and be patient as long as there are limits. But we balk when patience is required over a long haul. It's painful to persevere through a marriage that's forever struggling. Housekeeping routines that never vary from week-to-week. Even caring for an elderly parent can feel like a long obedience in the same direction.

If only we could open our spiritual eyes to see the fields of grain we're planting, growing, and reaping along the way. That's what happens when we endure.

Right now you may be in the middle of a long stretch of the same old routine. The beginning of your Christian life was exhilarating. But now there are miles behind you and miles to go. Your commitment to keep putting one foot in front of the other is starting to falter.

Take a moment and look at the fruit. Perseverance. Determination. Fortitude. Patience.

Your life is not a boring stretch of highway. It's a straight line to heaven. And just look at the fields ripening along the way. Look at the grains of righteousness. You'll have quite a crop at harvest, so don't give up! —Joni Eareckson Tada, *Holiness in Hidden Places*

When have you had to maintain a long obedience in the same direction?

"Be patient . . . until the Lord's coming. See how the farmer waits for the land to yield its valuable crop and how patient he is for the autumn and spring rains."

James 5:7 NIV

Sacrifice and Burned-Out Offerings

date:

In 1920, Edna St. Vincent Millay wrote a poem that accurately describes many of us:

> My candle burns at both ends:
> It will not last the night.
> But ah, my foes, and oh, my friends—
> It gives a lovely light.

It reminds me of that old hymn, "Let Me Burn Out for Thee." We believe that by exhausting ourselves in the service of God, we will somehow become nobler, more spiritual.

Perhaps we need to ask ourselves a hard question: Has *God* called us to "burn the candle at both ends," or is it burning due to motives that may be hidden even to ourselves?

Jesus gives us a clue to the secret incentives that may drive us. When you give alms, pray, and fast, Jesus instructs, do it privately. Those who are praised by others, Jesus says, "have already received their reward" (Matt. 6:2).

The Lord doesn't ask us to exhaust ourselves in outward service and work. God doesn't demand that we drain our inner resources to become more spiritual. Jesus offers rest, an easier burden than the one we impose upon ourselves. God offers grace and mercy, not a schedule so full we come to resent the Lord we claim to love and serve.

Of course we're called to fast, to pray, to give alms—both our money and our time and abilities—as a response to the love and grace that has been extended to us. But the sacrifice we need to draw us into relationship with God has already been accomplished. The era of burnt offerings is past. The time of grace is upon us. We don't need to burn the candle at both ends. —Penelope J. Stokes, *Beside a Quiet Stream: Words of Hope for Weary Hearts*

Is your candle burning at both ends? How can you rest in God's salvation instead of trying to earn it?

"So when you give to the needy, do not announce it with trumpets, as the hypocrites do . . . to be honored by men. I tell you the truth, they have received their reward in full."

Matthew 6:2 NIV

Many Sparrows

The birds of our neighborhood know we love them. We enjoy them so much that we have filled our garden with birdhouses, birdbaths, and feeders. God loves these little birds more than we do. They belong to Him. He cares for them long after our feeder is empty or the birdbath dries up.

The birds don't worry about their needs; they trust in God's provision and give thanks with a joyful song! God doesn't want you to worry about your needs either—your clothes, house, or food.

Your heavenly Father loves you. You are more valuable to Him than many sparrows. He has promised that if you will seek Him first—get to know Him, trust Him, and walk in His ways—He will always supply what is needed in your life. —Karla Dornacher, *Down a Garden Path To Places of Love and Joy*

Do you trust God to provide all your needs? What needs do you worry will not be provided?

date: ....

"So do not worry, saying, 'What shall we eat' or 'What shall we drink?' or 'What shall we wear?' . . . your heavenly Father knows that you need them [these things]. But seek first his kingdom and his righteousness, and all these things will be given to you as well."

Matthew 6:31–33 NIV

The River of Delights

date:

I passed through Nashville and spent an evening at the Opryland Hotel. I felt like a country girl come to the big city, exclaiming over everything I saw. A five-story waterfall fed into a river that meandered into a Delta town with a full-scale antebellum home perched on the levee and patio restaurants along the shoreline—all indoors, all created by some architectural genius.

It was unbelievable. But it wasn't real. Real rivers, you see, go somewhere. Real rivers sustain life. Real rivers move and change and take us places we hadn't anticipated going.

The river that flows from the heart of God into our hearts isn't a big show put on to attract tourists. It's as real in spiritual terms as the mighty Mississippi. The river of God's presence offers us abundant life, food for the spirit, quenching of the soul's thirst.

Has your heart grown weary? Lie on the bank and listen to the water. Let the breeze blow new energy into your being.

Does your soul feel grimy with the accumulated soot and smog of the world? Wash off in the shallows; feel the cool waters rush over you in a cleansing flood.

Are you thirsty? Drink deep. These waters will never run dry.

The river of God provides for our needs, but there's more. It's a river of *delights*—bright flowers along the banks, fish jumping in the rapids, sounds and sights and scents that bring us not merely *restoration*, but *rejuvenation*. Laughter. Joy. Renewal.

And a multitude of delights we haven't even begun to imagine. —Penelope J. Stokes, *Beside a Quiet Stream: Words of Hope for Weary Hearts*

Has your heart grown weary? Will you enjoy and indulge in the delights of the river of God?

"How priceless is your unfailing love! . . . [Men] feast on the abundance of your house; you give them drink from your river of delights. For with you is the fountain of life; in your light we see light."

PSALM 36:7–9 NIV

Prayer

"But when you pray, go into your room, close the door and pray to your Father, who is unseen. Then your Father, who sees what is done in secret, will reward you."
Matthew 6:6 NIV

Where do you often go to pray? Is it a special place of uninterrupted privacy?

"Pray continually; give thanks in all circumstances, for this is God's will for you in Christ Jesus."
1 Thessalonians 5:17–18 NIV

Do you pray continually throughout your day? When do you spend the most time praying to the Lord?

Joyfulness

date:

Life is difficult. We struggle with sin and self-denial. But no matter what trials assail us, no matter what sorrow of the soul comes upon us, we have this assurance: In Christ, the old has passed away, and all things have become new.

True joy, the kind of joy that endures despite all odds, is not founded on circumstance, but on the faithfulness of God. Happiness, that elusive state of feeling good about ourselves, comes and goes. When relationships are healthy, when love abounds, when the checking account is solvent, when we like our jobs and find peace at home, it's easy enough to be happy. But when the mortgage is due and there's no money in the bank, when our kids rebel and our spouses withdraw, when home is a place of chaos rather than harmony, happiness dissolves like an ice cube on a hot griddle.

We are called to be joyful people. "Be joyful always," Paul instructs us, "for this is God's will for you in Christ Jesus" (1 Thess. 5:16-18).

How can we be "joyful always"? By keeping our eyes focused on God, who is the source of our faith. By trusting the Lord's love and grace and goodness when the fig tree does not blossom and the cattle pens are empty. By looking beyond our circumstances to the faithfulness of the One who called us—to rejoice. —Penelope J. Stokes, *Simple Words of Wisdom: 52 Virtues for Every Woman*

Will you rejoice in the Lord today even if your circumstances aren't favorable?

"Though the fig tree does not bud and there are no grapes on the vine, though the olive crop fails and the fields produce no food, though there are no sheep in the pen and no cattle in the stalls, yet I will rejoice in the Lord, I will be joyful in God my Savior."

Habakkuk 3:17–18 NIV

Letter of Love

Once Joyce Landorf wrote her pastor a long letter, telling him she'd committed herself to cheering him ever onward. "You preach, I'll turn the pages!" she said in her letter.

Later she learned that her letter had arrived during one of the most difficult times of his life when he was about to wither from "pulpit despair" and the same week four disgruntled couples left their tiny 62-member church.

Landorf wrote, "Pastor Jim was not touched because my letter was clever or brilliant, but because *God* used the words to bring a healing. But God could not have used an *unwritten* letter."

—Cheri Fuller, *The Fragrance of Kindness*

Who do you know that might need an encouraging note? Would you be obedient to write such a letter if God leads you?

date:

"A word aptly spoken is like apples of gold in settings of silver."
Proverbs 25:11 NIV

Becoming the Garden

date:

We love gardens, don't we? We love the serenity, the quiet wonder of living beauty all around us, the miracle of bud and blossom and fruit. Our faith history begins in a garden—in Eden, that Paradise where our first mother and father walked with God in uninterrupted communion. Sin thrust them out of Paradise, and since that day, we have been trying to get back in. Back to the place of harmony with God, with others, and with all creation.

But God has something different in mind for us—not to go *back* to the garden, but to *become* the garden.

Imagine it—as we sink our roots deep into the Lord's love, by divine grace we can become, for ourselves and for those around us, a garden of wonder and spiritual nourishment. A place of tranquility and rest in the midst of a noisy, troubled world. A conservatory of serenity, where those beaten down by life can come to be healed and restored, empowered and cared for.

But to open the gate, we must live the password. We must give ourselves to God's purposes in our lives and let the Spirit create in us a place of healing, acceptance, and hope.

The gate stands open.

Come in. And bring others with you. —Penelope J. Stokes, *Beside a Quiet Stream: Words of Hope for Weary Hearts*

What do you need to give up or do to allow the Lord to till your heart into a beautiful garden?

"The Lord will guide you always and he will satisfy your needs in a sun-scorched land and will strengthen your frame. You will be like a well-watered garden, like a spring whose waters never fail."
Isaiah 58:11 NIV

Tolerance

As far back as history stretches, civilizations have systematically waged war, oppressed the underdog, and annihilated entire cultures in order to maintain their power and control.

date:

To our shame, the church is not immune: the Crusades, the Inquisition, slavery, and anti-Semitism all testify to the appalling effects of intolerance. In Jesus' day, the Pharisees tried to undermine his ministry, and even the disciples who followed him and listened to his teachings were not tolerant of everything he did. They reprimanded him for talking to a Samaritan woman, and tried to keep children from bothering him in the town square. They pushed aside the lame and the beggars and the prostitutes and the tax collectors—the very people Christ had come to save.

Jesus, however, both preached and modeled tolerance. The Messiah was an advocate for the poor, the homeless, the sick, the imprisoned, the outcasts of the world. Most of his earthly ministry was spent reaching out to people we probably wouldn't be comfortable welcoming into our churches.

Yet if we want to be imitators of Christ, we need to cultivate the virtue of tolerance. And tolerance is not merely political correctness or public forbearance, pasting on a false smile. It is an attitude of the heart, a recognition that all people, whether they are "like us" or not, are made in the image of God, precious in his sight, and worthy of honor.

We are not called to change people, to force them to see the light. We are not called to re-create others in our own image. We are called to love. —Penelope J. Stokes, *Simple Words of Wisdom: 52 Virtues for Every Woman*

What person or group of people could you be more tolerant towards?

"Whoever is not against you is for you."
LUKE 9:50 NIV

God Hears, God Sees

date:

Sending her children off to boarding school was the most difficult thing Lisa had ever experienced as a mother and a missionary in Southeast Asia. Her oldest child, Andy, went for the first time when he was just seven. She clung desperately to God's promises for assurance. Two years later, her second son, Timmy, left the "nest," and five years later her only daughter, Amber, left. Although the children attended a wonderful international school, it was still thousands of miles away from home!

Gradually, Lisa learned to trust that God would not only care for them but would bless them. Then just as she was getting the "trust thing" down pat, it was time for Andy to take the next step—go even farther away to a junior high school in the Philippines. The culture was different, and the family living dynamics were foreign to him. His classes were difficult, and he struggled to be accepted in a new social setting. About that time she was reading the Bible and came across one of God's names in Hebrew, *El Roi,* the God who sees. In another passage (Genesis 16:11) she read that the angel instructed Hagar to call her son *Ishmael,* which means "God hears." Like a warm, gentle hug around her troubled heart, Lisa knew God was watching over her son. God knew everything the boy was going through and was there to care for him, because He is *Jehovah Shammah,* the God who is present.

Lisa couldn't be with her son but God was. She couldn't be there to listen to his heartaches, to give him a hug and words of encouragement, but he wasn't alone. God was with him—the God who sees and hears and cares.

—Cheri Fuller, *Quiet Whipsers from God's Heart for Women*

Will you trust God to care for those you are unable to be near?

"Blessed are those who have learned to acclaim you, who walk in the light of your presence, O Lord. They rejoice in your name all day long; they exult in your righteousness. For you are their glory and strength. . . ."

Psalm 89:15–17 NIV

Diligence

"Whatever you do, work at it with all your heart, as working for the Lord, not for men. . . ."
Colossians 3:23 NIV

In your work do you go above and beyond since you are ultimately working for the Lord?

"We want each of you to show this same diligence to the very end, in order to make your hope sure. We do not want you to become lazy, but to imitate those who through faith and patience inherit what has been promised."
Hebrews 6:11–12 NIV

What can you do to make sure you stay diligent and don't become lazy?

Letters of History

date: ....

Letters become part of our history, and when they are preserved and passed down, they bless the next generations with a glimpse of who they are and where they've been.

A letter written by my husband's great-great-grandmother to her grandson (his grandfather Oliver) shared in just a few sentences a particularly "Fuller" trait of stoicism.

Describing the freezing winter of 1905 in Kansas she said, "I don't think we've ever had such a winter here before—lots of snow, deep on the ground, then the blizzard. Grandpa had his cap down over his ears and his collar turned up. He looked cold, and the tears were running out of his eyes, but he said he wasn't very cold."

You never know when the words you write today will become a part of tomorrow's history!

—Cheri Fuller, *The Fragrance of Kindness*

How can you preserve and pass down family letters or journals depicting your ancestors' traits?

"My son, keep your father's commands and do not forsake your mother's teaching. Bind them upon your heart forever; fasten them around your neck. When you walk, they will guide you; when you sleep, they will watch over you; when you awake, they will speak to you."

PROVERBS 6:20–22 NIV

Home Is Where the Heart Is

Over a lifetime of traveling, whether driving through cities, small towns, or farm country, I have never gotten over the attraction I have to houses at sundown. When the lights begin to go on and a soft glow washes from the curtained windows, cold architectural structures take on personality. They are not just buildings anymore, they are places someone calls "home."

I can't help wondering about the stories behind the walls. Who lives there? Are they singing? Are they yelling? Is there an awkward silence, or is there deep peace? Is there music playing? Is there a fire blazing in the fireplace? Is someone practicing piano lessons? Frying chicken?

For some of us, the house that shaped our memories was a large, rambling farm house, full of laughter, music, and love. Maybe a big oak table in that picture was the setting for great conversations, hours of homework, and boisterous family dinners.

For some of us, there are houses that hold painful memories of ugly sounds, bad dreams, and hateful words.

For all of us, it is important to sanctify the place we call home—to expel from that space any negative memories and to invite the Spirit of God to sweep it clean, making the rooms sweet and ready for fresh experiences that will foster growth and bring peace.

It is my hope that this blessing will encourage all who would like to sanctify and bless the place we call home—whether the home is new or whether you are making a new commitment to make your house a home.

—Gloria Gaither, *Bless This House*

How can you make your home a haven for your family and guests?

date:

"But as for me and my household, we will serve the Lord."
Joshua 24:15 NIV

Determination

date:

Philip Boit, a farmer from Kenya, isn't a very good cross-country skier. He's awkward on the snow, and sometimes falls down. But he gets up again and keeps going.

His Olympic debut was, in objective terms, a disaster. The race was lengthy and arduous, and he crossed the finish line long after the medals had been decided. Other skiers simply gave up, but he was determined. And with that trademark smile on his face, he vowed to be back in four years when the winter games convened again.

That kind of determination is a virtue we all might do well to emulate. Do you desire a deeper relationship with God? Go after it the way Philip Boit has sought Olympic glory.

Do you want to be a better friend to those closest to you? Determine to give yourself more freely—to be honest about your struggles and doubts. Let them share in your joy and sorrow. And make yourself available to support them in triumph and disaster.

Whatever our God-given goals, our dreams, our desires—they will remain inaccessible to us until we determine that we will not give them up without a fight. Nothing easily won is highly valuable. Relationships, education, spiritual and emotional growth—all take time and energy, investment of our very souls. The kind of determination that makes the effort worthwhile even if we don't win the gold.

For if we have determination, we will come back stronger tomorrow. More skilled next week. Further along next month. More ready for the challenge next year.

—Penelope J. Stokes, *Simple Words of Wisdom: 52 Virtues for Every Woman*

What area of your life could be improved if you were more determined?

"Ask and it will be given to you; seek and you will find; knock and the door will be opened to you."
Luke 11:9 NIV

Vacation or Holiday?

When Americans talk about taking time off from work, the word we most often use is *vacation.* The root: vacant. Empty. Void of activity. The British, on the other hand, favor a different term: *holiday.* A holy day. A day set apart.

date: ....

We may look at our crowded, overscheduled, stressed-out lives and say we need a vacation. But what we really need is a holiday, a holy day—a day apart with God.

In the lives of great men and women of faith, we discover an important principle about uninterrupted time with God. Moses met God in the desert, and there learned God's name and his own mission for freeing the Children of Israel from the bondage of Egypt. In the wilderness, God provided water from the rock (Exod. 3). Paul, after his conversion, spent three years in the wilderness in preparation for his ministry to the Gentiles (Gal. 1:17–18). Jesus himself, following his baptism, was "led by the Spirit into the wilderness" to face the Enemy's temptations and find strength for his calling as Messiah (Luke 4:1–14).

Moses and Paul and Jesus didn't wander into the wilderness by accident. God led them there, to a place of solitude where they could give the Lord their undivided attention.

Yet for most Christians, the wilderness raises unpleasant images of dryness, isolation, struggle, even death. We don't pray to be set down in the wilderness, and we rarely go there without resistance.

Only in the wilderness—in a place where the voices of distraction are silenced and the noisy shallow brooks are stilled—can we find the spiritual depth our souls long for.

Only in the wilderness can we truly experience a holiday with God. —Penelope J. Stokes, *Beside a Quiet Stream: Words of Hope for Weary Hearts*

Will your next day off be a vacation or a holiday?

"Teach me your way, O Lord, and I will walk in your truth; give me an undivided heart, that I may fear your name."
Psalm 86:11 NIV

PERFUME OF KINDNESS

date:

Letters have the magical capacity to encourage—not once, or twice, but as many times as the recipient pulls out the faded paper the words are written on and rereads them. Even if the stationery has faded and lost some crispness, the thoughts of the heart live on. They renew a sense of being loved and cared about—enough that someone would sit down, put pen to paper, and write the letter.

In our high-tech times of cellular phones and instant E-mail, letter writing may seem a lost art. Yes, E-mail is handy for keeping in touch with quick notes no matter where you are in the world, but the written note that expresses love or encouragement or praise or a simple hello is a gift from the soul.

Whether a scented piece of paper slipped into your husband's briefcase before his business trip, a yellow sticky note tucked into your child's lunchbox, or the simple words "I'm praying for you" on a floral card given to an elderly friend who's been under the weather, notes of kindness have the potential to lift the recipient's spirit, give hope, and fill the heart with encouragement that lasts and lasts.

In a most unique way, written words of encouragement touch other lives with a sweet perfume of kindness.

—Cheri Fuller, *The Fragrance of Kindness*

Will you ask God to show you someone who needs an encouraging note today?

"Reckless words pierce like a sword,
but the tongue of the wise brings healing."
PROVERBS 12:18 NIV

Hospitality

"Share with God's people who are in need. Practice hospitality."
Romans 12:13 NIV

How do you share with those in need?

"Offer hospitality to one another without grumbling."
1 Peter 4:9 NIV

When you have someone in your home, do you offer hospitality in a gracious way?

Honesty Backstage

date:

When the store clerk gave us too much change, Mother made us give it back. When other teens sneaked into the movies or the amusement park on a child's pass, Mother made us tell our true age.

When somebody lost something and I found it, my mother made me try to find the owner or turn it in to the Lost and Found.

When I flunked a pop quiz because I refused to cheat while friends did and got an "A," Mother complimented me on my decision.

When I helped someone else cheat because it was easier than being teased for being selfish with the answers, Mother punished me just as if the fault lay totally with me.

When I didn't know what to say in a baby-sitting situation about a child's behavior, my mother suggested the truth with tact.

The roots of honesty grow deep and early. They aren't easily pulled up in the winds of corporate bribes, political positioning, or customer finagling.

—Dianna Booher, *Mother's Gifts to Me*

Can you recall a time when were you honest and it was difficult?

"The Lord abhors dishonest scales, but accurate weights are his delight."
PROVERBS 11:1 NIV

Teachableness

We get our minds made up about what the Lord means and fail to listen—really listen—to what the Spriit is saying about our situation. Our prayers become sealed letters rather than open dialogues, and we cut ourselves off from the remote possibility that God may have something else in mind. We are sure—so very sure—that we know the mind of Christ.

But Jesus valued the teachable heart. "Unless you change and become like little children, you will never enter the kingdom of heaven" (Matt. 18:3).

Children eagerly absorb all that is taught to them. Like sponges, they soak up language, behavioral patterns, moral precepts, manners, and truth. They accept challenges with enthusiasm. They try on unfamiliar ideas. They grow.

The teachable soul responds to God's voice not with resistance, but with openness. If we're teachable, we will put aside our preconceived notions and consider the possibility that God just might be taking us in new directions. We will pray with a listening heart, ready to respond to the Holy Spirit's nudgings within us. We will keep an open mind when we read the Scriptures instead of assuming we already understand what the Word means.

And when we do, something wonderful happens. The burden of always being right is lifted from our shoulders, and we experience a freedom in our spiritual lives that we never imagined. No longer do we need to defend God's truth or convince others of the accuracy of our personal perspectives.

God is quite capable of leading others in the way they need to go. Our responsibility is to listen for ourselves, to be teachable—like little children. —Penelope J. Stokes, *Simple Words of Wisdom: 52 Virtues for Every Woman*

date: ....

Will you free yourself today by being teachable?

"Many nations will come and say, 'Come, let us go up to the mountain of the Lord, to the house of the God of Jacob. He will teach us his ways, so that we may walk in his paths.' "

MICAH 4:2 NIV

Chosen By God

date:

Kathy struggled with deep feelings of rejection. She was desperate to be included in whatever social function was going on—luncheon, party, or someone's birthday. If she heard about a gathering she hadn't been invited to, she felt as though an arrow was piercing her heart. Hurtful words would dominate her thinking. *"You're not accepted. You don't have enough money. You're not spiritual enough or smart enough to be included with other Christian women."*

One day as she mulling over a dinner party she had just heard about—and had not been invited to—she prayed, "God, it's not like people pick me out and say I'm not good enough or intentionally reject me. I know it's just that they're not choosing me, but it still hurts."

At that moment God whispered to her heart and said, "*But I chose you.*"

God chose me. God chose me. She pondered that thought. They were simple words, but they began to heal the wounded places in her heart. She looked for Bible passages on being chosen, and with each one, the reality that God had chosen her brought a new sense of security to her heart. As she read God also reminded her that those who are chosen of God should "put on tender mercies, kindness, humility, meekness, long-suffering; bearing with one another, and forgiving one another" (Colossians. 3:12-13).

Kathy suddenly realized that she could be the one to extend love and kindness to others. She could be the one to forgive and offer peace. From then on, whenever she heard about events she wasn't included in, her response was different. No longer was her heart wounded, for God's simple words had given her hope and happiness. —Cheri Fuller, *Quiet Whispers from God's Heart for Women*

How can you delight in being chosen by God today?

"For He chose us in Him before the creation of the world to be holy and blameless in His sight."
Ephesians 1:4 NIV

Spreading Enthusiasm

She was a shy, quiet girl with long, stringy blond hair. I didn't even know which child she was out of the 50, noisy fifth-graders I was working with for nine weeks in the "Writer in the Schools" program. I called her name and asked, "Would Brandy come up and read her marvelous poem entitled, 'My Hand'? Students, listen carefully because you're going to love the imagery and word choice in this poem."

She walked slowly up to the Author's Chair in our makeshift Reader's Theatre and read her poem aloud to a warm response.

"Share some of your other poems," the kids suggested. Slowly, Brandy began to blossom as the class poet.

A few days later I realized how much my few words of encouragement had meant to her when I received this note of thanks:

Dear Mrs. Fuller,

These few weeks have been the BEST days of my whole life! YOU brought out the person, the writer inside, that I didn't realize I had. I'll always remember you! And cherish you for what you did for me.

Your ENTHUSIASTIC student, Brandy

–Cheri Fuller, *The Fragrance of Kindness*

Who could you encourage with a few kind words?

date:

"The lips of the righteous know what is fitting. . . ."
Proverbs 10:32 NIV

Rivers in the Desert

date:

The desert, they say, has its own terrible beauty. I wouldn't know. I've always lived in green places. But I've seen photographs of the desert: arid waste places with not a sprig of growth in sight. I've witnessed time-lapse videos of the long-awaited rain when the dry ground soaks in the blessed moisture; the desert bursts into bloom as if by magic. It all happens so quickly, so unexpectedly.

Sometimes, in our spirits, it happens that way as well.

Some of us don't like being in the desert. When our spirits flag, our best efforts end in failure, and our relationships cause us no end of frustration, we don't really care what we can learn from the experience, or even how close we might draw to God in our solitude. We just want to go home.

But whether we like the idea or not, all of us need to spend time in the empty spaces. The desert holds vast possibilities. It gets us back to basics. It gives us the opportunity to experience God in a new way. Out there, alone, we see things more clearly. The stars seem closer, and the heavens more accessible. And when the rains do come, the miracle of growth astounds us.

Feeling a little dry? A little isolated, there in your desert? Want to escape, to get back to your green places, and as quickly as possible?

Take a little time to look around. The days in the desert—or weeks, or months, or even years—are not punishment, but preparation. Take time to focus on the Lord, to get direction, to hear God speak. —Penelope J. Stokes, *Beside a Quiet Stream: Words of Hope for Weary Hearts*

The next time you're in the desert will you see it as an opportunity to experience God in a new way?

"I provide water in the desert and streams in the wasteland, to give drink to my people, my chosen. . . ."
Isaiah 43:20 NIV

Purity

"Let us purify ourselves from everything that contaminates body and spirit, perfecting holiness out of reverence for God."
2 Corinthians 7:1 NIV

Do you ask God to purify your heart on a daily basis?

"Blessed are the pure in heart, for they will see God."
Matthew 5:8 NIV

How do you become pure in heart?

Mercy

date:

Our invitation to follow Christ includes a call to action. We are instructed to feed the hungry, clothe the naked, give shelter to the homeless, defend widows and orphans, minister to the imprisoned. We are challenged to live the truth even as we preach it. But we are not called to sacrifice ourselves upon the altar, or to demand such sacrifice from others.

What does the Lord require of us? "To act justly and to love mercy and to walk humbly with your God" (Mic. 6:8).

We live in a merciless world—a society of ever-increasing expectation. We're pushed to do more, to produce more, to make more money, to meet higher goals. And we transfer those expectations to our Christian lives. We say yes to everything. We demand that our pastors be superhuman, our youth leaders miracle workers. We drive them, and ourselves, into therapy or collapse or rage.

We need a little mercy. We need to concede our own humanness and that of our sisters and brothers. Once and for all, we need to realize that God does not want our sacrifices and our burnt-out offerings. The sacrifice of Christ was sufficient.

In modern terms, mercy means cutting ourselves and others a little slack. Admitting our human limitations. Taking a little time off. Giving ourselves and those around us the opportunity to refresh and regroup, to draw on the healing, restorative power offered to us in Jesus Christ. We are weary people, in need of God's rest. And the Lord has provided it for us if we'll only get down off the altar for a minute.

God calls it Sabbath. Mercy, not sacrifice. Awareness of God rather than burnt offerings. God is Lord of the resting time. —Penelope J. Stokes, *Simple Words of Wisdom: 52 Virtues for Every Woman*

How will you accept and rest in the mercy the Lord has shown you?

"For I desire mercy, not sacrifice, and acknowledgment of God rather than burnt offerings."
Hosea 6:6 NIV

A CHANGE OF HEART

At a time when she was busy with her flock of little ones, aged three, two, and six months, Connie began to realize that she and her husband, Stan, were not parenting the same way. He had a different temperament and gifts, and a distinctly different parenting style. But Connie was a professional; she had years of experience with children as a Child Life Specialist in hospitals. She'd taken many courses on child development. In fact, she had a master's degree in the field. She was sure *her way* was the right way and only way to handle their children. If only her husband would change and do things *her way.*

date: ....

One day in frustration, she sat down on her bed and began to pray about the conflicts they were having. "God, when are You going to show Stan that I'm doing this right, and he should come on board and do it my way?" she asked.

As clearly yet quietly as she'd heard anything from God, He whispered, *"If both of you were exactly the same, one of you wouldn't be necessary!"* She knew she didn't want to be the parent who wasn't needed, nor did she want Stan to be expendable.

With those few words from God's heart, a dramatic change took place in Connie's attitude. She began to value her husband's parenting style instead of criticizing it. She began to appreciate his gifts and unique way of relating to their kids, to celebrate their differences instead of being irritated by them. As a result, they had more unity and harmony as parents and a happy peace descended on their home. —Cheri Fuller, *Quiet Whispers from God's Heart for Women*

What attitude in your heart do you need to pray about and ask God to change?

"Create in me a pure heart, O God, and renew a steadfast spirit within me."
PSALM 51:10 NIV

The Power of Words

date:

A new pastor was called to a country church jokingly called "The Refrigerator" because its parishioners were known for being aloof and unfriendly to visitors and strangers.

When he observed their unfriendliness in action, he didn't criticize or berate them from the pulpit. Instead, whenever he got the chance, he talked about them as warm, friendly folks who could have a great impact on their community.

Over time, as they listened to his positive descriptions, they gradually took his words to heart and did become kind-hearted, friendly people who attracted new members like never before. —Cheri Fuller, *The Fragrance of Kindness*

Who will you encourage instead of berate to bring about change?

"Do not repay evil with evil or insult with insult, but with blessing, because to this you were called so that you may inherit a blessing."
1 Peter 3:9 NIV

Cycles and Seasons

It's autumn in the mountains—bright blue-sky days with temperatures in the 60s; crisp, star-studded nights dropping into the 40s. The Blue Ridge Parkway and most of the rural highways are crowded with leaf-lookers: tourists straining to find the brightest maple tree, the most magnificent panorama of color climbing down the mountainsides.

But this fall, they may go home disappointed. The dry summer has taken its toll on fall colors and fruit. Withered leaves already litter the roadways, and the vibrant reds and oranges we brag about are few and far between.

But the old-timers aren't worried. Our trees are strong. The oaks and maples have deep roots. They'll come back next year. And so will the leaf-lookers, making their annual journey to the mountains.

There's a spiritual lesson in the browning trees on the hillside. Sometimes, in our relationship with God, drought seems to take its toll. The fruit we bear is less than perfect. Our leaves—the evidence of the Lord's grace in our personal lives and in our relationships with others—seem withered and colorless.

But one bad season is no reason to give up. Here in the mountains, we don't go digging up the apple trees or burning the maples off the slopes just because the fall harvest of Granny Smiths and the flaming color haven't lived up to our expectations. We wait. We trust. Next year will be better.

Spiritual life, like physical life, has its cycles.

Has it been a bad year? Don't despair. Don't give up. The fruit will come "in its season." Withered leaves will sprout again. Spiritual prosperity will come once more.

—Penelope J. Stokes, *Beside a Quiet Stream: Words of Hope for Weary Hearts*

date:

How do you trust God when you go through a dry and unfruitful season?

"Because of the Lord's great love we are not consumed, for his compassions never fail. They are new every morning; great is your faithfulness."

LAMENTATIONS 3:22–23 NIV

A Compact with Conscience

date:

I arrived home with my purchases, one of which was a bag containing cosmetic items. I had my friend unpack mascara, moisturizer, foundation and—"What's that?" I said as she held up a small square box. "I didn't buy anything else." Inside was a pressed powder compact. "Where did that come from?"

"Maybe the woman at the counter slipped this in as a gift?" Since I had already taken one step in justifying my actions, the next came easier: "Taking this back to the mall would be such a hassle for me."

The whole thing could have been easily solved with a phone call to the cosmetics department, but I got distracted. The next day when the urge to call resurfaced, it seemed less urgent. I felt guilty, but not enough to take it back. With each passing day my lack of initiative seemed less sinful than it actually was in the sight of God. I chose to believe that sin—at least in this case—wasn't quite as sinful as God says—and that I wasn't quite as bad as I, in fact, am.

A few nights later, however, I stumbled across Hebrews 3:13 in my quiet time: "Encourage one another daily . . . so that none of you may be hardened by sin's deceitfulness." I sighed, realizing that I was a casualty of sin's deceitfulness. The compact went back to the makeup counter the next day.

Every time we cover up sin, we suppress our conscience; that is, a knowledge of ourselves as God knows us. We cannot argue with our conscience—it will never change its mind. It will only become less forceful and more faint. And when it does, we are the ones who become damaged.

—Joni Eareckson Tada, *Holiness in Hidden Places*

How can you safeguard yourself from being hardened by sin's deceitfulness?

"Dear friends, I urge you, as aliens and strangers in the world, to abstain from sinful desires, which war against your soul."
1 Peter 2:11 NIV

Honesty

"An honest answer is like a kiss on the lips."
Proverbs 24:26 NIV

Do you give others and God honest answers?

"Truthful lips endure forever, but a lying tongue lasts only a moment."
Proverbs 12:19 NIV

Can you think of an example of when truthful words have endured over lies?

DEDICATION

date:

Jerusalem had been conquered, its walls destroyed, its people carried off into slavery. One of those people, a prophet named Nehemiah, was serving as cupbearer to King Artaxerxes when the call of God came to him: Go and rebuild the walls of Jerusalem.

This was Nehemiah's call, but it obviously wasn't a job Nehemiah could do alone. He needed help.

The job got done. The wall was rebuilt, the gates restored, because each worker committed to the space in front of his own house.

It's easier, sometimes, for us as Christians to proclaim our dedication to the larger work of God—to the salvation of nations, to evangelistic outreach in far-off places. But real dedication to the Lord's purposes often means getting dirty in the ditches that border our own homes.

It's not a glamorous call, this dedication to the everyday. Serving lunch in a soup kitchen or spending the afternoon in a nursing home doesn't win Nobel prizes. Providing refuge for an abused wife, or offering a day's respite for an AIDS caregiver doesn't hold much in the way of drama or excitement. Dealing with broken relationships in our own families doesn't win us any accolades.

It's emotional and spiritual bricklaying.

Still, the walls need to be shored up. Relationships need to be healed. The environment needs a good scrubbing. People need the touch of a hand and the light of a friendly face. Children are homeless. Old men are hungry. Single mothers bear the weight of the world on their shoulders.

We are called, like Nehemiah's helpers, to restore the walls in front of our houses.

I'll do mine if you'll do yours. And before we know it, the walls will stand strong again. —Penelope J. Stokes, *Simple Words of Wisdom: 52 Virtues for Every Woman*

What needs to be done in front of your house?

"The priests made repairs, each in front of his own house."
NEHEMIAH 3:28 NIV

Grace's Discriminatng Ears

s a professional church soloist, I strive for accurate intonation and pronunciation, good breath-control and projection, and such familiarity with the score that I can sing nearly from memory. But until one life-changing experience, I always thought I fell extremely short of my aspirations.

date:

One Sunday, all professional decorum melted as my high C collided with the organ's piercing C-sharp. Though it was my error, mid-song I had no recourse but to sustain the glaring wrong note.

After the service, Grace, a beautiful, radiant woman, lavished me with undeserved praise. Embarrassed by her compliments, eyes downcast, I lamented, "But Grace, didn't you hear that awful note I caterwauled?"

Without hesitation, she gently encouraged, "Yes. But how many right notes did you sing?"

I was dumbfounded. How many right notes had I sung? Hundreds? Thousands? With God's grace, my right notes far surpassed the wrong, but I'd never noticed them until her comment.

That one wrong note sung so many Sundays ago, literally changed my life because it fell on Grace's discriminating ears. —Cheri Fuller, *The Fragrance of Kindness*

Will you focus on the many right notes instead of the few wrong ones today?

"And God is able to make all grace abound to you, so that in all things at all times, having all that you need, you will abound in every good work."
2 Corinthians 9:8 NIV

Trees by the Riverside

date:

The city is under a ban: no washing cars or watering lawns. Those of us with private wells watch our pump gauges and pray that the underground springs will hold out until it rains again.

In spiritual terms, too, drought can be frustrating, even frightening. We've all experienced it—times when we pray, but our supplications seem to bounce off the ceiling. Times when the scriptures remain silent, answers refuse to come, and the presence of God seems very far away.

We long for the rain, the refreshing of God's Spirit, the hope that's renewed with a sense of the Lord's nearness. We force ourselves to keep on praying. We fast and beg and storm the gates of heaven for some sign that the Lord has not abandoned us.

God, who created, redeemed, and loves us, hasn't forsaken us. This time of spiritual dryness will pass, just as winter passes into spring, just as drought eventually is relieved by the rainfall.

Our nourishment doesn't have to come from above, in signs and wonders, in miracles. It can come from below, where our roots go deep into the silent springs of God's grace.

If we depend upon the rain, we are likely to become frustrated and disappointed, rootless, like a tumbleweed that dries up and blows away at the first breath of wind. But if we sink our roots into the subsoil of God's love, if we look not to circumstances but to the certainty of God's faithfulness, we can endure drought and still bear fruit.

In time, the rains will come again. But until they do, you will stand firm. —Penelope J. Stokes, *Beside a Quiet Stream: Words of Hope for Weary Hearts*

Will you look to God for comfort and security instead of circumstances during a time of spiritual drought?

"But blessed is the man who trusts in the Lord, whose confidence is in him. He will be like a tree planted by the water that sends out its roots by the stream. It does not fear when heat comes; its leaves are always green. It has no worries in a year of drought and never fails to bear fruit."

Jeremiah 17:7–8 NIV

How to Treat a Man

Mother demonstrated how to treat a husband to make him love and cherish her. She's been practicing with the same man for 55 years now.

On occasion, she coddles him—through colds and fever and with favorite casseroles. As if he were a king on his throne, she serves him bedtime snacks of popcorn and leftover pudding in front of the nightly news.

On occasion, she guides him like a child: She lays out ties to match his suits, and tells him when he needs a haircut. At other times, she does his bidding as if he were the parent, patiently running his errands to the dry-cleaners and the hardware store.

She isn't afraid to speak her mind to him about what investments will prove best for the long haul—whether they should sell the rental property or if they should donate to the local fund-raiser. On the other hand, where his mistakes or shortcomings are concerned, she knows to hold her tongue in front of the kids and friends.

Mother has learned the fine art of negotiating. If they go to his favorite vacation spot this year, she gets to redecorate the kitchen next year.

She capably and charitably makes demands on his time. She knows when to obligate him to attend a child's piano recital, and when to let him roam free to hunt and fish with his buddies. She insists that he help with the housework and preparations for guests. She, in turns, helps clean the garage and wash the car.

She respects his judgment, praises him in front of family and friends, and follows his leadership in important family decisions.

In short, she accepts his authority without diminishing her own. The heart of her husband does safely dwell with her. —Dianna Booher, *Mother's Gifts to Me*

date: ....

How could you honor your husband today?

"However, each one of you also must love his wife as he loves himself, and the wife must respect her husband."
EPHESIANS 5:33 NIV

Gifts from God

date:

Children are a gift from God! They are tiny packages filled with tremendous potential, given to bring great blessing—as well as a challenge here and there! God gives them to us, not to be possessed or controlled, but to be loved and nurtured.

Each little bundle is created with the greatest care in the mother's womb, woven carefully in God's own image. No two children are exactly alike. Each child has a distinct and unique personality with strengths and weaknesses, gifts and abilities, desires and dreams to be nurtured and molded with love, discipline, and instruction. God has a perfect plan for each child's life—a future with purpose and hope.

Just as proper nutrition is needed for children to develop strong and healthy bodies, the pure milk of God's Word is vital to nourish the heart and character of every child. And God uses a parent's love not only to teach and instruct but also to wrap a child's heart with the warmth of comfort, protection, and blessing.

—Karla Dornacher, *Love In Every Room*

Do you view children as tiny packages filled with tremendous potential? Do you nourish your child's heart with God's Word?

"Like newborn babies, crave pure spiritual milk, so that by it you may grow up in your salvation, now that you have tasted that the Lord is good."
1 Peter 2:2–3 NIV

Confidence

"In him and through faith in him we may approach God with freedom and confidence."
EPHESIANS 3:12 NIV

Do you approach God's throne with confidence?

"Let us then approach the throne of grace with confidence, so that we may receive mercy and find grace to help us in our time of need."
HEBREWS 4:16 NIV

Does confidence in God help you during your times of need?

Plant Seeds of Greatness

date:

What a powerful impact a grandma's encouraging words can have! When Luciano Pavarotti was a little boy, his grandmother scooped him up into her lap and said, "You're going to be great, you'll see." His mother wanted him to be a banker. But he took a different direction—teaching elementary school, and singing only occasionally.

Then his father began to urge him to quit teaching and study music. At age 22, he did. Giving up his teaching position, he became an insurance salesman so he would have time for voice lessons.

Although Pavarotti credits his father for steering him toward his first love of music, he credits his grandmother as being the source of his inspiration. "No teacher ever told me I would become famous. Just my grandmother."

—Cheri Fuller, *The Fragrance of Kindness*

Who needs to hear some inspiration from you today?

"The tongue of the righteous is choice silver. . . ."
Proverbs 10:20 niv

ADVENTURING WITH GOD

Circumstances don't always turn out, up close and personal, the way they looked on the brochure. Disappointments come, right along with the wonderful surprises. Difficulties catch us off guard. But we learn. We grow. We change. And when we look back, we can usually say that the situations that brought pain also brought new insight, deeper understanding, a closer relationship with God.

date: ....

Attitude is everything. We can see life as a dismal maze that keeps us going around in circles. Or we can look beyond the difficulties and see the adventure.

Adventure is never without its danger—in part, that's what makes it exciting, exhilarating, challenging. We stretch ourselves, go beyond the limitations that we've always accepted, find out what we're made of. And whether we succeed or fail, we become something more than we thought we were in the first place.

The disciples discovered what it meant to adventure with Jesus. Sometimes Jesus fed 5,000 with a little boy's lunch; sometimes his disciples were so hungry they gleaned the fields along the way. The crowds gathered around, sometimes listening, sometimes threatening their lives. But even when the crucifixion had been accomplished and evil seemed to have won the day, the adventure wasn't over.

Because adventuring with God isn't about circumstances—it's about character. What happens to us doesn't matter nearly as much as what happens in us. The ups and downs of life all work in concert to make us into the people God has created us to be.

Journeying with God is an adventure that will last a lifetime—and beyond. —Penelope J. Stokes, *Beside a Quiet Stream: Words of Hope for Weary Hearts*

What adventures have shaped your character?

"We also rejoice in our sufferings, because we know that suffering produces perseverance; perseverance, character; and character, hope."
ROMANS 5:3–4 NIV

Kindness

date:

Ronny was running the race of his life, the Special Olympics, with his mom and dad and hundreds—maybe thousands—of people watching from the stands. He could see the finish line, and no one was ahead of him.

Then Ronny turned and looked over his shoulder. A boy named Curtis, the new friend Ronny had met just that morning, was right behind him and gaining ground. At just that moment, to Ronny's horror, Curtis stumbled and went down.

Ronny stopped in his tracks. He looked at the finish line, and then back at Curtis. And without a second thought he turned back, helped Curtis to his feet, and together they crossed the finish well back in the pack.

Whatever his limitations, Ronny comprehended something essential about life. He understood that winning isn't the most significant thing in the world. That being kind is important, even if you lose the race.

Remember the Good Samaritan? He had nothing to gain and everything to lose when he stopped to help that mugging victim. He was a hated Samaritan, an outcast. The religious people had all passed by. Still, he showed kindness. He went out of his way, spent his own money, rearranged his busy schedule, to help a man he had never met. And Jesus used him, not the religious leaders, as the example of neighborly kindness and compassion (Luke 10:29-37).

I suppose a random act of kindness is better than none at all. But God calls us to more than random kindness. God calls us to *clothe* ourselves with it, to wrap it around us so that kindness is the first thing people touch when they reach in our direction. —Penelope J. Stokes, *Simple Words of Wisdom: 52 Virtues for Every Woman*

Are you wrapped in kindness?

"He who despises his neighbor sins, but blessed is he who is kind to the needy."
PROVERBS 14:21 NIV

Content with Quiet

Yelling at the top of our lungs, we hit the doorway after school every afternoon with, "Moooootheeeeer, I'm hoooooommme." Sometimes just for the fun of it, Mother would tuck herself into a nook to hide. Then when we'd go lunging through the house looking for her and she'd step out and yell "boo." I suspect she had enormous amounts of fun each day in the quiet before the storm.

date:

Although we've long since dropped the "boo" part, I still stop by for a visit and find her enjoying the solitude. There's rarely any music playing in the background. The television is always off. She's not talking to friends on the phone. Instead, she's quietly working on one of her pet projects—flower arranging, painting ceramics, refinishing furniture, or learning to do spreadsheets on the computer.

Unlike those who seem uncomfortable when they find themselves alone, she always discovers enjoyable ways to spend her time and use her mind. She taught me to be content with my own company.

Not to have to depend on others for peace of mind or food for thought grants great freedom. —Dianna Booher, *Mother's Gifts to Me*

Are you content with your own company?

"The fruit of righteousness will be peace; the effect of righteousness will be quietness and confidence forever."
ISAIAH 32:17 NIV

Encouraging Words Are a Blessing

date:

Mary Kay Ash is well known for the powerful effect of her encouraging words—not just to large audiences or to the hundreds of "Mary Kay" cosmetics sales representatives she mentors, but even to less visible people, such as the staff in hotel kitchens and the maids cleaning the guest rooms. For years she has stated that God didn't create any nobodies—only somebodies—and everyone has something wonderful about them.

Whenever she attended a Mary Kay event at a hotel, she insisted on entering through the kitchen. There she would greet workers with a big smile that made them feel important. "Hi! How are you?" she'd say to each person. If they hesitantly responded, "F-f-fine," she'd say, "No, you're great!" Each day, for as long as the event lasted, she was there, repeating her warm greetings.

Hotel managers said she did more for their employees' morale and performance in those few moments than the managers had been able to do in years. Mary Kay's fragrance of kindness was sent out to bless others wherever she went. —Cheri Fuller, *The Fragrance of Kindness*

Will you speak words of kindness to those you encounter today?

"Do not withhold good from those who deserve it, when it is in your power to act."
Proverbs 3:27 NIV

Desires

"Those who live according to the sinful nature have their minds set on what that nature desires; but those who live in accordance with the Spirit have their minds set on what the Spirit desires."

Romans 8:5 NIV

Do you find that your desires change depending on what your mind focuses on most?

"You open your hand and satisfy the desires of every living thing. The Lord is righteous in all his ways and loving toward all he has made."

Psalm 145:16–17 NIV

How has God opened his hand to satisfy your desires? Have you thanked Him?

The Tension of the Unknown

date:

Some of us find security in savings balances, stock purchase plans, and retirement accounts. But what if the market crashes, or the accountant embezzles the 401k funds? Some of us put our trust in relationships. But what if my spouse becomes interested in someone else, or my friends move away? Some of us bank on education, experience, and marketable skills. But what if I have to start over, to go back to college, to change careers in midlife?

The truth is, we can never escape the tension of the unknown. We may be faithful, responsible adults, but we can neither know nor control what will happen tomorrow. We can never be sure, except in hindsight, where our decisions and directions will take us in the long run.

"Follow me," Jesus said to a lot of different people and received a lot of different responses. Some dropped what they were doing and followed him. Some said, "Okay, Lord, but first I need to say good-bye to my family. I need to take care of my elderly parents. I need to pick up my last paycheck. I need to leave a forwarding address."

If we intend to follow Christ, however, we need to realize that we can't always wrap things up neatly, tie up loose ends, have answers to all our questions. Being in relationship with God is a journey of faith.

Faith means stepping out onto the water when we don't understand what can possibly hold us up.

Faith means resting in the assurance that, although the future may be unknown to us, it's not in the least unfamiliar to the One who leads us. A future filled, not with answers, but with hope. —Penelope J. Stokes, *Beside a Quiet Stream: Words of Hope for Weary Hearts*

Is your faith and hope in the One who holds your future?

"Now faith is being sure of what we hope for and certain of what we do not see."
Hebrews 11:1 NIV

A Quiet Calm beneath the Waves

A warm breeze touched my cheek the other day and took me back to sunny childhood memories of camping in the sand dunes near Ocean City, Maryland.

date:

After the sun was high and hot, my sisters and I would don our bathing suits and head for the water. It was nothing for us to spend an entire afternoon in the ocean, playing catch with the waves. The deafening sound of powerful breakers thrilled, yet frightened me. Yet when I swam beyond the breakers, I was amazed at how subdued the crashing waves sounded. When I dove beneath the surface, the underwater acoustics made the thunderous roar seem distant and gentle.

There's a majestic and powerful beauty on the surface of the ocean; there's even more beauty when you dive beneath the waves. Even as a kid with a face mask on, I'd dive and discover a world of endless calm—luxuriant seaweed swaying gracefully, colorful shells, small fish darting here and there—a world that's quiet and deep.

When you dive beneath the surface things of God, you also discover an endless calm—a world of divine life that is quiet and deep. There, in the depths, God will reveal a quiet and gentle kind of interior beauty.

The Lord is so generous! Even when we choose to live only on the surface of things, where we're often tossed this way and that, God still reveals Himself through thrilling displays of His power. But there's much more to God than what you see—what we all see of Him—on the surface.

When we dive deeper into God's heart, all the turmoil of our daily lives—the problems that crash around us like huge waves—seem somehow distant.

—Joni Eareckson Tada, *Holiness in Hidden Places*

Will you dive deeper instead of living on the surface?

"The Spirit searches all things, even the deep things of God. For who among men knows the thoughts of a man except the man's spirit within him? In the same way no one knows the thoughts of God except the Spirit of God."

1 Corinthians 2:10–11 NIV

Words of Hope

date: ....

Numb from the stress of a 12-hour workday and the responsibility of caring for her girls at night, Marcia didn't have the strength to go on. The intense pressure piled up until she felt herself breaking into a million little pieces. Desperate for help, she called a local hospital. "I feel like I'm having a nervous breakdown," she said. "Could I come there if I can't make it through the night?"

She went instead to the Great Physician. Opening her Bible to Isaiah 61:2–3, Marcia read that Christ had come to heal brokenhearted people like her, that He could turn her mourning into joy and exchange the heaviness she felt for a thankful attitude.

As she read those words, God whispered, *"I've been with you all along, Marcia, even when you weren't aware of My presence. When there's no one else, I'm right here with you. I am your Helper."* The words were like healing salve poured over her aching heart, and for the first time she realized the enormous strength that was available to her in Christ. She knew with confidence that God would be with her in all the challenges she faced.

Through His guidance, she left a position in commercial real estate, which took her away from her daughters until after dark every night, and started a house-cleaning business. Not only did she make more income, but she was able to be home for the girls after school.

Looking back, Marcia realized that had she wasted her energy on worry and emotional distress, she would never have accomplished so much. God's words of hope late one night made all the difference. —Cheri Fuller, *Quiet Whispers from God's Heart for Women*

Have you ever realized the enormous strength available to you in Christ?

"I can do everything through him who gives me strength."
Philippians 4:13 NIV

Meekness

In the real world, meekness does not seem to be a virtue. The meek are weak, spineless, doormats who let other people walk all over them. Then I read Numbers 12:3: "Now the man Moses was very meek, above all the men which were upon the face of the earth" (KJV).

date: ....

Moses? Meek? Surely not Moses, the Deliverer of Israel, who lifted his rod and parted the sea, delivered water from the rock, stood before God and brought the Commandments down from Mount Sinai?

Then I took another look at Moses—specifically that fascinating scene at the Burning Bush. Chosen to bear the news of liberation to God's people, Moses asked the Lord to choose someone else—not because he was a weakling or a coward, but because he knew his own limitations. Moses knew himself. He was aware of his strengths and weaknesses. And yet, when God called him, he removed his shoes and bowed down in obedience.

Meekness is the outward manifestation of humility, the active response of a soul committed to God's purposes. The heart that knows its dependence upon God can strike bravely into the unknown, counting always on his faithfulness to provide whatever is needed.

We don't have to be afraid of our shortcomings. They are as much a part of God's plan as our strengths and gifts. If we held within ourselves all that was necessary to fulfill his purpose, we wouldn't need the miracle of God's presence.

The place where you stand—wherever the Lord has put you—is holy ground. Take off your shoes. Bow down. Acknowledge your limitations, and trust God to be God.

—Penelope J. Stokes, *Simple Words of Wisdom: 52 Virtues for Every Woman*

Have you acknowledged your limitations to God?

"Blessed are the meek, for they will inherit the earth."
MATTHEW 5:5 NIV

Godly Housekeeping

date:

There's order and there's disorder—and there's somewhere in between. To be a perfectionist in your housekeeping is not only no fun, it's not healthy for you or your family. On the other hand, neither is being a slob. There is, however, a certain degree of orderliness and cleanliness necessary to create a pleasant, comfortable, and safe home.

Most important, remember that whatever you do, be it dishes, laundry, sweeping, or cleaning, do it with your whole heart to bless—not impress!

Determine to let the focus of your housekeeping chores be to bless the Lord, your family, and your guests. Let God work through your hands to bring beauty and order into their lives. This will give your family a sense of stability and comfort, and will make your guests feel comfortable and welcome.

Use your housekeeping time as an opportunity to give thanks for the many blessings you have! Be thankful for running water, a roof over your head, hands to work with and a heart to love with!

A home with a little dust and a lot of laughter will win the heart of God every time! —Karla Dornacher, *Love in Every Room*

Do your housekeeping chores bless the Lord and others? How can you glorify God even through your housework?

"Whatever you do, do it all for the glory of God."
1 Corinthians 10:31 NIV

ENCOURAGEMENT

"Therefore, encourage one another and build each other up, just as in fact you are doing."
1 THESSALONIANS 5:11 NIV

How could you encourage and build up at least one person in your church today?

"May our Lord Jesus Christ himself and God our Father, who loved us and by his grace gave us eternal encouragement and good hope, encourage your hearts and strengthen you in every good deed and word."
2 THESSALONIANS 2:16–17 NIV

Do you behave as someone who has eternal encouragement through Christ?

Entertaining Angels

date: ....

In biblical times, hospitality was a matter of life and death. God's people were commanded to be hospitable to strangers—to provide food and water and shelter to them, lest they die in the hostile desert climate.

I'd like to think that God's definition of hospitality—rather than being limited to gourmet dinner parties—extends to the care and nurture of souls. To those times when we set aside our own agenda to put on a pot of coffee and listen to the struggles of a sister or brother who's going through a hard time. To the hours we spend on the phone comforting a grieving friend.

These are the life-and-death matters of modern society. For the most part, the people who travel through our daily lives aren't in danger of dying from exposure or malnutrition or dehydration. But they do need spiritual sustenance—the bread of truth, the water of grace, and the encompassing shelter of God's love.

"Do not forget to entertain strangers," Hebrews 13:2 reminds us, "for by so doing some people have entertained angels without knowing it."

No, Martha Stewart I am not. I can barely cook, and I'm not very adept at entertaining large groups of people. But I like to believe that somewhere along the way I've given comfort to an angel or two—or at least weary souls who needed a safe place to rest on their journey through the wilderness. —Penelope J. Stokes, *Simple Words of Wisdom: 52 Virtues for Every Woman*

What could you do today to provide hospitality to someone?

"We ought therefore to show hospitality to such men so that we may work together for the truth."
3 John 8 NIV

LETTING GO

Our son was in the hospital fighting for his life. The doctor had called us out into the hall after examining our six-year-old and said, "We've done everything we know to do for Justin. Something inside his body has got to rally." He had suffered a severe asthma attack the day before.

date:

My heart raced and fear overwhelmed me. My husband sent me home to "pull myself together" since I was a nervous wreck and only making things worse. Dashing through the driving rain in the parking lot, I tried to find our car. Finally, soaked and shivering, I gave up and went back into the hospital to wait for the storm to let up.

Finding refuge in the chapel, I was drawn to a large white Bible by the altar. In the quiet I prayed, *Lord, I've put my hope in the wrong things. That's why I'm so afraid; I've trusted you in some areas of my life, but I've clung to my kids, trying to keep them safe.*

Quietly an inner voice whispered to my heart. *"Cheri, where is your faith? Trust in me . . . be still."* Just then, lightning caused the chapel lights to flicker off and on, and thunder boomed outside. The raging storm reminded me that God was the Creator of the whole universe. If He could command a thunderstorm, surely He could handle my son's life. I bowed my head and gave Justin back to God. As I sat in the silent chapel a huge weight began to lift off my heart. The icy fear that had gripped me melted away. I knew that Justin was safe and cared for, that I could trust God whatever happened. Justin did defeat that battle with asthma, and though he faced many others in the years to come, his illness never again left me panicked and despairing. My heart was at rest. God was in control.
—Cheri Fuller, *Quiet Whispers from God's Heart for Women*

What do you need to let go of and trust God to handle?

"Why are you downcast, O my soul? Why so disturbed within me? Put your hope in God, for I will yet praise him, my Savior and my God."
PSALM 42:11 NIV

Encouraging Words Inspire Courage

date:

A young Japanese woman, Atsuko was thrilled with the opportunity to attend college in California. It was a dream come true. But when she arrived on the West Coast, she was overwhelmed with culture shock. She found that people were stressed and harried. Students struggled with their own problems, and no one had time for her. Atsuko felt totally alone.

One of her most difficult classes was volleyball, something that seemed to come naturally to the other students but not to her. One afternoon the instructor told Atsuko to hit the ball to her teammates so they could knock it over the net. Suddenly she froze. Terrified, she feared humiliation if she failed. But a young man on her team somehow understood what she was going through. He walked up to her and whispered, "Come on, Atsuko. You can do it!"

"You'll never understand how those words of encouragement made me feel. Four little words: *You can do it.* I felt like crying with happiness." Atsuko was able to knock the ball over the net and made it through volleyball class with flying colors.

Even after returning to Japan and pursuing a career, she never forgot those encouraging words from a classmate. And when things are difficult or seem impossible, she reminds herself of his four simple words: *You can do it.* And she does! —Cheri Fuller, *The Fragrance of Kindness*

Who needs to hear you say "You can do it!" today?

"A happy heart makes the face cheerful,
but heartache crushes the spirit."
Proverbs 15:13 NIV

THANKFULNESS

Whatever happened to thankfulness? When did we lose track of the importance of ongoing "thanksgiving"—not just a cursory nod toward the Giver of all good gifts during a hasty blessing over the turkey, but a deep spirit of gratitude, a true awareness of the blessedness of our lives?

date:

Of all the inner virtues important to the development of Christlikeness, I believe that thankfulness is one of the most neglected and underrated. Of course I'm thankful—I say grace over my meals, don't I? I give my tithe, attend church, sing "God is so good."

Thankfulness has little to do with how much we own. A heart of gratitude is based, instead, on an understanding of the source of our spiritual and emotional riches.

All we require, in order to cultivate a grateful heart, is a little bit of time. Time to reflect on the outpouring of Christ's love that is evident in our lives. Time to consider what our existence might be like apart from the grace and mercy and direction of Almighty God. Time to remind ourselves what really matters. Time to look into the eyes of those we love and see our Savior's generosity reflected there.

Thanksgiving is not a holiday—it is a holy way of life. It is a new perspective that guards us from greed and self-centeredness, that tenderizes our hearts and renews our minds.

Every day is Thanksgiving to those who know God's spiritual bounty. —Penelope J. Stokes, *Simple Words of Wisdom: 52 Virtues for Every Woman*

Will you turn thanksgiving into a way of life?

"Enter [God's] gates with thanksgiving and his courts with praise; give thanks to him and praise his name. For the Lord is good and his love endures forever; his faithfulness continues through all generations."

PSALM 100:4–5 NIV

Constancy

date:

My dad had a telescope, and he would let me look through it at the night sky. He didn't know much about astronomy, but he knew enough to convey to his daughter a sense of wonder at the immensity and constancy of God's creation.

"See the Big Dipper?" he said, pointing. "OK, now follow from there—that's the North Star. Back in the old days, before compasses and radar, sailors navigated by that star."

I didn't understand. If you were on the other side of the world, wouldn't that star be in a different place? But no, Daddy said, it was always there, indicating North. The Polestar.

It was a constant, like the sun coming up in the east or Venus rising at dusk. A fixed marker in an ever-spinning world.

The world needs a little constancy. An anchor. A sure direction.

What does it mean to be the North Star for the spiritual universe? It means holding fast to the truth of God's mercy and grace. It means being faithful to God and to others. It means founding our lives, our relationships, and our actions on the bedrock of Christ's sacrificial love.

All around us, people are cut off from their moorings, adrift on a sea of uncertainty. Any port can look like home to a sinking ship. Perhaps it's time to set aside our negative theologies, our pet doctrines, the differences that divide us from the rest of God's people, and let one constant truth illuminate like a beacon: God's love endures forever.

Welcome the travelers. Hold out the Word of Life.

Love is the Polestar that draws people home to God, the never-changing mark that guides them into a safe harbor.

—Penelope J. Stokes, *Simple Words of Wisdom: 52 Virtues for Every Woman*

Do others see God's love in your life as you hold fast to Him and His truth?

"Do everything without complaining or arguing, so that you may become blameless and pure, children of God without fault in a crooked and depraved generation, in which you shine like stars in the universe as you hold out the word of life. . . ."
PHILIPPIANS 2:14–16 NIV

HUMILITY

"And what does the Lord require of you? To act justly and to love mercy and to walk humbly with your God."
MICAH 6:8 NIV

Do you walk humbly with God?

"Your attitude should be the same as that of Christ Jesus: Who, being in very nature God, did not consider equality with God something to be grasped, but made himself nothing, taking the very nature of a servant, being made in human likeness. And being found in appearance as a man, he humbled himself and became obedient to death—even death on a cross!"
PHILIPPIANS 2:5–8 NIV

Is your attitude like Christ's, the ultimate example of humility?

Releasing Those You Love

date:

It's amazing how a little thing can cause a big conflict. A little thing such as my teenage daughter's hair! She wanted to be creative—to try a shorter style, dyed burgundy. I envisioned a horrid red hue spoiling her long, lovely blond hair, and since I was paying for her beauty shop expenses, I thought I ought to have a *little* input. Naturally, she disagreed, and tension grew between us over the hair issue.

Strangely, tension also grew between the Lord and me. Frustrated, I prayed, "Lord, what do you want me to do? You know what she'll look like with those colors!"

One day soon after my prayer God whispered distinctly to my heart, *"Release her . . . and her hair."*

Finally, one afternoon when Alison was in the kitchen, I turned to her and said, "Ali, your hair is yours to do with whatever you want. So is your room. And though we'd prefer that you keep it clean, there is going to be no more nagging or picking up after you."

I was comforted one day when I heard Dr. James Dobson say, "I'm convinced the pulling away of adolescents from their parents is *divinely inspired*." With relief, I realized Alison's attempts to be more independent were entirely normal. It meant that I needed to let go—and entrust her continually to her heavenly Father.

When I released Alison and let go of control, she began experimenting with her own hair and even colored and cut her friends' hair. Right away she showed tremendous talent, and this year she's attending hair design school. Now she's cutting and highlighting my hair . . . and doing a beautiful job, I might add! —Cheri Fuller, *Quiet Whispers from God's Heart for Women*

Is there someone you need to let go of and entrust to God?

"Do not exasperate your children; instead, bring them up in the training and instruction of the Lord."
Ephesians 6:4 NIV

Celebrate Communion

For me, the Lord's Supper is always a powerful visual symbol. Maybe it's because we actually handle the bread and lift the wine to our lips. Yet as the plate of crackers is passed, we're ever so careful to aim for our cracker without touching any of the others. Our fastidious care also seems symbolic: We go to such extraordinary efforts to live our lives totally isolated from each other, even though we are *one* in Christ.

date: ....

I thought about this when I watched Teddy, an autistic teenager, reach toward the communion plate. He groaned with delight (he can't speak) and leaned his large frame forward. His hand grabbed, and before his mother could stop him, he held up a fistful of pieces of cracker. "Teddy, no!" his mother hoarsely whispered.

Teddy guffawed and proudly held up a squeezed mash of crackers. Unlike the rest of us, he felt no shame in touching other people's crackers.

I thought of that when my friend sitting next to me reached into the plate to get crackers for both of us. Then, after the pastor invited us all to participate, she lifted one piece to my mouth and then, the other piece to hers. I can't take communion by myself. I'm a little . . . no . . . a lot like Teddy. I'm forced to depend on another Christian to handle my bread for me.

I'm glad about that. It makes me feel connected. It's a happy symbol of how closely I must live my life with fellow believers. I can't live my life alone and isolated.

Communion celebrates the body of Christ, broken on the cross. Communion celebrates the Body of Christ, the Church. Communion is a celebration of unity.

—Joni Eareckson Tada, *Holiness in Hidden Places*

Do you celebrate the body of Christ when you take communion?

"For whenever you eat this bread and drink this cup, you proclaim the Lord's death until he comes."
1 Corinthians 11:26 NIV

White Water

date:

How we face the future is a matter of attitude—whether we see it as welcome surprise or looming disaster. Inevitably, life brings us difficult times—storms, rough water, white water rapids. Even the disciples, who had Jesus with them on a daily basis, encountered such difficulties.

They were out on the lake in their small fishing boat when a storm kicked up—a raging tempest that threatened to swamp the craft and drown them all. The wind was against them, and they couldn't get back to land. So where was Jesus when they needed help? Up in the mountains praying. And then, in the darkness of night—about the time the disciples had decided there was no hope at all—Jesus came, walking to them on the water. "Take heart!" Jesus says. "It is I; do not be afraid" (Matt. 14:22–27).

Don't be afraid. Jesus spoke those words before he reached the boat, before the winds died down, while the disciples still feared for their lives. *Don't be afraid.*

We need to remember those words when we round the bend and see terrifying rapids ahead, when storms crash around us and darkness closes in and the Lord is nowhere to be found. *Don't be afraid.* Even when God seems far away, even when you can't hear the whisper of comfort over the roaring of the waves, don't be afraid.

The storm is part of the journey, too. It can be an adventure rather than a threat, an exhilarating experience of the presence of God. For Jesus still walks on the surface of the storm, still calms the tempest around us—or the one that rages in our hearts.

Your future is in good hands. Don't be afraid.

—Penelope J. Stokes, *Beside a Quiet Stream: Words of Hope for Weary Hearts*

Do you view life as an adventure, knowing God is in control?

"Which of all these does not know that the hand of the Lord has done this? In his hand is the life of every creature and the breath of all mankind."

Job 12:9–10 NIV

Trust

Seeing is believing, the world tries to tell us. But not to God. From a faith perspective, believing is seeing. The Bible is full of exhortations to trust. "Command those who are rich in this present world not to be arrogant nor to put their hope in wealth, which is so uncertain, but to put their hope in God," Paul tells Timothy (1 Tim. 6:17). And for the church in Rome, Paul prays: "May the God of hope fill you with all joy and peace as you trust in him, so that you may overflow with hope by the power of the Holy Spirit" (Rom. 15:13).

The power of trust lies in the ability to turn over control of our lives and our destiny to One who knows far more about the future than we do. It's not weakness to trust, but strength of spirit. It is not naivete, but the utmost wisdom. For God is trustworthy. Even if we are faithless, 1 Timothy 2:13 says, God remains faithful, for the Lord cannot act contrary to the Divine Nature.

Trust in God sets us free to live authentically, to act courageously, to forgive readily. It gives us the power we need to persevere, to repent, to obey, to show compassion, to treat those around us with tolerance and respect. Trust infuses hope and joy into our daily interactions, honesty into our dealings, patience into our waiting. Trust gives us power to commit our way to One who sees the path around the bend.

If you trust, you won't be sorry.

Step out onto the invisible bridge.

God is waiting on the other side with wonders your heart cannot begin to imagine. —Penelope J. Stokes, *Simple Words of Wisdom: 52 Virtues for Every Woman*

Do you trust God and step out even when you can't see what's ahead?

date: ....

"Do not let your hearts be troubled. Trust in God; trust also in me."
John 14:1 NIV

Making Time for Friends

date:

We all seem to struggle with not having enough time! How do we ever find time to enjoy and invest in our friendships? My friends and I are so thankful for our telephone visits, but we still need face-to-face encounters—complete with hugs.

The most important investment of your time needs to be with your Best Friend. Jesus should be the first one to whom you run when you have a problem, and the first one with whom you celebrate blessings! I have found that when I spend time with Him in the morning, He has a way of fitting in all that I need during the day, including other friends.

Take a moment to look at your busy schedule. What do you normally do by yourself that you might be able to do with a friend? In days gone by, women got together for quilting bees, canning, and food preserving. Surely there's something in your life that can be done in the company of other women.

Bible studies and prayer groups offer a chance to grow spiritually as well as connect with like-minded women. Walking with friends combines physical exercise with inspiration and encouragement. Why not get together and mend socks, sew quits for the homeless, read to one another, or even go shopping?

Look in your life for opportunities to connect with other women—and then do it! —Karla Dornacher, *The Blessing of Friendship: A Gift from the Heart*

What could you ask a friend to do with you today?

"Two are better than one, because they have a good return for their work: If one falls down, his friend can help him up."
Ecclesiastes 4:9–10 NIV

Knowledge

"The fear of the Lord is the beginning of wisdom,
and knowledge of the Holy One is understanding."
Proverbs 9:10 NIV

On what do you base your knowledge?
In what areas do you increase your knowledge?

"We know that we all possess knowledge. Knowledge puffs up, but love builds up.
The man who thinks he knows something does not yet know as he ought
to know. But the man who loves God is known by God."
1 Corinthians 8:1–3 NIV

Does your knowledge of God "puff you up," or
does it increase your love for Him?

Believe in Your Children

date: ....

Billy Graham says his mother was one of his greatest encouragers. In his book *Facing Death,* he explained that his mother had always told him to "preach the gospel, and keep it simple." Two weeks before she went to be with the Lord she admonished him with the same words and he responded, "Mother, I'm going to preach His birth, death, and resurrection. I'll preach it till Jesus comes."

His mother squeezed his hand and said, "I believe it!"

Having a mother who believed in him and encouraged him meant the world to this man whose life has impacted millions. "What a blessing it is for parents to believe in their children," Graham says.

—Cheri Fuller, *The Fragrance of Kindness*

How have your parents believed in you? Do you support and believe in your children? Do you tell them often?

"Everything is possible for him who believes."

Mark 9:23 NIV

God Is My Copilot?

I still laugh when I read that bumper sticker: *God Is My Copilot.* Oh, really? And you consider that a good idea? Besides, the way some people drive, you'd think God was lying down on the job, taking a nap in the backseat.

But don't we often act as if God holds the position of honorary consultant in our lives? We go to the Lord for advice now and then, but we aren't obligated to accept it. We've had some experience at living, and we've got a good idea what is best for us. It's okay for the Lord to paddle in the front of the canoe, but we'll do the steering.

If God is my copilot, I might want to re-evaluate the chain of command.

It's just human nature: When we steer the boat, we don't take chances. It's more comfortable to keep to the shoreline, where the current's gentler and the risks are minimal.

When God is at the helm, we find ourselves facing challenges we'd never dreamed of, opportunities that stretch our faith to the limit, and ports we've never even heard of.

It's a scary prospect, letting the Lord take over the pilot's position. But we don't grow in faith unless we abandon the rudder to One who knows far better than we do where we're going and what we'll discover along the way.

And in the long run, it's much less hazardous to allow God to steer the ship. The Lord we serve is a competent commander, able to lead us on a quest that will change our lives.

So pry your fingers off the controls. A grand adventure awaits you. It won't be what you've expected. It will be something far more exciting. It will set your heart racing and bring you to a depth of trust you could never imagine possible.

—Penelope J. Stokes, *Beside a Quiet Stream: Words of Hope for Weary Hearts*

date: ....

Will you acknowledge God as the pilot of your life?

"Yet I am always with you; you hold me by my right hand. You guide me with your counsel, and afterward you will take me into glory."
PSALM 73:23–24 NIV

SERVANTHOOD

date:

The world is full of invisible people. All those workers behind the scenes who make things run. Yet, modern society values fame—movie stars and football heroes. But God has a different value system. God's applause is reserved for the invisible ones.

Jesus showed us the way. On the night before he was betrayed, he met with his disciples to celebrate the Passover. Before the feast began, he took water and a towel and washed his followers' dirty feet. "I have set you an example," Jesus said, "that you should do as I have done for you. I tell you the truth, no servant is greater than his master" (John 13:15-16).

Christ calls us to servanthood. To take up the mundane, thankless tasks that no one else wants to do. But it's hard to give ourselves to invisibility when we'd love to see our name in lights.

Make no mistake—Christ, too, was tempted by the seduction of stardom. The devil offered him fame and fortune, even a way out of the suffering that was to come (Luke 4:1-13). And Jesus turned him down.

How did Jesus do it? "Jesus knew that the Father had put all things under his power, and that he had come from God and was returning to God" (John 13:3).

Christ understood who he was, where he had come from, and where he was going.

These are the keys to servanthood. If we're assured that we come from God and are called by God, we can be content to be invisible. If we are certain that our future lies with God, we don't have to exalt ourselves, for our ultimate exaltation is already accomplished in Jesus Christ.

—Penelope J. Stokes, *Simple Words of Wisdom: 52 Virtues for Every Woman*

Are you content to be invisible since your future lies with God?

"Jesus said to them. . . . 'I am among you as one who serves.' "
LUKE 22:25–27 NIV

Keeping Sabbath with a Friend

When it comes to Sundays, I was raised right. My parents always enforced *no shopping*! When I was a kid, there were no malls. Five-and-dimes, as well as Sears, shut their doors on Sundays. Today it's a different story.

date: ....

For the most part, I steer clear of Sunday purchases. If I do go to the mall, I will open my wallet for a cup of Starbucks.

When my friend Mary Jean came for a visit, I took her for a meander through the mall after church. We sat, sipping our cafe lattes, and talked. I told Mary Jean about Bonnie, a young lady living at Magnolia Gardens Nursing Home. "Bonnie's neuro-muscular disease has advanced to the point where she lies in bed all day," I told Mary Jean. "We could spend some time praying for her today."

For a long moment, we said nothing. Then our eyes met, and we said simultaneously, "What are we doing here?"

We made a beeline for the parking lot. We pulled into the driveway of the little nursing home and hurried down the dimly lit hallways.

Bonnie's eyes lit up when she saw us. She couldn't communicate much through her stiffened smile. Breath and words didn't come easily. We sang to Bonnie and occasionally sat quietly, enjoying the birds chirping outside the window. At the close of our visit, I asked if Bonnie would like to repeat the Lord's Prayer with us. We united our hearts and spoke to our Father.

Mary Jean did many things during her visit. But the highlight was that marvelous chance to keep the Sabbath with a friend in need. There will always be a sale at Nordstroms, but there won't always be an opportunity to "redeem the time." Especially on a Sunday. Especially since Bonnie passed on to glory just a few months later.

—Joni Eareckson Tada, *Holiness in Hidden Places*

How do you usually spend your Sundays?

"If you call the Sabbath a delight and the Lord's holy day honorable, . . . then you will find your joy in the Lord. . . ."

Isaiah 58:13–14 NIV

The Bend Beyond

date:

You can't watch television nowadays without seeing advertisements for free psychic readings. Gullible people—even well-known celebrities—tout the empowering benefits of a glimpse into the future.

All of us are tempted, from time to time, with the seduction of seeing what's around the next bend.

The fact is, we can *never* know what tomorrow will bring. Divine wisdom has withheld that information from us—for our own good. If we did know what waited for us in the future, we'd try to change our destiny—or we'd be completely overwhelmed by what we saw. Instead of letting us know the future, God gives us something even better: The presence of One who is able to guide us.

"Trust in the Lord with all your heart," Proverbs 3:5–6 exhorts us, "and do not rely on your own insight. In all your ways acknowledge him, and he will make straight your paths."

Trust. That's the key to what lies before us. Not enlightenment, but trust. Trust enables us to navigate the river without being frantic about what lies beyond the next bend. We put our faith in a God who understands the risks and the outcome. A God who is all-knowing, all-wise, and all-loving.

No matter what lies around the bend, no matter what risks we must take, no matter what the outcome, the God who created us and loves us journeys with us.

We may not know the future, but we know the One who knows the future. We trust—and that is enough.

—Penelope J. Stokes, *Beside a Quiet Stream: Words of Hope for Weary Hearts*

Are you trusting the Lord with your future?

"Find rest, O my soul, in God alone; my hope comes from him. Trust in him at all times, O people; pour out your hearts to him, for God is our refuge."
Psalm 62:5, 8 NIV

Salvation

"It is by the name of Jesus Christ of Nazareth. . . . Salvation is found in no one else, for there is no other name under heaven given to men by which we must be saved."
Acts 4:10–12 NIV

Do you seek salvation from anyone or anything other than Christ?

"For God did not appoint us to suffer wrath but to receive salvation through our Lord Jesus Christ. He died for us so that, whether we are awake or asleep, we may live together with him."
1 Thessalonians 5:9–10 NIV

How can you thank the Lord for sparing you from wrath and for freely offering salvation through Christ?

Righteousness

date:

Being right isn't the same thing as being righteous. The Pharisees found that out the hard way when they tried to justify themselves as keepers of the law. "The truth will set you free," Jesus told them (John 8:31). But they couldn't get their minds around the concept. They were children of Abraham; they didn't need to be set free.

The local rumor mill, clearly, had done its work. Wasn't this Jesus the one born out of wedlock? Who was he to be telling them that they needed to be set free? Who was the righteous one here? "Abraham is *our* father," they sneered. "*We* are not illegitimate children."

And the Pharisees were right—at least technically. They were, indeed, descendants of the patriarchs; they kept the law; they could claim Abraham as their father. But Jesus was talking about a different kind of parentage—the legacy of the soul, the inheritance that comes through faith.

The Pharisees kept the Jewish commandments religiously, every jot and tittle. But they were not righteous in God's sight. Righteousness is a matter of the heart, not the mind. It is based on faith, on surrender to the truth, not on keeping the law.

The virtue of righteousness is the state of being in right relationship, vertically with God and then horizontally with those around us. If we're righteous, we are liberated by the truth rather than being constrained by legalism. And yes, we "do right," but as an outgrowth of our relationships with God and others, not as proof of our adherence to the law. —Penelope J. Stokes, *Simple Words of Wisdom: 52 Virtues for Every Woman*

Do you base your righteousness on "doing the right things" or on your heartfelt faith in and surrender to God?

"'I [Paul] do not set aside the grace of God, for if righteousness could be gained through the law, Christ died for nothing!'"
GALATIANS 2:21 NIV

Fence of Protection

One summer, while living in Alaska, we tilled a small plot of ground for a vegetable garden. More than one well-meaning neighbor stopped by to muse over the fact that we had no fence around our garden and in Alaska, that most likely meant "free lunch" for a visiting moose.

date:

However, my enthusiasm for gardening and lack of funds led me to trust God to be the "fence of protection" around our garden. Much to the amazement of our neighbors, we found mooseprints in the garden twice and chased out one lost cow, but nothing was eaten!

Your life is of far greater value than a small patch of dirt and a few peas or cauliflowers!

You don't need to be afraid of the "predators or pests" of life—those circumstances that try to discourage you and eat away at your peace of mind. God has promised to be your protection. His strong outstretched arms will keep you safe. —Karla Dornacher, *Down a Garden Path To Places of Love and Joy*

How has the Lord protected you from the "pests" of life—those circumstances that try to rob you of your peace of mind?

"For the Lord loves the just and will not forsake his faithful ones. They will be protected forever. . . ."
PSALM 37:28 NIV

THE INS AND OUTS OF GOD'S WILL

date:

When I traveled to the Cotswolds years ago, I got my first glimpse of an English hedge maze. It was a marvel of cocreation between nature and the gardener. Negotiating a maze is an entertaining game, but it's a debilitating way of life.

And too often that's our image of God's will—a near-impossible labyrinth. The Lord sees the right way, of course, but doesn't tell us. And so we search frantically, fearful that choosing the wrong way may endanger our spiritual lives—or even our souls.

The Bible, however, does not portray God as a cunning adversary, but as a loving Creator. The search for God's will is not a puzzle to be solved, but a life to be lived.

The familiar passage in Romans 8:28 tells us that "all things work together for good for those who love God, who are called according to his purpose." But let's not stop there. What is the purpose of God? Verse 29 tells us: that we might be "conformed to the image of his Son."

The prime directive of the Christian life is not that we "find God's will and do it," but that we become like Jesus. Like Jesus—who went through life touching those who were in pain, healing the sick, speaking words of hope and liberty to those who lived in despair. Like Jesus—who kept his eyes fixed on the One who had sent him. Like Jesus—who sought, first and foremost, to please God.

If our hearts long for the fulfillment of God's purpose, we need not fear making some fatal mistake. The river will bring us to decisions to be made and new directions to take. But we can make these changes fearlessly, with confidence that we will learn and grow from the journey. And growth, after all, is God's will for us in Christ. —Penelope J. Stokes, *Beside a Quiet Stream: Words of Hope for Weary Hearts*

How are you becoming like Jesus?

" 'For I know the plans I have for you,' declares the Lord, 'plans to prosper you and not to harm you, plans to give you hope and a future.' "
JEREMIAH 29:11 NIV

Respect

Aretha Franklin made a fortune out of a single word: "R-E-S-P-E-C-T," she sang. Why, was the song "Respect" such an enormous hit? I think it was because she touched a nerve in many women—the desire to be respected rather than just wanted.

date: ....

If truth be told, that's the virtue that we as Christians neglect when we seek to minister to those around us.

God has called us to be agents of reconciliation to a troubled, dying world. The problem is, we sometimes approach the troubled and dying as if we have all the answers, and they've never even considered the right questions.

That's not the way God intends for us to reach out. First Peter 3:15 admonishes us. "Always be prepared to give an answer to everyone who asks you to give the reason for the hope that you have. But do this with gentleness and respect."

We show disrespect to others when we insult them by our holier-than-thou attitudes. We disrespect them when we demean their suffering, tell them to believe and stop doubting.

Now, we're not always conscious of being disrespectful. But if we want to help people find direction and guidance, we need to be conscious. Conscious of the way Christ dealt with others, of his tenderness and acceptance. Conscious that he, who knew much more than we do about the human heart, allowed people to find their own way to faith.

Respect draws people to the truth. When we respect them, amid all their doubts and struggles, we give them the liberty to make their own decisions in their own time. When we honor their search, we honor the image of Christ within them. And we demonstrate our own trust in God, who is capable of leading people where they need to go.

—Penelope J. Stokes, *Simple Words of Wisdom: 52 Virtues for Every Woman*

How have you shown respect or disrespect to someone you've ministered to?

"Show proper respect to everyone. . . ."
1 Peter 2:17 NIV

Chattering the Batter

date:

I started playing girls' basketball on the school team in the fourth grade. Two nights a week during season, followed by volleyball, and then cheerleading for football season. My brother played football in the fall, basketball in the winter, baseball and track in the spring. That meant that for most seasons Mother had a game commitment at least four nights a week, not to mention practice and tournaments.

Did she go grudgingly? Hardly. During football season, she yelled at the wide receivers when they dropped the ball, applauded the defense when they forced a safety, and booed the refs for not calling clipping. During basketball season, she dreaded a tie ball when my opponent was six feet tall, hoped for a one-and-one shot when I got fouled, and spotted a double dribble a mile away. During baseball season, she had her own opinions about when it was wise to bunt, yelled at the runner to tag up after a pop fly, and needled the batter on a three-and-two count.

In short, she spoke the language. She understood the importance of supporting our interests and joining in our activities wholeheartedly. When there was a rough spot in our relationship, she always knew how to reconnect the conversational crosswires with things that interested us.

—Dianna Booher, *Mother's Gifts To Me*

How do you connect with your children or with others? Do you "speak their language" and get to know the things that interest them? How do others connect with you?

"How good and pleasant it is when brothers live together in unity!"
Psalm 133:1 NIV

Belief

"Jesus replied, . . . 'If you believe, you will receive whatever you ask for in prayer.' "
Matthew 21:21–22 NIV

Do you really believe that your prayers will be answered? If no, then why not?

"If you confess with your mouth, 'Jesus is Lord,' and believe in your heart that God raised him from the dead, you will be saved. For it is with the heart that you believe and are justified, and it is with your mouth that you confess and are saved."
Romans 10:9–10 NIV

As Christians, why is it important to confess what we believe in our hearts?

The Hand That Knows

date:

The path of salvation is a narrow one, but not so narrow that you must walk it alone. It is the perfect width for the Master Gardener to walk beside you as your Father and your Friend. Though the way may be difficult at times, the path before you is an everlasting path of promise, and God will never let go of your hand.

When you cannot see ahead of you and you've lost your sense of direction, don't hold hands with doubt and confusion—hold more firmly to the only hand that knows the Way.

Let God lead you beside still and quiet waters, where He will restore your peace and give rest to your soul.

—Karla Dornacher, *Down a Garden Path To Places of Love and Joy*

What or who do you hold onto when you've lost your way in life? What or who leads you?

"For I am the Lord, your God, who takes hold of your right hand and says to you, Do not fear; I will help you."
Isaiah 41:13 NIV

PENITENCE

Remember the movie *Love Story*? You're sure to remember the one line from the movie that makes most people laugh: "Love means never having to say you're sorry." And just what kind of love would that be?

date: ....

Love—whether it's with your spouse, your kids, or your God—means you'd better learn to say "I'm sorry." And fast. Penitence is the cornerstone of real relationship.

Take David, for example. The King of all Israel. A fellow the Bible calls "a man after God's own heart" (Acts 13:22). But David was far from sinless. In 2 Samuel 11, David lusts after Bathsheba, has her husband Uriah killed off in battle, and then takes her for his own. In the very next chapter, the prophet Nathan confronts the king with his sin.

When Nathan reveals his sin, David doesn't try to make excuses. He says, "I have sinned against the Lord" (2 Sam. 12:13). David's sin is forgiven, even though he has to live with the consequences he has brought upon himself.

The virtue of penitence doesn't mean that we despair and make sin our primary focus in life. But it does mean that we own up to our sin, whether we have violated our relationship with God or offended someone else.

We don't need to confess for God's sake. The Lord knows more than we do about what's in our hearts, and the sacrifice of Christ has already paid the penalty. But for our own sakes—and for the sake of others we may have hurt—we need to come clean about it. What we hide festers and contaminates us. What we reveal purifies and heals.

Those three little words—*I love you*—are rendered even more powerful by three more: *I was wrong.*

—Penelope J. Stokes, *Simple Words of Wisdom: 52 Virtues for Every Woman*

To whom do you need to confess your wrongs today?

"If we confess our sins, he is faithful and just and will forgive us our sins and purify us from all unrighteousness."

1 JOHN 1:9 NIV

Words for Success

date:

Many years ago, there were two groups of aspiring writers at the University of Wisconsin who began meeting regularly as a support group. One group named themselves "The Stranglers," and lived up to their name—they critiqued each others' writing abrasively and rarely offered an encouraging word.

The other group, "The Wranglers," encouraged all efforts, however feeble. Praise flowed freely in this group and biting words of criticism were never spoken.

Interestingly, 20 years later, not one person in the critical group had made it as a professional writer. But over half of the encouraging "Wranglers" were successful writers, even nationally known. Among that group was Marjorie Rawlings, author of the award-winning American classic, *The Yearling.*

—Cheri Fuller, *The Fragrance of Kindness*

Can you ever remember a time when you regretted having said a kind word to someone? How have kind words contributed to your successes in life?

"How sweet are your words to my taste, sweeter than honey to my mouth!"
Psalm 119:103 niv

Where the Current Flows

I was born and raised in the relatively flat lands of the Deep South, and I know—or thought I knew—that rivers flowed south—down, toward the Gulf of Mexico.

date: ....

But not in the mountain ranges of North Carolina. Here the rivers run south, north, east, west out of the higher ranges. These are not straight-arrow streams pointing toward the ocean, but twisting, winding serpents of water, subject to powers beyond their natural tendencies. Eventually, they do turn south and head for open seas, but not before they confuse even the most competent navigator.

The northbound river reminds me of what it can be like to negotiate God's will.

Somehow, we always think we should know which direction God is leading us. We've got it figured out. And then a force beyond our comprehension begins to change the rules. Where are we going, anyway? Who's in charge here?

We want to know. We want God to speak clearly and plainly, telling us our destination up front so that we can get on with the business of being obedient.

We're Christians, after all. We have the mind of Christ, or so the Bible tells us. We're supposed to be able to discern where God's leading us. And from there on, it's pretty simple. We take a ruler, draw a line between point A and point B, and bingo! We're on our way. Everyone knows, after all, that the shortest distance between two points is a straight line.

But not on God's river. —Penelope J. Stokes, *Beside a Quiet Stream: Words of Hope for Weary Hearts*

How do you try to discern where God is leading you in life? How can you trust Him and know that His path will often change directions?

"The one who trusts will never be dismayed."
Isaiah 28:16 NIV

WHAT A FRIEND WE HAVE IN JESUS

date: ....

We all want so much to be loved and accepted. The fear of rejection, of not measuring up, can sometimes cause us to try to be something or someone we're not, just so we can fit in. Or it can cause us to never risk entering into a relationship at all.

What a friend we have in Jesus! You don't ever have to be afraid of Him leaving or rejecting you. He knows everything there is to know about you—He knows you're not perfect—and He still loves you and accepts you for who you are!

The more we are able to grasp this truth, to find our value and security in Jesus alone, the more able we are to accept ourselves and others.

God's love sets us free to be who He designed us to be. It also releases us from the fear of rejection and the need to live up to someone else's expectations.

Jesus is our example of a perfect friend. His perfect love is our standard.

We are called to love our friends as Jesus loves us. They need to be free to be all God designed them to be, and to know they are loved—even when they're not perfect!

—Karla Dornacher, *The Blessing of Friendship: A Gift from the Heart*

Where do you find your value and security—in Jesus' love for you or in others' expectations of you? Do you love your friends the way Jesus loves you?

"And so we know and rely on the love God has for us.
We love because he first loved us."
1 JOHN 4:16, 19 NIV

Sin

"For the wages of sin is death, but the gift of God is eternal life in Christ Jesus our Lord."
Romans 6:23 NIV

Do you understand that your sin deserves death, but instead God gives us eternal life in Christ?

"God made him who had no sin to be sin for us, so that in him we might become the righteousness of God."
2 Corinthians 5:21 NIV

How do you respond to the fact that Jesus, who was perfectly holy and without sin, became your sin in order to atone you before God?

The Gift of One's Self

date:

I was sitting in bed the day before Christmas with a broken right arm and elbow, surrounded by gifts that hadn't been wrapped, a "To-Do" list I would never get done, and a house that desperately needed cleaning since family members were coming for Christmas and our son's wedding. I'd been up most of the night in pain. The day was overcast and gloomy, but my heart was even gloomier. How was I going to make even the most basic preparations for Christmas?

Suddenly, the telephone rang. "We're on our way over, so make a list of what you need done and we'll do it!" Susan said from her car phone. In a short while she and Marilyn, friends from our House Church, arrived and swooped in like Mr. Clean, putting things in order, vacuuming, dusting, and cleaning the kitchen. "What's next?" they asked when that was done. I pointed at the pile of unwrapped gifts.

Just then Connie walked in and joined them in wrapping presents and fashioning lovely bows to adorn them. When all the work was complete, we brewed a pot of Christmas tea, brought out a tin of cookies, and sat by the fire chatting and reading Christmas stories aloud. Their gift of time had encouraged my heart beyond words. These dear friends had certainly shown to me that the best gift is truly the gift of one's self. —Cheri Fuller, *The Fragrance of Kindness*

How could you make yourself a gift to someone who needs you today?

"Be devoted to one another in brotherly love. Honor one another above yourselves."
ROMANS 12:10 NIV

A Christmas Blessing

It was one of those Christmases when the schools didn't dismiss until late December. Amy was teaching and the frenzy of giving finals had left her little time to enjoy the season. She planned to join her husband and three-year-old daughter who had traveled to her mother-in-law's home, where they would spend the holidays. Amy considered herself a veteran flyer, but she was relieved to have one of the back seats, statistically the safest seats on the plane.

date: ....

Amy was just dozing off when the captain announced that they would be going through some turbulence. *No problem* Amy thought as she cinched her seat belt tighter.

No one was ready for the terrible jolt that caused the plane to drop suddenly. Amy had never experienced turbulence like this. Anxiety was heightened when all the lights went out. She gripped her seat and closed her eyes, "Please, Lord, don't make my little girl spend this Christmas without her mother. Please let all of us reach our loved ones safely."

From somewhere in the front of the plane, came a giggle. With the next jolt the giggle turned into a little girl's hearty laugh that only a child can produce. Soon the child's laughter infected all the passengers. People were laughing and were almost disappointed when the captain announced they were clear of the turbulence.

When they landed safely a short while later, Amy was one of the first to get off the plane. She never did catch a glimpse of the little girl with the infectious laugh, but was sure God had sent the child to ease their burdens and replace their fears with peace. A Christmas gift from heaven you might say. —Cheri Fuller, *Quiet Whispers from God's Heart for Women*

When have you received a Christmas gift from heaven?

"But the angel said to them, 'Do not be afraid. I bring you good news of great joy that will be for all the people. Today in the town of David a Savior has been born to you; he is Christ the Lord.' "

LUKE 2:10–11 NIV

A Prompting from the Spirit

date: ....

Rush from work. Meet Judy at *Hamburger Hamlet.* Scarf down Chicken Caesar. Exit restaurant. Oh yes, pray with Judy before heading in different directions. After our "Amen," she headed for her car. I was heading to my church to speak to our women's group.

As I pulled out of the parking space, I noticed a woman. I wonder who she is? *That baseball cap and her scraggly hair.* I sensed a powerful urge to ask her to come hear me speak.

Cars were backing up behind me. "What am I supposed to do, God? Roll down my window, yell and say, 'Hey, I think you ought to follow me to church!' That's ridiculous!"

All the way to church I berated myself for not inviting the woman to come. As I was pulling into the church parking lot, I was surprised to see Judy.

After I left the restaurant, the woman approached Judy and asked who I was. So Judy invited her to come hear me speak.

There in the church parking lot I heard her story. "My husband and I were at the cancer clinic and we stopped to eat on our way home." Joyce—that was her name—continued. "I've had breast cancer for four years and two hours ago I learned that the cancer is now in my brain. It's inoperable. You looked so happy. I don't know where to turn. "

Suddenly I understood the scraggly hair under the baseball cap—chemotherapy. I also understood why the Holy Spirit had urged me to invite her to come hear me speak.

That night, Joyce and her husband had an opportunity to bow their heads and pray to accept Jesus as their Savior.

This week you'll hear God's still, small voice whisper, "Say something to her, invite him, make that call." You'll be tempted to brush it off—but don't. The prompting may never pass your way again. Neither might that person.

—Joni Eareckson Tada, *Holiness in Hidden Places*

Will you listen to God's prompting today?

"Be very careful, then, how you live—not as unwise but as wise, making the most of every opportunity. . . ."
Ephesians 5:15 NIV

Faithfulness

A lot of us harbor a deeply rooted misconception about faithfulness. We assume that, in order to be faithful, we must rid ourselves of doubt, we must have victory over the struggle. We cite the story of Thomas, that disciple whose single claim to fame was that he doubted the resurrection. His very name is used to characterize someone who questions—a Doubting Thomas.

date:

But Thomas wasn't the only one who doubted. He was just honest enough to verbalize his doubts. When Mary Magdalene and the other women came from the tomb on Easter morning to tell the apostles about the resurrection, the men "did not believe the woman, because their words seemed to them like nonsense" (Luke 24: 11). Even when Jesus appeared to them (Luke 24:36-37), they thought they were seeing a ghost.

Still, poor old Thomas gets the brunt of the criticism. But when he finally does see Jesus, he receives not judgment, but acceptance—and gentleness and understanding. "Put your finger here," Jesus says, "and see my hands. Reach out your hand and touch my side. Stop doubting, and believe" (John 20:27).

Stop doubting, and believe. Christ's words do not represent condemnation, but invitation. Thomas spoke his doubts openly, honestly, and Christ answered them. Jesus reached out to him and drew him in.

Faithfulness is not a matter of gritting your teeth and hanging on. It's a matter of trusting the Lord enough to be candid about your doubts. It's about having enough faith in the character of God to question. So go ahead, ask your questions. Your faith will be stronger for it. —Penelope J. Stokes, *Simple Words of Wisdom: 52 Virtues for Every Woman*

What questions do you have for God? Will you ask him so He can increase your faithfulness?

"What if some did not have faith? Will their lack of faith nullify God's faithfulness? Not at all!"
Romans 3:3–4 NIV

Sixty Seconds of Stillness

date: ....

Once, in a church I attended, a young intern was serving as worship leader. When the time came in the service for silent reflection and confession, she invited the congregation to sit in quietness for a moment and allow God to speak in their hearts.

Then she waited. Completely at ease and composed, she stood before the altar as silence descended over the group.

Feet shuffled. Bulletins rattled. A few people coughed. A few eyes opened, and people began to shift uncomfortably in their seats.

She waited a little longer.

At last she went on with the pastoral prayer, and sighs of relief ascended from every corner of the sanctuary.

After the service I asked her how long the "silent prayer time" had gone on.

"I timed it," she said with a grin. "It was 52 seconds."

Less than a minute! Not even 60 seconds of silence in the presence of God, and an entire congregation grew restless.

Perhaps we're all uncomfortable with silence. Maybe that's why we fill our environments with distracting sound—why we fill our "quiet" times with a multitude of words.

But just as emotional intimacy cannot be based on superficiality, so an intimate relationship with God cannot be based on spiritual small talk. Sooner or later we've got to "be still" if we are to "know that God is God."

And how do we learn to be still? By waiting through the disturbing, self-conscious moments until our hearts and minds grow comfortable with silence. It takes practice.

You don't need words to get through to God. All you need is a mind attuned to the Lord's voice, a soul willing to wait.

—Penelope J. Stokes, *Beside a Quiet Stream: Words of Hope for Weary Hearts*

How often are you quiet and still before the Lord?

"That we may live peaceful and quiet lives in all godliness and holiness. This is good, and pleases God our Savior. . . ."
1 Timothy 2:2–3 NIV

COMMANDMENTS

"We know that we have come to know him [God] if we obey His commands. If anyone obeys His word, God's love is truly made complete in him."
1 JOHN 2:3, 5 NIV

Do you know the Lord and show it by obeying what he commands?

" 'The most important one [commandment],' answered Jesus, 'is this: . . . Love the Lord your God with all your heart and with all your soul and with all your mind and with all your strength. The second is this: Love your neighbor as yourself. There is no commandment greater than these.' "
MARK 12:29–31 NIV

Do you value these commandments above all others?

Fairness

date:

Human beings have a strong, built-in sense of fairness—any four-year old can tell you that. It's not fair for her to get a cookie if I don't get one. It's not fair to let her take my doll away. The problem is, we often see fairness from only one side—ours. And when the judgment goes against us, we claim unfairness.

Jesus told the story about a landowner who needed laborers. He went to the marketplace early in the morning and hired men, agreeing on a fair day's wages. At noon he went back and hired more. Again at three o'clock. And at five.

When the day was over, the laborers who had worked the least were given the agreed-upon wage, so the ones who had worked all day expected more. But they received the same amount as those who had only worked an hour. "It's not fair!" they complained. "You have made them equal to us who have borne the burden of the work and the heat of the day" (Matt. 20:1-16).

Don't we do the same thing? We see God blessing someone who isn't nearly as "mature" or "spiritual" as we think we are, and we mutter under our breath that it's unfair. We look at other people's behavior and judge the condition of their heart.

We need to accept the truth that only God is capable of seeing the heart and judging rightly. The Lord tells us not to judge, and for good reason. We can see only the outside. We can never know how far a person has come just to get to the place we designate as "immature." Our responsibility is to look up to God, not down on others.

Fairness doesn't necessarily mean that the cookies are divided evenly. It means that we trust God to do the dividing.

—Penelope J. Stokes, *Simple Words of Wisdom: 52 Virtues for Every Woman*

Do you leave the judging of others up to the Lord?

"There is only one Lawgiver and Judge, the one who is able to save and destroy. But you—who are you to judge your neighbor?"
James 4:12 NIV

Our Authors

Dianna Booher has almost singlehandedly changed the way corporate America communicates. The author of 37 books, Dianna helps women achieve the proper balance in their work, home, and spiritual lives. Excerpts from *Mother's Gifts to Me* (Nashville: J. Countryman).

Karla Dornacher is an accomplished artist who combines warm inviting images, calligraphy, and devotional text to reveal how even life's most mundane tasks and surroundings can direct us to God's love. Excerpts from *Love in Every Room* (Nashville: J. Countryman), *Down a Garden Path To Places of Love and Joy* (Nashville: J. Countryman), and *The Blessing of Friendship: A Gift from the Heart* (Nashville: J. Countryman).

Cheri Fuller derives her greatest joy from encouraging others. The best-selling author of more than 20 books, Cheri has helped countless Christian women build a strong prayer life and overcome worry. Excerpts from *Quiet Whispers from God's Heart for Women* (Nashville: J. Countryman) and *The Fragrance of Kindness* (Nashville: J. Countryman).

Gloria Gaither, the gifted author and song-writer, is always eager to share her insights on finding eternity in the moment, nurturing families, and discovering the joys of discipleship. Excerpts from *Bless This Child* (Nashville: J. Countryman), *Bless This House* (Nashville: J. Countryman), *Bless This Marriage* (Nashville: J. Countryman), and *By This Fire: Fireside Moments at the Gaither House* (Nashville: J. Countryman).

Penelope J. Stokes is a former college professor who left the halls of academe to become a full-time writer and editor. She has written 12 books, including a popular fiction trilogy set on the home front during World War II. Excerpts from *Beside a Quiet Stream: Words of Hope for Weary Hearts* (Nashville: J. Countryman) and *Simple Words of Wisdom: 52 Virtues for Every Woman* (Nashville: J. Countryman).

Joni Eareckson Tada is a quadriplegic who showed the world that with God all things are indeed possible. Despite her disability, Joni has written 23 books, is an accomplished painter, and has her own national radio show. Excerpts from *Holiness in Hidden Places* (Nashville: J. Countryman).

prayer list

Prayer Requests

prayer list

Prayer Requests

favorite scripture

favorite scripture

dates to remember

January

Occasion	Date

February

Occasion	Date

March

Occasion	Date

April

Occasion	Date

dates to remember

May

Occasion	Date

June

Occasion	Date

July

Occasion	Date

August

Occasion	Date

dates to remember

SEPTEMBER

Occasion	Date

OCTOBER

Occasion	Date

NOVEMBER

Occasion	Date

DECEMBER

Occasion	Date

thoughts & inspirations

Thoughts & Inspirations

thoughts & inspirations

THOUGHTS & INSPIRATIONS

thoughts & inspirations

Thoughts & Inspirations

Thoughts & Inspirations

thoughts & inspirations

Thoughts & Inspirations

Thoughts & Inspirations